STEALING SECRETS

HOW A FEW DARING WOMEN DECEIVED GENERALS, IMPACTED BATTLES, AND ALTERED THE COURSE OF THE CIVIL WAR

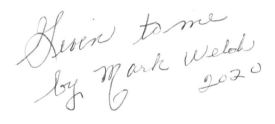

Given to me by Mark Welch 2020

Acw

H. DONALD WINKLER

CUMBERLAND HOUSE™

Published by Cumberland House, an imprint of Sourcebooks, Inc.
P.O. Box 4410, Naperville, Illinois 60567-4410
(630) 961-3900
Fax: (630) 961-2168
www.sourcebooks.com

Library of Congress Cataloging-in-Publication Data

Winkler, H. Donald
  Stealing secrets : how a few daring women deceived generals, impacted battles, and altered the course of the civil war / by H. Donald Winkler.
      p. cm.
  Includes bibliographical references and index.
1. United States--History--Civil War, 1861-1865--Participation, Female. 2. United States--History--Civil War, 1861-1865--Women. 3. United States--History--Civil War, 1861-1865--Secret service. 4. United States--History--Civil War, 1861-1865--Biography. 5. Women spies--United States--Biography. 6. Women spies--Confederate States of America--Biography. I. Title.

  E628.W57 2010
  973.7082--dc22

                              2010025638

          Printed and bound in the United States of America.
                POD 10 9 8 7 6 5

To my friend
Robert T. Redd,
a Virginia gentleman
and a beloved educator

For a spying enterprise that requires real finesse, a woman will be likely to accomplish far more than a man. She is quicker-witted, less easily imposed upon, and can more easily deceive other people.

—*Loreta Velazquez, Confederate Spy*

CONTENTS

ACKNOWLEDGMENTS

I am indebted to a number of individuals and institutions for hard-to-find information about and photographs of several spies featured in this book.

The chapter on Antonia Ford and Laura Ratcliffe could not have been written without the assistance of Karla and Charles W. Vernon III of Vienna, Virginia; Susan Inskeep Gray, curator and visitor services manager for the Fairfax Museum and Visitor Center; and Bill Etue, a Civil War tour guide. Mrs. Vernon studied the life of Antonia Ford intensely for a year and coproduced the 2009 docudrama, "Spies in Crinoline." She provided me with magazine articles and news clippings, information from the Willard Family Papers at the Library of Congress and from the City of Fairfax Historic Collection, and Civil War–era photographs of Antonia Ford, Joseph Willard, the Willard Hotel, the original Fairfax Courthouse, and the Gunnell House, among others. Her husband, Charles, shared his expertise of Washington divorce law in the 1860s and his recent discovery of adultery charges against Joseph Clapp Willard, the man Antonia married.

Thanks, too, to Charles V. Mauro, for permission to reproduce his photograph of the cover page of the album that Jeb Stuart gave to Laura Ratcliffe, and to photographer Susan Bock at www.art2die4.net for her tinted photograph of Jeb Stuart.

For information on Lottie and Ginnie Moon, I thank Valerie E. Elliott, head of the Smith Library of Regional History in Oxford, Ohio, the hometown of the

Moon family. She also provided rare photographs of the Moon sisters and of the Oxford Female Institute.

For material on Nancy Hart, I am grateful to Terry Lowry, historian of the West Virginia State Archives and History Library, who provided numerous newspaper and magazine clippings.

For the excellent photograph of the dining room at the Confederate White House, I am indebted to Ann Drury Wellford, manager of photographic services for the Museum of the Confederacy, and photographer Katherine Wetzel.

No spies were more difficult to document than Olivia Floyd and Sarah Slater. And no one could have exceeded the helpfulness given to me by two special ladies: Anita Warnes, circulation manager of the Library of the College of Southern Maryland at La Plata, and Sheila R. Smith of the Society for the Restoration of Port Tobacco. Ms. Warnes provided copies of two lengthy articles written by historian James O. Hall for the *Maryland Independent* in 1975 and extensive information from the files of the Southern Maryland Studies Center and the Historical Society of Charles County (the latter with the assistance of its president, Joyce B. Candland). Ms. Smith mailed to me a never-before-published photograph of young Olivia Floyd and other materials that answered several questions I had about her. Two other photographs for the chapter about Olivia came from A. J. McDonald, director of the St. Albans Museum in Vermont.

To all of the above, I am deeply appreciative of their willingness to go far beyond the call of duty to respond to my numerous questions and requests.

Special thanks also go to Betty Webb of the Anna Porter Public Library in Gatlinburg, Tennessee. She provided scores of books through the interlibrary loan program, including some that were more than a hundred years old.

Finally, I would be remiss if I did not thank my wife, Azile, for always being available when I needed her help and advice. She has been my best critic and my staunchest supporter.

INTRODUCTION

The stories of women spies are filled with suspense and seduction, treachery and trickery, romance and bravery. Women took enormous risks and achieved remarkable results—often in ways men could not. A quiet Quaker schoolteacher reported information to a Union commander that led to an important victory. Two women provided intelligence that prevented Confederates from breaking the Northern blockade of Southern ports. A teenage girl rushed intelligence to a marching army. Those with social connections invited enemy officers to parties where loose lips let slip critical information. Others galloped on horseback through enemy lines with information concealed in their bodices. They used disguises. They created ciphers. They intercepted military dispatches. They carried secret messages, medicines, and supplies on the rings of steel wires that puffed out a hoop skirt. And they provided accurate information about the enemy's fortifications, plans, troop size, and movements.

But the most potent tools in their arsenals were physical charms, flirtations, and the powers of feminine persuasion.

A twenty-three-year-old lady cultivated a sweet and subdued voice and hired a phrenologist to help enhance her ability to win friends and influence powerful figures. Spies charmed cabinet-level secrets out of lovesick admirers and bewitched countless officers. Allan Pinkerton, head of the Union Intelligence Service, wrote of the "almost irresistible seductive powers" of Confederate spymaster Rose Greenhow, a widowed mother of four. Pinkerton said that her "forceful, compelling style and abiding attractiveness to men were the underpinnings of her success." They made her an extremely dangerous enemy of the Federal government.

Not all of the women and teenage girls who spied in the Civil War were sexy and gorgeous, but many of them were. And that gave them a huge advantage in fulfilling their clandestine missions. Of course, they also were clever, devious, daring, and passionately committed to a cause.

Another advantage female spies initially had over their male counterparts was that they were less likely to be searched. It was a time when men prided themselves on being chivalrous, but as the war went on, women were searched more completely, even strip-searched. Mary Chesnut, a prominent Southern diarist, wrote: "Women who come before the public are in a bad box now. False hair is taken off and searched for papers. Pistols are sought for. Bustles are suspect. All manner of things, they say, come over the border (across the lines) under the huge [hoop skirts] now worn. So they are ruthlessly torn off. Not legs but arms are looked for under hoops."

Unlike soldiers, spies are defined as criminals in military law. A captured soldier becomes a prisoner of war, but a captured spy usually faces death. Captured women usually were confined in decrepit, unsanitary prisons for several months, and then ordered never to return to enemy soil. At first, a gentleman could not bring himself to order a teenager or a prominent socialite to be shot or hanged, and so women escaped such punishment early in the war. Later on, at least two women were sentenced to hang. One was rescued at the last minute; the other's sentence was commuted.

Despite the danger, women spies stayed active. The fate of more than one battle was decided, not by the valor of the soldier, but by movements generals were able to make through information these spies furnished. Several commanding officers testified, in hearty terms of approbation, to the efficiency and fidelity of the women spies who aided them.

To their credit, they had broken out of the confines of "a woman's place" in nineteenth-century America to participate in a profession perilous in the extreme. As the grave marker of Union spy Elizabeth Van Lew states, female spies "risked everything that is dear to man—friends, fortune, comfort, health, life itself."

One of my distant cousins, a Civil War Yankee, benefited significantly from the clandestine activity of a pretty Southern belle. She was Bettie Smith of Wartrace, Tennessee. He was 2nd Lt. John Coker of the 155th Illinois Volunteer Infantry. In March 1865 he became separated from his unit, which served in garrisons along the line of the Nashville and Chattanooga Railroad. Not feeling well, the twenty-one-year-old officer sought assistance at the Smith farm. Apparently John Coker and Bettie Smith were instantly attracted to each other. She nursed him back to health.

One day Bettie heard horses approaching the house and glanced out the window to see Confederate cavalrymen. For her protection, and Coker's, she lowered him down a cistern behind the house. What happened next is unknown. Presumably, they asked her if she had seen any Yankees, and she said no. After they left, she raised Coker from the cistern, and a few days later he rejoined his unit. After being mustered out on September 4, 1865, he returned to Wartrace and married the Tennessee girl who had saved him. They settled in southern Illinois. He became a lawyer, an assistant U.S. marshal for Hamilton County, and a judge of the U.S. Court of Claims in Washington, D.C.

Learning about John and Bettie and other relatives who served the North and South spurred my own interest in studying and writing about the Civil War. The seeds had been planted on my tenth birthday when my grandfather gave me an 1861 Springfield rifled musket—the most widely used model in the Civil War.

My 2008 book, *Civil War Goats and Scapegoats*, focused on blundering generals—men who failed. This time I wanted to write a success story about Civil War women who made a positive difference. A few books currently in print deal with the broader subject of women nurses, soldiers, scouts, and spies. I chose to limit this work to women who spied and to cover them in greater depth than they previously have been accorded in one volume.

The project has been far more difficult than I anticipated when I started it a few years ago. Existing materials contain many inconsistencies and errors. Much of the misinformation comes from exaggerated claims and from testimony given at the trial of the Lincoln assassination conspirators and at congressional hearings. For example, in 1866, a congressional committee was determined to prove, through a Confederate agent (James Fowle), that two Rebel female spies were the same person:

> Q. Mr. Fowle, did you know Miss Olivia Floyd (a militant secessionist in Port Tobacco, Maryland)?
> A. I did know her, I think, but I did not know her by that name. It was Mrs. [Sarah] Slater, but I will not be certain of that.

Sarah Slater has been aptly described many times as "the mysterious woman," and that she was, always wearing a thick veil over her face as she spied for the Confederacy. But she was not Olivia Floyd.

Then, in 1988, three highly respected scholars produced a groundbreaking book on the assassination that contained the following line: "Sarah Slater was an exotic young French-speaking Confederate agent also known as Kate Thompson." I could not find any supportive evidence for this assertion. Sarah did use an alias on at least one occasion to protect her identity, but it was not Kate Thompson. The best-known woman of that name was the wife of Jacob Thompson. He headed the Confederacy's clandestine activities operating out of Canada. Kate remained at their home in Mississippi until near the end of the war, when she and her husband fled to Europe. At least one writer believes that Jacob once used the alias Kate Thompson, but this is questionable.

These examples illustrate the difficulty in researching and writing about spies who, by the nature of their profession, serve best when known only to their confidential spymasters. Their success and survival depended upon secrecy. They did not carry any information about themselves. One tiny mistake could mean incarceration or death. They left no paper trails that could reveal their identities, occupations, or missions.

The chronicling of Civil War intelligence activities is further complicated by the lack of official records, the lack of access to records, and the questionable truth of other records. Judah P. Benjamin, the Confederacy's secretary of state, burned all the intelligence records he could find just before Federal troops entered Richmond in 1865. On the Union side, Allan Pinkerton's Secret Service records were lost in the 1871 Chicago Fire. And some individuals involved in intelligence gathering burned their personal papers. Thus the identities of many Civil War spies remain secret.

Government historians worked from 1864 to 1927 to compile the 128 volumes that contain the official records of the Union and Confederate armies and the thirty-one volumes that print similar accounts for the two navies. Captured Confederate records dealing with covert activities are included in these government publications, but the Union side was withheld from the public.

I have read and used primary sources where available, including the memoirs and diaries of women who served as spies. Some of these works have been heavily embellished, and the challenge was to separate fact from fiction. Where feasible, I have used the actual words of the spies to provide firsthand accounts and help readers visualize these remarkable ladies.

Also, I have conferred with historical organizations that have files on spies from their area, and I have scoured manuscripts and other materials in national and state archives. Rare, previously undiscovered newspaper clippings have been especially helpful. Several scholars, tour guides, and local historians have shared with me information and photographs never before published. And I have talked and corresponded with other individuals and groups knowledgeable about the subjects being investigated.

I feel that I have gotten to know most of the spies I have written about. They are fascinating, spirited individuals with stories at times so unbelievable that the reader will be forced to admit that truth is indeed stranger than fiction.

—H. Donald Winkler
Gatlinburg, Tennessee

1

REBEL QUEEN OF WASHINGTON SPIES

Rose Greenhow*

At least once a week—always at night—an elegant horse-drawn black carriage stopped at 398 West 16th Street, four blocks from the White House. A well-dressed, tall, stocky man with white hair stepped out of the carriage and entered the narrow but stately brick house. Neighbors in this fashionable section of the city stared through their lace curtains. They recognized the gentleman as James Buchanan, president of the United States. And as the visits continued throughout his presidency from 1856 to 1860, they gawked and gossiped. The president usually stayed well past midnight. What, they asked, was going on? What dubious role was the quiet lady of the house playing in national politics or in the president's personal life?

The lady he visited ever so frequently was a beautiful widow, Rose O'Neal Greenhow, the grande dame of Washington society, the "queen" of the Democratic administration, a cherished adviser to the president—a woman who would later write casually of her tête-à-têtes with the chief executive.

Rose's influence with Buchanan dated back to 1845, when Buchanan was secretary of state and Rose's late husband served under him. Now,

---

* Note: In this chapter, direct quotes from Allan Pinkerton are from his book, *The Spy of the Rebellion*. Direct quotes from Rose Greenhow are from her memoir, *My Imprisonment and the First Year of Abolition Rule at Washington*.

Rose was in her early forties, and Buchanan, known as "Old Buck," was in his midsixties. He was the only president who never married.

Newspapers described Rose as "the most persuasive woman ever known in Washington" and "a woman of almost irresistible seductive powers" who would do anything to get ahead. Whether or not she seduced the president is up for debate. Some thought he was devoid of sexuality; others said he was homosexual. But, unquestionably, he liked being around this accomplished, witty lady with sleek black hair, long legs, slim

Rose Greenhow, a very merry widow of a State Department official, developed an extensive Confederate spy network of forty-eight women and two men. She acquired verbatim reports of Lincoln's cabinet meetings and minutes of private conversations among Union generals.

waist, and ample bosom. So did countless other prominent men. Her fresh charm, vigor, and physical appearance generated a strong magnetic force that drew men of all ages to her. She was personally acquainted with all of the capital's leading men, and many of them had partaken of her hospitality. Her home became their rendezvous. Some called her "the Wild Rose."

Reaching Elite Circles

Rose had worked her way upward from a modest beginning. She was born around 1814 on a farm in Montgomery County, Maryland. Neighbors said she was high-spirited like her father, John O'Neal, a wheat and tobacco farmer and owner of fifteen slaves.

After O'Neal's sudden and tragic death, his widow, Eliza, and their five daughters fell on hard times. Desperate, she sent her two oldest daughters—Rose and Ellen—to live with their uncle and aunt, Henry and Maria Hill. Rose was about fourteen years old at the time.

The Hills ran the Congressional Boarding House across the street from the Capitol. It was a lodging for many congressmen and other VIPs. Rose quickly became their pet. She learned the ways of Washington—protocol, customs, places, subjects—and she forgot nothing. The Hills' most prestigious boarder, John C. Calhoun of South Carolina, served as vice president under two consecutive administrations (John Tyler and Andrew Jackson) and would become a U.S. senator for seventeen years. A strong advocate of slavery and states' rights, he called slavery "a positive good" rather than "a necessary evil." He claimed, "All societies are ruled by an elite group which enjoys the fruits of the labor of a less-privileged group."

As a teenager, Rose saw him often at the lodging house, and he became her mentor. She worshiped him. She would later speak fervently of the South's need to strike out for its rights. She said: "I am a Southern woman, born with revolutionary blood in my veins (related to the Lees, Randolphs, and Calverts), and my first ideas on State and Federal matters [were shaped] by the best and wisest man of this century."

At age seventeen she attracted her first important social escort—the gallant Cave Johnson of Tennessee, a future postmaster general. He introduced Rose to Washington society. On his arm she attended parties and receptions at all the right places. When women learned she was a nobody, they snubbed her. But men gave her a second chance. She conversed well, and she listened intently.

Next came a highly respected Virginian, Dr. Robert Greenhow. Although he was fourteen years older than Rose, no one dared gossip about the attention he paid her. Educated at William and Mary, Columbia, and the Sorbonne, he held medical and law degrees and had assisted Thomas Jefferson in obtaining anatomical castings for the fledgling University of Virginia. He was one of the three highest-paid officials in the U.S. State Department (at a thousand dollars a year), where he served as librarian and translator.

At age thirty-five in 1835 he was perhaps Washington's most eligible bachelor. That status ended on May 26 when he married Rose. The wedding was her first-class ticket to the elite circle of Washington society—a circle in which Rose was no longer snubbed. Even those who had once resented her now recognized her as "a leader, famous for her beauty, her brilliant conversation, her aptitude for intrigue, and her 'royal' manners." She had a knack for sizing up who was really important—not an easy task—and she built a network of powerful contacts.

The Greenhows attended posh diplomatic receptions, threw a party to honor Chief Justice Roger B. Taney and had tea with former first lady Dolley Madison, who for fifty years was the most important woman in America's social circles. Dolley took a special interest in Rose, and Rose tried to model herself after Dolley.

Fifteen years later, the Greenhows had moved to San Francisco. After Rose returned to Washington to see their older children, her husband fell six feet off of an elevated sidewalk, disabling his left leg and causing internal injuries. He died a few weeks later, on March 27, 1854. Rose filed a damage suit against the city of San Francisco and won a judgment of ten thousand dollars. And after lobbying influential friends, she received forty-two thousand dollars from Congress to make up for Robert's "salaries and incidental expenses" as a staff member of the Federally financed California Land Commission.

Rose plunged into politics and urged her close friend James Buchanan to run for president in 1856. Rose's support was partly personal. Buchanan was a Northern Democrat with Southern sympathies. The likely Republican candidate was John C. Frémont. His wife, Jessie, was Rose's social rival. If Frémont became president, Rose's social status would go into a freefall.

Although Buchanan didn't want to run, he received the nomination on the seventeenth ballot and accepted it. He defeated Frémont in the general election, carrying every slave state except Maryland and five Northern states. And because of Buchanan's close relationship with Rose, she became one of Washington's most powerful women.

Although Rose was closely associated with the Democratic administration, some of her best friends were Republicans—Sen. William H. Seward of New York, a future secretary of state, and Sen. Henry Wilson of Massachusetts, a future vice president.

Further contributing to Rose's social status was the marriage of her niece and namesake, Rose Adele Cutts, to Sen. Stephen A. Douglas, who would be Lincoln's chief rival for the presidency in 1860. Rose Cutts was a granddaughter of Dolley Madison.

Soon, Rose Greenhow was known as the go-to person for promotions or favors from legislators, army officials, and government personnel. She arranged meetings between interested parties in her new house on Sixteenth Street. She got results, and the people she helped became indebted to her.

Rose's reign as queen of the Democrats ended when Abraham Lincoln was elected president in 1860. South Carolina seceded from the Union, followed by six other states of the Deep South—Mississippi, Florida, Alabama, Georgia, Louisiana, and Texas—and four states of the Upper South—Virginia, Arkansas, North Carolina, and Tennessee. Jefferson Davis resigned from the Senate and was elected president of the Confederate States of America. Old-time Southerners in Washington packed up their belongings and rode south with their slaves to join the new Confederate government.

Among those who did not leave was Rose Greenhow. A Southerner to the bone, she once bragged that "no drop of Yankee blood ever polluted my veins." She wept in the Senate gallery on January 21, 1861, when Davis, one of her many influential friends, said farewell to the Senate.

Rose would remain in Washington and serve the South.

She Would Do "Anything"

Virginia Governor John Letcher laid the foundation for Confederate espionage work in Washington. He put in motion a spy nest by telling Col. Thomas Jordan, a Virginia-born West Point graduate, to recruit Rose Greenhow. Sometime in the spring of 1861, while still a U.S. Army officer, the handsome man with a dark beard called on Rose and asked her to be an agent. What was needed, he said, was quick, dependable information about troop movements, army supplies, and communications between governmental and army officials.

Rose accepted the mission enthusiastically. Unsparing in her denunciation of the "Abolition North," she openly declared that "instead of loving and worshipping the old flag of the Stars and Stripes," she saw "in it only the symbol of murder, plunder, oppression, and shame."

Jordan asked her what she would do to aid the Confederacy.

"Anything," she replied.

She said that, before the war, she had "employed every capacity with which God has endowed me, and the result was far more successful than my hopes could have flattered me to expect." She said she would do the same for the Confederacy.

Now in her midforties, Rose still radiated sensuality. At night, when she let down her hair, it extended below her waist. With her feminine wiles, she anticipated no problems in cajoling military secrets from those in the know.

That night, before Jordan left the house, he gave Rose a simple, twenty-six-symbol cipher code and told her to use his cover name, Thomas John Rayford, for sending him reports. He challenged her to gather in her own way information from the enemy—her former friends. Remember the admonition, he said, "All's fair in love and war."

Then he crossed the river into Virginia and shortly became the adjutant general (chief of staff) for Brig. Gen. P. G. T. Beauregard. A native of Louisiana and the hero of Fort Sumter, Beauregard had just arrived at Manassas, Virginia, from Charleston to take command of the Confederate Army of the Potomac. Sixty miles to the west, Brig. Gen. Joseph E. Johnston headed a Confederate army about half as large as Beauregard's. If their forces were combined, they would total about thirty-four thousand men. But there was no point in bringing them together unless they knew where they would be attacked.

Because the cipher was critical to her mission, Rose practiced writing the strange symbols for hours at a time. She was determined to get them right.

Rose sometimes used a word code in her espionage. For example, in a letter, she wrote, "Tell Aunt Sallie that I have some old shoes for children, and I wish her to send someone downtown to take them, and to let me know whether she has found any charitable person to help her take care of them." What the letter actually meant was: "I have some important information to send across the river and wish a messenger immediately."

Getting ciphered reports to Jordan involved an ever-changing "Secret Line," the name for the system used to get letters, intelligence reports, and other documents across the Potomac and Rappahannock rivers and into the hands of Confederate officers and officials. Rose's Secret Line began with a courier to whom she would entrust her reports. The courier would pass them to the next link in the chain of men and women who slipped in and out of taverns, farms, and waterfront docks along routes that connected Washington and Baltimore to the Confederacy.

Before long, Rose created the largest network of spies to exist during the Civil War, reaching as far as New Orleans and Boston. It included dentists, physicians, architects, clerks, professors, government workers, servants, and cooks. Her accomplices—she called them scouts—observed military movements around the capital and tapped official sources for military secrets.

In Washington, her closest conspirator was a young unmarried woman, Lillie Mackall. Lillie's bland and shy personality concealed a courageous woman who would do anything Rose asked. She was hardly noticeable as she listened outside government offices and made contacts with others in the network.

Among Rose's spies of high social status were banker William Smithson, who led a double life as Charles Cables, and Rose's dentist, Aaron Van Camp, who transmitted cipher messages. Not to be overlooked was Rose's boisterous eight-year-old daughter, Little Rose, who could curse with the best of them.

Meanwhile, pressure mounted in Washington for the Federals to attack the Confederates in northern Virginia. The press raised the cry, "On to Richmond!" The urgent questions for the Rebels were: When would they start? Where would they strike first? Answers to these questions would determine Confederate strategy.

To command the Union forces in and around Washington, Lincoln turned to Brig. Gen. Irvin McDowell. Paris-educated, the general spoke fluent French and played Mozart sonatas with the style of a professional pianist. Although he had never commanded troops in combat, he was an imaginative strategist. He brought together the recruits scattered around Washington and drilled them incessantly. By midsummer of 1861 the pressure to attack had reached a boiling point. While the troops were unready and inexperienced, Lincoln believed that Confederate forces were equally ill prepared. He ordered McDowell to launch an offensive against Beauregard and secure the important railroads thirty miles southwest of the capital at Manassas Junction, Virginia. Lincoln expected a quick victory, with McDowell then marching on to conquer Richmond.

In early July 1861 Rose Greenhow learned about Lincoln's order and McDowell's plan for a surprise attack, the size of the Union army going south, and the route of march. She probably finagled the information during her intimate contacts with Henry Wilson. As chairman of the Senate Military Affairs Committee, he was privy to many of the nation's vital secrets. After the war, Rose's spy supervisor, Colonel Jordan, said he was aware of their intimacy early in the war and that he had "induced her to get from Wilson all the information she could." Jordan said that Wilson was Rose's source for McDowell's orders to advance on Manassas.

Observing "officers and orderlies on horses...flying from place to place [and] the tramp of adorned men...heard on every side," Rose prepared a cipher dispatch telling of the intended advance. Her messenger was Bettie Duvall. Bettie was a beautiful, well-bred sixteen-year-old Southerner. On July 9 she disguised herself as a country girl selling sweet cream and buttermilk at the city market. Taking the reins of a farm cart, she headed out through Georgetown, riding by the headquarters of the 1st Massachusetts Infantry. She rumbled along a dirt road for several miles without interruption. As night approached she stopped at a plantation near Langley owned by the family of a friend. The next morning she abandoned her country attire and her cart and changed into a stylish riding habit. Borrowing a saddle horse, she cantered off toward the village of Fairfax Court House, which was about ten miles from Manassas Junction.

On the way, she came upon a Confederate outpost near Vienna and asked to see Brig. Gen. Milledge Bonham. He had just relinquished command to Beauregard, but Bonham had remained as his top aide. The soldiers escorted Bettie to Bonham's headquarters at Fairfax Court House.

"No, I won't see her," Bonham told the pickets. "She's probably a female spy dispatched by the Federals to assess our strength."

One of the soldiers asserted that she was prepared to take her message to Beauregard himself. He then added, "And she is very pretty."

Bonham relented. "Bring her in."

"I was very startled," Bonham later wrote, "at recognizing the face of a beautiful young lady, a brunette, with sparkling blue eyes, perfect features, glossy black hair." Bonham, a former U.S. congressman from South Carolina, remembered seeing her in the spectator gallery, where Southern ladies often gathered.

When Bonham agreed to forward her message to Beauregard, Bettie took out her tucking comb from a knot of hair at the back of her head. She shook loose her locks, releasing what Bonham described as "the longest and most beautiful roll of hair I have ever seen." Calmly, she "took then from the back of her head, where it had been safely tied, a small package, not larger than a silver dollar, sewed up in silk." In the packet was a note that, deciphered, said: "McDowell has certainly been ordered to advance on the sixteenth. R.O.G." (R.O.G. stood for Rose O'Neal Greenhow.)

With this message, Beauregard knew he would be attacked in less than a week. At once he began preparations and sent a courier to Jefferson Davis to urge immediate concentration of the scattered Confederate forces. Davis, however, hesitated, wanting more specifics.

But Bettie had successfully completed her mission.

One day before the predicted advance, Beauregard secretly sent a Washington native, George Donnellan, to call on Rose for confirmation. Donnellan and Rose were well acquainted, as he had once served as a clerk in the Department of the Interior.

When he reached her house, he knocked on the door, and after Rose had been awakened by a maid, he handed her a cipher from Jordan. "Trust bearer," it said.

She quickly scribbled a note in cipher: "Order issued for McDowell to move on Manassas

Bettie Duvall hid this coded message in a small silk purse tucked in her long hair, which she wound around her head.

tonight." She also advised that the Federals, fifty-five thousand strong, would advance via Fairfax Court House and Centreville.

Rose gave the message to Donnellan. By the time he had finished a quick breakfast and hidden the note in the hollowed-out heel of his boot, Rose's agents had arranged "lightning express" travel back to Beauregard. They used buggies, a ferry, and cavalry couriers. The dispatch was in Beauregard's hands that night.

Where did Rose get the information? She later said she "received a copy of the actual order to McDowell!" She had not used her powers in vain among the army's officers or in bed with Senator Wilson.

Beauregard telegraphed President Davis, and this time Davis ordered reinforcements from Johnston's twelve-thousand-man army sixty miles northwest in the Shenandoah Valley. Johnston loaded his army onto trains for the rush to aid Beauregard.

At midday on July 17, Rose received Jordan's reply: "Yours was received at eight o'clock at night. Let them come; we are ready for them. We rely upon you for precise information. Be particular as to description and destination of forces, quantity of artillery, etc."

She already had the information, and she sent a messenger back with the news that the Federals intended to cut the Manassas Gap Railroad in an effort to hold off Johnston's movement.

Right on Rose's schedule, McDowell's army marched toward Manassas on the afternoon of July 16. The army was joined by a jubilant party-minded group of Washington celebrities and their wives, many of whom had packed picnic baskets in their buggies.

On July 21 the Federals forded Bull Run near Manassas and assaulted the Confederates. The Southerners fell back, and the Federals appeared to be on the verge of victory. But the tide of battle shifted as Johnston's troops became engaged and a Virginia brigade commanded by Brig. Gen. Thomas J. Jackson stood unmovable "like a stone wall," giving birth to Jackson's permanent nom de guerre. Then, screaming the Rebel Yell, Johnston's reinforcements counterattacked, and McDowell's army turned and ran. The panicky retreat became a rout.

Rose heard the news of the Confederate victory in New York City, where she had spent the weekend. Upon returning to Washington by overnight train, she

Confederates won the First Battle of Manassas thanks in part to coded messages Rose sent to General Beauregard. Confederate President Jefferson Davis later thanked Rose for making the victory possible.

found and savored a message awaiting her from Colonel Jordan: "Our President and our General direct me to thank you. We rely upon you for further information. The Confederacy owes you a debt."

In the days immediately following the battle, Confederate sympathizers in the capital believed that their victorious army would march into Washington and take it. "Everything about the national capital betokened the panic of the Administration," Rose wrote in her memoir. "Preparations were made for the expected attack, and signals were arranged to give the alarm....A part of the plan was to cut the telegraph wires connecting the various military positions with the War Department [and] to make prisoners of [generals], thereby creating still greater confusion. Measures had also been taken to spike the guns in Fort Corcoran, Fort Ellsworth, and other important points, accurate drawings of which I had furnished to our commanding officers."

But Beauregard did not attack Washington, and wealthy Southerners continued to leave the city. Several army friends advised Rose to leave. "No," she said emphatically. She later wrote: "I resolved to remain conscious of the great service I could render my country...my position giving me remarkable facilities for obtaining information."

Rose sent at least nine more coded messages to Beauregard. Most included military information about the defenses and fortifications around Washington— the comings and goings of troops, railroad operations, and locations of hidden batteries. Other messages included items from newspapers with coded notes written in the margins. But Rose grew careless. She kept copies of some reports in her home—something a professional agent would never do. Even worse, she retained one report as she first wrote it and as she had encrypted it. Anyone finding it could crack the code and use it to transmit false information to Confederate commanders.

Meanwhile, Rose expanded her spy network to forty-eight women and two men, and more and more secrets flowed through the network to the Confederacy. Washington officials began to wonder if anything could be kept secret.

Rose was acquiring verbatim reports of Lincoln's cabinet meetings and minutes of private conversations of Maj. Gen. George B. McClellan, McDowell's successor. McClellan once explained his plans at a war council, and the next day they were known to the enemy. McClellan later said that the Rebels knew his

Dolley Madison, wife of America's fourth president, was Rose Greenhow's role model.

John C. Calhoun, the fierce-eyed former vice president from South Carolina, was Rose's mentor.

plans better than Lincoln or the cabinet. Four times he had been compelled to change them.

Although Rose frequently asserted that she had no intention of leaving Washington, she made a different statement to a friend, Martha Morris of Ohio, whose husband had taken a job in Lincoln's State Department. "I expect to be in Richmond soon," Rose reportedly told Martha, according to her memoir. Martha wrote that Rose had a risky escape plan—that she had stitched secrets about Union troop movements into the lining and cuffs of a gown and sewn a pearl-and-ivory tablet and contraband for Confederate soldiers into her voluminous quilted underskirt. She also intended to hide maps of Federal forts in twists of her waist-long hair.

Had she really planned to escape, she waited too long.

Someone—a lady who preferred not to be identified—suspected Rose was seducing Federal officials in return for military intelligence. She reported unusual activity around Rose's house to Thomas A. Scott, a recently appointed assistant secretary of war.

Scott brought in Allan Pinkerton, head of Lincoln's new Intelligence Service. His assignment was to find "secret traitorous organizations" and Confederate spies. Specifically, he was instructed to place Greenhow under surveillance. "Watch her house and every person entering or leaving," he was ordered.

Pinkerton used the name Maj. E. J. Allen, one of several aliases.

Pinkerton, aged forty-one, pioneered undercover work and surveillance as founder of America's first detective agency in Chicago in the 1850s. He foiled an alleged assassination plot earlier that year in Baltimore, while guarding Lincoln on his way to be inaugurated.

Pinkerton found and stopped many leaks in the Union government, but he paid particular attention to Rose Greenhow's residence. On the stormy night of August 22, he saw a Federal officer enter the house. Unable to see inside because of the home's elevated windows, Pinkerton removed his boots and stood on the shoulders of two agents. By turning the slats of the exterior blinds, he was able to see the entire parlor. Shortly, the visitor entered the parlor to await Rose. He was a tall, handsome man about forty years of age.

In the full glare of the gaslight he looked like an ideal soldier, but as Pinkerton watched him closely he noticed a troubled, restless look on the officer's face, and he appeared ill at ease as he shifted nervously in a chair.

When Rose entered the room, the officer's countenance changed. He smiled as he gazed upon her.

They sat at a table in the rear of the room, but their conversation was conducted in such low tones that Pinkerton could only catch fragments of their sentences. He heard enough, however, to convince him that this trusted officer was betraying his country.

The officer took a map from an inner pocket of his coat. Pinkerton recognized it as a plan of the fortifications in and around Washington. The officer pointed out particular points and positions. Then the two of them left the room, holding hands, and were gone for more than an hour. When Rose and her companion reentered the parlor, the officer went directly to the front door. They kissed, and he left.

Pinkerton, forgetting to put on his boots, followed him. When the officer glimpsed Pinkerton, he broke into a run, and the two of them raced through deserted rain-swept streets straight to the door of a provost-marshal station.

The officer reached the station first and vanished into a doorway. Four soldiers with bayonets then rushed out. They grabbed Pinkerton and marched him to the guardhouse.

About thirty minutes later, Pinkerton was taken upstairs to face the captain of the guard. To Pinkerton's astonishment, the captain was the man he had been following. Pinkerton later wrote: "He was pacing excitedly up and down the floor. Stopping immediately in front of me, he glared fiercely at me for some minutes without uttering a word." The captain then demanded his name.

"E. J. Allen," Pinkerton replied, using his pseudonym.

"What is your business?"

"I decline to answer any further questions."

"Take him back to the guardhouse," ordered the captain. Pinkerton later described it as "a most filthy and uncomfortable place" filled with drunken soldiers and common prisoners of the streets. "My clothes were still wet, and I shook like an aspen and my teeth chattered like castanets....One might more readily imagine that I had been fished out of the Potomac than that I was the chief of the Secret Service of the government."

Later that night, Pinkerton bribed a guard to carry a message to Thomas Scott in the War Department. A few hours later a sergeant appeared at the prison door and called for E. J. Allen. The sergeant took Pinkerton to the captain's office. The captain said to him: "The secretary of war has been informed of your arrest, and you will be conducted to him at once, and then we shall see if you will remain silent any longer."

At the War Department, Pinkerton was ushered into Scott's private office. Pinkerton briefed him on the events of the previous evening.

Scott rang a bell on his desk, and the officer who had imprisoned Pinkerton was admitted. Scott asked for details about the arrest of E. J. Allen. The captain replied that he had been visiting some friends, and while he was returning to his post late at night, he noticed that he was being followed. Afraid of being robbed, he had arrested the man.

"Did you see anyone last night who is hostile to our government?" Scott asked.

"No sir, I did not," he replied.

"Are you quite sure of that?" Scott inquired.

"I am, sir."

"In that case, you are under arrest. Surrender your sword at once."

"Mama's Been Arrested!"

On the same day that Pinkerton was freed from his incarceration—August 23—Rose was taking a leisurely stroll. One of her scouts passed her on the sidewalk and whispered that she was being watched. A second member of her spy ring then passed, and Rose told him: "Watch from the corner. If they arrest me, I'll raise my handkerchief."

Nonchalantly she walked to her house. Before she could enter it, Pinkerton stepped up. "You're Mrs. Greenhow, aren't you?"

"Yes. Who are you and what do you want here?"

"I've come to arrest you."

"Prove your authority!"

"It is verbal authority from the War Department and the State Department."

Rose signaled her agent by raising her handkerchief to her lips. She turned to Pinkerton in an icy rage: "I have no power to resist you, but had I been inside my house I would have killed you before submitting to this illegal process."

Pinkerton ordered her to open the door. He and another agent escorted her into the house.

She recalled later: "Men rushed into my chamber, into every sanctuary. They searched everywhere!"

Detectives dismantled beds, checked footboards and headboards, knocked apart chairs and tables, and removed photographs from their frames. They found Rose's small leather diary with several pages of notes about military operations. They also found a seven-page copy of orders from the War Department giving the organizational plan to increase the size of the regular army. Inside the kitchen stove they found singed scraps of incriminating letters.

Pinkerton wanted to keep the arrest a secret. He instructed his men to lay low. But the back door had been left unguarded, and eight-year-old Little Rose—Rose's daughter—ran outside and screamed, "Mama's been arrested! Mama's been arrested!"

Detectives ran after her. With her head start, she had time to climb a tree, and from one of its limbs, she hung over the garden wall and called out to the neighbors: "Mama's been arrested!" The detectives eventually pulled her down, but she had accomplished her mission.

At 3:00 p.m., Rose's chief assistant, Lillie Mackall, and her sister showed up at the house to check on their friend. Detectives seized them. Frightened, Lillie hugged Rose and wept. "I did not know what they had done with you," she said. Then, in a whisper, Lillie reminded Rose that they had left some of Colonel Jordan's letters in the library, as well as a dispatch of their own they had planned to send to Jordan that day. Perhaps it was too late. Maybe the

Federal agents seized this coded letter from Rose's house on August 23, 1861.

detectives had already found the papers. Rose had either to secure them or burn down the house during the night.

Rose also worried about documents in her pockets and feigned an illness so she could dispose of them. "The heat is making me sick," she told a guard. "I must change my dress."

The guard nodded his approval, and she darted upstairs to her boudoir and shut the door. She pulled several documents from her pockets and threw them into the fireplace. One contained the cipher code.

The guard, however, sensed his mistake, went upstairs, rapped on her door, and walked in. As he entered, Rose grabbed a revolver from a drawer and aimed it at his head. Reacting swiftly, the detective seized it. Then a female detective came in to conduct a strip search.

"I was allowed the poor privilege of unfastening my own garments," Rose reported, "which one by one were received by this pseudo-woman and carefully examined, until I stood in my linen." When the search was finished, Rose dressed herself and went downstairs.

When she looked out the window, Rose gasped. Two of her agents were coming down the street. She waved them away, her hand making forward thrusts. A detective grabbed her arm so hard that he bruised it, but the alerted agents successfully fled. Other visitors weren't as lucky. Throughout the day and evening, everyone who came by the house was arrested.

Later that evening, Pinkerton needed to run an errand, so he left the house, leaving several detectives to stand guard. Not having anything better to do, the detectives discovered the brandy cabinet and began drinking. This gave Rose and Lillie a chance to go to the upstairs bedroom. When the guard there took a break, Rose tiptoed into the library, took a book from a shelf, and removed incriminating documents from its hollow interior.

When the guard returned, the two ladies were lying on the bed. While he stood at the door, Rose slipped the message for Jordan under the sheet to Lillie, who later succeeded in forwarding the message to the spymaster.

Rose was placed under house arrest. Other women were arrested the same day and also incarcerated in Rose's house. When the news was made public, the press called the home "Fort Greenhow." It was officially named "the House of Detention for Female Rebels." Detectives remained there for a week. They unpacked stored boxes of fine china and crystal, examined every drawer and shelf, flipped through books in the library, and removed charred but legible strips of paper remaining in the fireplaces. In the books they discovered Rose's drawings of fortifications. The charred paper scraps, when pieced together, formed cipher messages and bits of letters with military information.

HOUSE OF DETENTION FOR FEMALE REBELS   CORNER OF K AND SIXTEENTH STREETS   WASHINGTON

In August of 1861, the Federals turned Rose's home into a makeshift prison for women spies.

Clearly, Rose had been careless. And not just in her handling of traitorous material. Detectives also found a bundle of thirteen steamy love letters tied together with a yellow ribbon and marked: "Letters from H., not to be opened—but burned in case of death or accident." They were from an unidentified congressman infatuated with Rose—a political bigwig with access to the kind of information Rose wanted. One message was written on congressional stationery and dated January 30, 1861. It spoke of spies who might be watching them and of the need for secrecy. Here are excerpts from four letters:

For the last few days every movement and act of mine have been watched with Hawk-eyed vigilance. For your sake more than my own I have been compelled to be cautious. But tomorrow at 10 a.m. I will see you at all hazards. H.

You know I love you—and will sacrifice anything. I have feared bringing you into trouble—for I repeat to you that spies are put upon me, but I will try to elude them tonight, and once more we can have a happy hour in spite of fate. H.

We are...considering the Pacific Railroad Bill....I will not fail you to-night, and will bring you the thing of which we spoke last night. Bless you always. H.

You know that I do love you. I am suffering this morning; in fact I am sick physically and mentally, and know nothing that would soothe me so much as an hour with you. And tonight, at whatever cost, I will see you. Yours, H.

The letters are believed to be from Rose's intimate source of military secrets, Senator Henry Wilson of Massachusetts, who lived with his ailing wife, Harriet, in a boardinghouse for congressmen. As noted earlier, the powerful chairman of the Senate Military Affairs Committee was sharing more than tea and crumpets with a Confederate spy.

Pinkerton, however, did not follow up on Wilson. The letters apparently were slipped to the secretary of the Senate for safekeeping and are now stored at the National Archives. The Senate has a long history of taking care of its own.

Other materials found in the house implicated key members in Rose's band of conspirators: dentist Aaron Van Camp; government clerks William Walker and F. Rennehan; George Donnellan, who had carried a message to Manassas; and banker William Smithson. Pinkerton watched them closely. He believed they would trap themselves.

A week after Rose Greenhow's informal imprisonment, the home of her close friend and neighbor Eugenia Phillips was raided by Federal officials. Her letters and other papers were ransacked, and she and two of her daughters and a sister were imprisoned in the attic of Fort Greenhow. They were not allowed to speak to Rose.

Among the Phillipses' powerful Federal friends in Washington was Edwin M. Stanton. He had worked with Eugenia's husband on legal cases before the Supreme Court and was about to become Lincoln's secretary of war. Stanton arranged for the Phillips family to return to the South, out of reach of Federal authorities. The Phillipses were given three days' access to their home to pack their belongings and prepare to leave the capital.

When Rose learned of this situation, she saw an opportunity to communicate with Jefferson Davis. She wrote a note and placed it in a ball of pink worsted yarn. She gave the ball to Little Rose with instructions on what to do with it on her daily walk—supervised by a guard. So as Little Rose walked past the Phillips residence, she tossed the ball of yarn through an open window, shouting lightheartedly, "Here is the yarn you left at my house, Mrs. Phillips." The gullible guard thought nothing of it.

Eugenia knew she hadn't left any yarn and immediately understood that the ball must contain a message.

On their way south, the Phillipses went through Richmond and delivered the yarn to President Davis. He unwound it and found the cipher dispatch.

Back in Washington, Lillie Mackall's dedication and loyalty to Rose Greenhow prompted her to ask to be taken into custody and imprisoned at the house. From then on, said Rose, they were "inseparable," and Lillie served as an extra pair of eyes for her.

One day Lillie noticed and disposed of a blotter Rose had used on a dispatch to Jordan at Manassas. The words were clearly visible.

Eventually, Union officials realized that Lillie was transmitting messages for Rose, and they ordered her to leave Fort Greenhow, an unusual demand. She objected—an unusual response—but was forced out. That winter Lillie caught a severe cold. She died on December 12 at age twenty-two.

When Rose heard of Lillie's death, she was heartbroken. She sent a note to her onetime friend, Secretary of State Seward, requesting permission to attend the funeral. Seward replied through the provost marshal: "Her correspondence with [Beauregard] renders improper all interference in her behalf."

Around October 10, Ellie M. Poole of Virginia was added to the list of female spies housed at Fort Greenhow. She had been arrested in Wheeling, West Virginia, for sneaking documents into the city by hiding them in the lining of her guitar case. Her stay at Fort Greenhow was short. Although suffering from a severe attack of rheumatism, she escaped through the basement and took refuge in a neighboring house, staying just ahead of searching Federal officials. A few months later, Ellie was captured in Vincennes, Indiana, by the relentless Federal detective Delos Thurman Blythe. She was incarcerated in the Old Capitol Prison until her release in June 1862.

Rumors reached Rose that she might be tried for treason. "Let it come," she responded. "There will be rich revelations."

A number of congressional and high government officials lost sleep over the possibility.

Magically Sending Out Messages

Although Federal agents restricted Rose's writing materials, sealed her windows, and cut off all apparent avenues of communication with possible co-conspirators, Rose somehow continued the flow of information in and out of the house. In her memoir she wrote about "peculiar square" dispatches to President Davis, a "bird" that flew to Confederate territory, and "a vocabulary of colors, which though not a very prolific language, served my purpose."

To get some messages out, Rose seduced her guards. She smiled at them and flattered them. When the detectives were replaced with a detachment of McClellan's headquarters guard—the Sturgis Rifles—Rose selected one of them for personal attention: Lt. Nathaniel E. Sheldon. Before long he was providing her with writing paper and allowing her to have periods of privacy. He even intervened when the prison doctor, a heavyset man named Stewart, announced he was going to inspect her "sanitary condition" daily.

Pinkerton worked persistently for weeks to secure evidence against Rose's top spies, especially the dentist Van Camp and the banker Smithson. Shortly, Union forces captured a blockade-runner and found letters incriminating both of them. Then they caught an army physician trying to escape to the Confederacy. He told officials that Van Camp provided the horse and buggy he used. Pinkerton arrested the whole bunch.

Incoming mail to Rose received careful scrutiny. When they inspected a cake that had been sent to her, officials discovered treasury notes that were obviously intended to help her buy her way out.

One letter Rose sneaked out of Fort Greenhow was addressed to Secretary of State Seward. She demanded to know why she had been arrested without a warrant and kept captive in her own house and why her property had been seized. She also was able to have a copy of the letter sent to the Richmond newspapers. They published it in full.

That stunt, however, resulted in more restrictions. Her windows were nailed shut. No one was allowed to talk to her. She was not allowed to see any newspapers. And her friend Lieutenant Sheldon was prohibited from having any personal communication with her. Still, she transmitted a second letter to Seward, this one even more inflammatory than the first, and it, too, was published in Richmond. Here are portions of it:

> *You have suspended the law throughout the land, and, by your secret police, hold the assassin's knife at the throats of your own people. The mist of fanaticism, which makes them for the present but blind instruments in your hands, will pass away; and he who raises the whirlwind does not always ride upon it into a harbor of safety....We may not successfully compete with you in the open field, but we will then defeat you by stratagem. And beware lest you drive us to secret organization, or you in your day may experience that the vengeance of man is swifter than that of Heaven. No, Sir, you cannot subdue a people endowed with such a spirit of resistance; and although we may yet wade through oceans of blood, we will achieve our independence, or leave our whole Southern land one howling wilderness, and a monument to all future times of the crimes of your party.*

Seward and several War Department officials grew wary. They decided to move her to the Old Capitol Prison, a dingy brick building across the street from the Capitol. The Old Capitol Prison had once been her aunt's boardinghouse. There, Rose had spent her teenage years, succumbed to the secessionist enchantments of John C. Calhoun, and attended to Calhoun during his dying hours. But this was a different place now. It was a filthy place with spider webs, grimy walls, and an overwhelming stench. The prison housed accused spies, Yankee deserters, blockade-runners, captured Confederate soldiers, and civilians of questionable loyalty.

Rose and Little Rose were led to their cell by the prison's superintendent, William P. Wood. In it was a straw bed swarming with bedbugs, a wooden table and chairs, and one glass.

Little Rose looked up at Wood and boldly said, "You have one of the hardest little rebels here you ever saw, but if you get along with me as well as Lieutenant Sheldon, you will have no trouble!"

Rose disliked the other women in the prison. She wrote that associating with them was "but a shade less obnoxious" than sharing a bench with the black prisoners. Actually she shared a section of the prison with blacks and complained bitterly about it. She wrote, "The language which fell upon my ear, and

The Old Capitol Prison. Today, the Supreme Court building stands on the site.

sights which met my eye, were too revolting to be depicted—for it must be remembered that these creatures were of both sexes, huddled together indiscriminately, as close as they could be packed."

For several weeks Rose and Little Rose were not permitted outside. When Rose was finally allowed to exercise in the yard, she antagonized her jailers with haughty theatrics. One day, for example, she leaped into a cart. While male prisoners pulled her around, she shouted, "I'm off for Dixie!" Her declaration would soon come true.

Rose should have been tried for espionage, but Federal authorities rejected that option, fearing

Rose and eight-year-old Little Rose in front of the window to their room in the Old Capitol Prison. Boards were nailed across the window to prevent Rose from passing messages to couriers on the outside.

potential scandals. She knew too much about them, and on trial, she would have implicated and embarrassed numerous top-ranking Union officials and civil servants. In court, "Wild Rose" could make or break the career of almost any man in the city. No, she wouldn't go on trial.

Instead, she appeared before a commission in March 1862. One of its two members was Maj. Gen. John A. Dix, a prominent figure often seen in Rose's company in the prewar years.

Rose took her place at a long table, midway between the commissioners.

There is no record of any witnesses for or against her. The evidence seems to have consisted solely of the papers found in her house. She summed up the hearing in her memoir:

"You are charged with treason."

"I deny it."

"You are charged, madam, with holding communication with the enemy in the South."

"If this were an established fact, you should not be surprised at it; I am a Southern woman."

"How is it, madam, that you have managed to communicate, in spite of the vigilance exercised over you?"

"That is my secret!"

"What is the source of your military information?"

"If Mr. Lincoln's friends will pour into my ears such important information, am I to be held responsible?"

That was the essence of it, along with her refusal to take the oath of allegiance to the Union. The commission sentenced Rose to be exiled to the Confederacy.

Secret Mission to Europe

When Rose arrived in Richmond, she was welcomed as a conquering heroine by Confederate leaders. Jefferson Davis supposedly heaped praise on her: "But for you, there would have been no [victory at] Bull Run." That was the proudest moment of her life, she wrote in her memoir.

Davis instructed Secretary of State Judah P. Benjamin to give her twenty-five hundred dollars out of the Secret Service's funds for her "valuable and patriotic services." And that summer they sent her on a special mission to Europe, so secret that its purpose is still unknown. What is known is that she met with

Napoleon III at the Tuileries Palace and Queen Victoria in London, attended weekend parties at the homes of Lady Franklin and Lady Gray, and was invited to discuss politics over tea at the residence of the eminent British essayist, historian, and philosopher Thomas Carlyle.

Among England's royalty, she met Lord Granville, leader of the House of Lords. A widower, Granville had lost his wife in 1860 and was seeking a new mate. Supposedly, Rose Greenhow was to become that mate. They had an openly romantic relationship in England.

Years later, Rose's European address book surfaced in England with a note written next to a name by one of Rose's daughters and intended for a granddaughter. It read: "If your grandmother had not died, you would have been his granddaughter. He was mummy's chum and [she planned to] marry him."

The note was attached to the name of Baron Wharncliffe, who was one of two Granvilles in the book. Since he was married and ten years younger than Rose, the note writer probably mistook him for the other Granville.

Rose delivered correspondence from President Davis to the senior Confederate official in England, and a few days later that official gave up his post. Shortly thereafter Rose wrote a twelve-page letter to Davis. Its bottom line was that sentiment had turned against the South in both England and France.

While in England, Rose secured a publisher for a memoir she had written about her imprisonment. It was published before she left Europe. The *New York Times* called the book "as bitter as a woman's hate can make it....Many may wonder, not that she was treated with such severity, but that she got off so easily."

Perhaps her most important personal business in Europe was finding a suitable school for her beloved Little Rose. She placed her in the Convent of the Sacred Heart in Paris. It was a Catholic boarding school. She would live with two hundred students from across Europe.

After remaining abroad for more than two years, Rose Greenhow boarded the blockade-runner *Condor* on August 10, 1864. Its ports of call were Bermuda, Halifax, and Wilmington, North Carolina—the last if it could run the Union blockade.

Undoubtedly, her plans were to return to England later that year, marry Lord Granville, and remain in England. She would not have left her future husband in London and her darling Little Rose in Paris and risked her life to run the blockade unless she had very important business to discuss face-to-face with Jefferson Davis.

The *Condor* was a three-funneled steamer, newly built, and on her first trip as a blockade-runner. She was commanded by a veteran of the Crimean War, Englishman Augustus Charles Hobart-Hampden, variously known to the blockade-running fleet as Captain Roberts, Hewett, or Gulick.

After dark on September 30, the *Condor* fought heavy gales as she arrived opposite the mouth of the Cape Fear River, the entry to Wilmington, and stole swiftly through the blockade. She was almost in the mouth of the river, only two hundred yards from shore, when suddenly there loomed in the darkness a vessel dead ahead.

The captain was frightened. He was sure it was a Federal gunboat. He swerved his ship sharply, and she drove hard on New Inlet bar. Actually, the ship he saw was the wreck of the blockade-runner *Nighthawk*, which had been run down the previous night.

Dawn was near breaking, and a real Union gunboat, the USS *Niphon*, began to close in.

At Confederate Fort Fisher, a short distance off, the commander realized the *Condor's* plight and shouted an order: "Fire at the Yankees. Keep them back!" The guns held back the Federal ship, and for a while the passengers were safe.

Meanwhile, Rose and two other passengers—both Confederate agents—debated their options. Then she went topside to find the captain.

"You must lower a lifeboat for us!" she demanded. "You must do it for us!"

"Too risky," replied the captain, shaking his head.

"We'll take our chances," she exclaimed.

Reluctantly, the captain agreed. The two agents joined Rose as a lifeboat was lowered toward the rough water.

Two hundred yards. That's all they had to cover.

The little boat rocked back and forth, back and forth, then spun about, pitched high on a powerful wave, sank in a low trough of water, and overturned. The three had to swim for the shore.

Rose, however, was weighted down by her heavy black-silk dress and a bag of gold sovereigns worth more than two thousand dollars, which she had fastened around her waist. The money, much of it from her book royalties, was believed to be destined for the Confederate treasury. A good swimmer, Rose would have made it to shore had it not been for the weight of her bulging belt. The weight forced her downward, and she drowned, carrying with her not only the gold but also anxiously awaited dispatches. The other agents succeeded in getting ashore.

Rose's body washed up on the beach the next day. A Confederate soldier stumbled upon it and stared at the bag of gold. He ripped it from her, and pushed her body back into the river.

A few hours later the body washed up again and was recovered by a search party. When the soldier who had taken the gold realized

This cipher, found on Rose's body after she drowned, provides a key to the messages she sent to Confederate commanders.

he had robbed the body of a Confederate hero, he confessed and surrendered the treasure.

Searchers found a copy of her book, *My Imprisonment*, hidden on her person. There was a note inside the book, intended for her daughter, Little Rose. It is not known how the writing was legible after being submerged for so long; it is possible the note was wrapped in protective materials. It read: "London, Nov. 1st 1863: You have shared the hardships and indignity of my prison life, my darling; And suffered all that evil which a vulgar despotism could inflict. Let the memory of that period never pass from your mind; Else you may be inclined to forget how merciful Providence has been in seizing us from such a people."

On October 1, Rose O'Neal Greenhow was buried in Oakdale Cemetery in Wilmington with full military honors. A Confederate flag was wrapped about her coffin. The minister spoke of "the quiet sleeper, who after many storms and a tumultuous and checkered life, came to peace and rest at last."

Every Memorial Day since her interment, a leaf of laurel leaves has been placed upon her grave for her contributions to the Confederate cause. A simple marble cross, erected by the Ladies' Memorial Society, bears the inscription: "Mrs. Rose O'N. Greenhow, A Bearer of Dispatches to the Confederate Government."

President Davis grieved over the loss of his valuable spy while powerful men who had known her all too well in Washington breathed more easily, knowing their reputations could no longer be soiled by the devious grande dame.

While many Southern leaders praised Rose and her activities, perhaps the greatest tribute came from the abolitionist Massachusetts senator Charles Sumner, who said, "She was worth any six of Jeff Davis's regiments."

VANISHED WITHOUT A TRACE

Sarah Slater

Sarah Antoinette Slater was called "mysterious," "the French woman," and "the lady in the veil." She was all three plus one more: a clever Confederate agent.

Sarah was so mysterious that she was misidentified by her enemies and by other Confederate agents. A congressional committee believed she was Olivia Floyd. They were wrong. Three prominent historians said she was also known as Kate Thompson. The real Kate Thompson would have resented that. A fellow agent introduced Sarah as Mrs. Brown, an alias Sarah used.

Sarah Slater *was* Sarah Slater. And she had an interesting background, daunting missions, and a disappearing act second to none.

She came from solid American stock—Grandfather Ebenezer Gilbert of Middletown, Connecticut, who fought in the American Revolution—and parents with just enough French blood to give her the courage of Joan of Arc. Sarah's grandfather married a pretty French girl from Martinique. Their son, Joseph Gilbert (Sarah's father), married an equally attractive eighteen-year-old French girl, Antoinette, born in Trinidad. Joseph and Antoinette lived in Martinique about eight years before moving to Middletown, Connecticut. Sarah Antoinette Gilbert was born there on January 12, 1843. She had three brothers and one sister.

Sarah would become so effective and elusive in her Civil War espionage work that she probably would be unknown today if Louis J. Weichmann hadn't opened a door to detectives during the early morning hours of April 15, 1865.

Union Secretary of War Edwin M. Stanton.

Only hours earlier, President Abraham Lincoln had been shot by John Wilkes Booth at Ford's Theatre in Washington, D.C. Secretary of War Edwin M. Stanton and the superintendent of the Washington city police, A. C. Richards, both knew that John H. Surratt Jr. was one of Booth's close associates. Around 2:00 a.m. Richards acted on his own initiative and sent four detectives to the boardinghouse of Surratt's mother, Mary Surratt. But John Surratt was not there. In fact, he was nowhere near Washington on April 14.

Louis Weichmann, a twenty-two-year-old War Department clerk and friend of John Surratt, was one of Mrs. Surratt's boarders. He responded to the knocks at the door and faced the four city detectives. Weichmann's involvement in or knowledge of the conspiracy against Lincoln is unclear. He apparently sought to join the earlier plot to kidnap Lincoln but was turned down by both Surratt and Booth because he could neither ride nor shoot.

According to Weichmann, he told the detectives that Surratt was in Montreal, Canada, and he volunteered to do all he could to assist them. He joined the detectives in a search of the Surrattsville area and later accompanied them to Montreal to look for Surratt. They could not find him.

Weichmann, as part of his "tell-all" testimony, linked both John Surratt and his mother, Mary, to the conspiracy. But he also stated that a mysterious Mrs. Slater, who had visited the boardinghouse, was close to Booth, the Surratts, and the other conspirators. That information caught Stanton's attention.

Weichmann told officials that Slater was a French-speaking Confederate agent from North Carolina who carried dispatches to the Confederate organization working out of Montreal. He said she had been to Mrs. Surratt's boardinghouse twice in recent weeks, and once had remained all night. But, he added, none of the boarders ever got a good look at her, "as she always wore a [thick] veil over her face."

"Find her!" ordered Stanton. He believed she was involved in the plot to kill Lincoln and had carried dispatches about the plot between Richmond and Montreal.

Her name came up dozens of times during the 1865 conspiracy trial and the 1867 trial of John Surratt. But no witness could give her first name, and several of them weren't sure that Slater was her real name. "The government did its best to find out who the woman was, but was unable to find her," Weichmann later wrote.

If they did their best, as Weichmann asserted, their best was pathetic. Had they read two Hartford, Connecticut, newspapers in June 1865 or visited the town of New Bern, North Carolina, they could have learned much about Mrs. Slater.

Her father, Joseph Gilbert, taught French at a high school in Middletown, Connecticut, and manufactured pills. In 1858, when Sarah was fifteen, her parents separated. Mrs. Gilbert took Sarah and her brother Robert with her and moved to Hartford and then to New York City. While the children were only in the Big Apple a few months, Sarah learned enough about the area to enhance her later service to the Confederacy as a courier and spy operating through the city to Canada.

Meanwhile, Sarah's father migrated south to Kinston, North Carolina, with the two other sons. About two years later Sarah and Robert joined them there, and, almost immediately, Mr. Gilbert and the two sons who were there with him packed up their belongings and relocated to Goldsboro, about twenty-five miles west of Kinston. Sarah and Robert, apparently very close and not wanting to remain with the family, went the opposite direction—twenty-five miles east—to New Bern, a busy little seaport. It was the winter of 1860–61. War loomed on the horizon.

At New Bern, Sarah boarded in the home of J. L. Pennington, publisher of the *Daily Progress*. Within days of her arrival, he introduced her to Rowan Slater, who operated a dancing and waltzing academy in New Bern. Pennington was Slater's friend and a patron of the arts.

Sarah was then eighteen years old. Rowan, twenty-six, was an accomplished musician and a graduate of Trinity College (now Duke University). He was from an old and highly respected family in Salisbury, North Carolina, near Charlotte. After college, Rowan became a traveling instructor in stringed instruments and ballroom dancing. He settled in New Bern in the early spring of 1859 and opened his academy.

Sarah, known as "Nettie" to Rowan and her friends, soon fell in love with the musician.

Then, on April 12–13, 1861, the Confederates bombarded Fort Sumter in Charleston Harbor, starting the Civil War. Sarah's three brothers took up arms

New Bern, North Carolina, was Sarah's home when she was 18. There she met her future husband, Rowan Slater.

for the Confederacy. Rowan closed his academy on April 26. Sarah, with no other members of her family in New Bern, joined her father in Goldsboro in the spring of 1861. Rowan Slater also moved to Goldsboro and secured a position as a purchasing agent.

Two months later, on June 12, 1861, Sarah and Rowan became husband and wife.

Sometime between April and July 1863, Sarah and Rowan took up residence on a Slater farm just outside Salisbury, the family seat of the highfalutin Slaters. One relative remembered driving to the farm for a watermelon get-together on a Sunday afternoon. But farm life was not the kind of life that the cultured Sarah Antoinette had envisioned for herself. So six months after Rowan enlisted in the 20th North Carolina Infantry, Sarah left the farm and went to Richmond, Virginia, the Confederate capital. Rowan never saw her again.

Stanton's investigators could have uncovered all of this background material easily in 1865, but what happened next was much harder to document.

In Richmond in mid-January 1865, Sarah Slater met with two North Carolina congressmen—Burgess S. Gaither and James G. Ramsay. She asked them to persuade Maj. J. H. Carrington, the provost marshal of Richmond, to issue her a pass through Confederate lines so she could go to New York City and live with her mother. The congressmen supported her request. In their letter to Carrington they said: "She has lost her only brother in the Confederate Army, and we have no hesitation in vouching for the loyalty of this lady and her high social position and hope she will meet with no difficulty in passing the lines of our army."

Carrington endorsed the request, but he forwarded it to Secretary of War James A. Seddon for action.

There was one misstatement in the Gaither-Ramsay letter.

Sarah had three brothers in the army, not one, but the one she referred to—Pvt. Frederick G. Gilbert—died of natural causes at the age of seventeen. Sarah did not mention the other two brothers because they had been convicted of persuading other soldiers to desert the army. Gen. Robert E. Lee had set aside the conviction, and the two brothers left a camp near Kinston and were last seen heading for New Bern, then in Union hands. That's the last that was heard of them. Both were dropped from the Confederate army rolls.

Seddon undoubtedly gave Sarah's request careful, personal attention. He even met with her and questioned her. She was barely twenty-two. He liked what he saw. She was beautiful, unafraid, spunky, and daring—qualities that would be highly useful on the Richmond-Montreal courier route. Union officers would be too swayed by her beauty and personality to even consider her being an enemy agent. Further, Sarah's fluency in French would enable her to blend in with the Montreal population. If caught she could claim French citizenship and appeal to French diplomatic representatives for help.

Having nothing better to do, and intrigued by the excitement of spy work, Sarah accepted the offer to carry dispatches to and from Montreal. Seddon needed her to convey some documents immediately. A crisis was brewing in Canada. The Confederacy's Canadian office had been turned into a terrorist organization, and its agents were carrying out complex covert operations and attempting to foment a rebellion by the antiwar parties in the North.

In one instance, twenty-one Confederate soldiers in civilian clothes had robbed banks in St. Albans, Vermont, and would have burned the town had they not been chased back to Canada by the infuriated villagers. Fourteen of the raiders were caught and imprisoned and faced extradition to the United States if they could not prove they were soldiers on a mission. Extradition, however, meant death by hanging.

Documents were needed from Richmond to establish their military status. The usual underground channels and relays of couriers could not be used. These documents had to be delivered to a Montreal court by the same hand that had received them from official sources in Richmond. Seddon needed a new face on the route, and Sarah seemed perfect for the mission.

She was on her way on January 31, 1865.

From Richmond, Sarah Slater traveled to the Rappahannock River ferry at Port Royal, Virginia, and on to a Confederate signal corps camp near the mouth of Mattox Creek on the Virginia side of the Potomac River. Augustus "Gus" Howell, one of the most effective Confederate agents operating in southern Maryland, met her there. They were rowed across the wide river at night and put ashore in Maryland. From there, in-place Confederate agents rendezvoused with them and provided food, shelter, and transportation. Sarah and Howell probably took a stagecoach from Leonardtown, Maryland, to Washington. Howell accompanied her all the way to New York City, arriving there about February 12–13. He then came back to Mary Surratt's boardinghouse in Washington to await Sarah's return from Canada.

Sarah traveled by train to Montreal and registered at the St. Lawrence Hotel at 3:00 a.m. on February 15, 1865. The hotel, Montreal's best, was the unofficial headquarters of the Confederate operation in Canada. Here, the so-called Canada Cabinet of the Confederacy conducted business. John Wilkes Booth met with the group four months earlier, probably to plan a kidnapping of President Lincoln.

After only a few hours' sleep, Sarah, heavily veiled, entered the Montreal courtroom, clutching a large envelope in her hand. She claimed to be a Kentucky widow, and she handed the package to the Confederate counsel. When the packet was opened, he found copies of commissions and other official papers that sanctioned the St. Albans raid. Thus extradition was denied, and the raiders were freed.

Sarah met with high-ranking Confederate officials at the St. Lawrence and was given urgent dispatches to deliver to Secretary of State Judah P. Benjamin in Richmond. During her return trip, she linked up with John Surratt in New York City, and he accompanied her to Washington. In the capital city he secured a horse and buggy, and near dusk Sarah and Surratt drove up to his mother's boardinghouse. Gus Howell came out and got into the buggy with Sarah. Within moments, they headed for Port Tobacco, near the Potomac River in southern Maryland.

George Atzerodt, one of Booth's co-conspirators, had ridden down to Port Tobacco to row them across the river to Virginia.

Once in Virginia, Sarah continued to Richmond and made the urgent delivery.

She embarked on two more missions to Canada in March and April. She broke up the first trip by staying in Washington at Mary Surratt's boardinghouse on the afternoon and night of Wednesday,

Confederate Secretary of State Judah P. Benjamin worked closely with Sarah Slater and John Surratt.

March 15. Louis Weichmann had to give up his room to Sarah that night. She supposedly kept to herself all evening and left for Canada early the next day. While she was in her room, three of Booth's conspirators were in another room, sitting on a bed amid spurs, bowie knives, and revolvers.

Two days later, Booth's team attempted to capture Lincoln as he rode in his carriage to a hospital for invalid servicemen. Lincoln, however, changed his schedule at the last minute, and the kidnapping went awry.

Sarah arrived in Montreal on March 17 with dispatches from Secretary of State Benjamin for Jacob Thompson and Brig. Gen. Edwin G. Lee. Thompson, a Mississippian who had been secretary of the interior in the James Buchanan administration, headed the Confederacy's team of clandestine operatives in Canada. Lee, a second cousin of Robert E. Lee, was the ranking military official. Lee, however, was preparing to take over the Canadian apparatus. Thompson was in deep trouble with the Canadian government over the St. Albans raid and other covert operations, and he was about to be charged with violating Canada's neutrality.

Sarah departed Montreal on March 23 with their responses for Judah Benjamin.

These exchanges reflect not only the turmoil in Canada but also the frantic situation in which the Confederate government found itself. Robert E. Lee was under siege at Petersburg, Virginia. Union Gen. William T. Sherman was advancing up the Carolinas. And the Confederate Congress was in a fit of contention with President Jefferson Davis. It was symptomatic of the need to blame someone for the crisis encompassing all of them.

From New York, Sarah took an overnight train to Washington, traveling with John Wilkes Booth. Conspirator George Atzerodt, who was quite taken with Sarah, said in his confession after the assassination, "Mrs. Slater went with Booth a good deal....She stopped at the National Hotel [where Booth resided]."

When the train reached Washington at seven thirty in the morning, Booth went straight to the hotel. John Surratt picked up Sarah in a rented four-seated carriage pulled by two white horses. He drove to his mother's boardinghouse, and Mary Surratt stepped into the carriage. They proceeded to her tavern at Surrattsville, Maryland, some ten miles south of the Navy Yard Bridge. There, Gus Howell was supposed to meet them and escort Sarah to Richmond with the Montreal dispatches. But Federal cavalry had raided the tavern the night before (March 24), and Howell had been arrested by the commanding detective, Sgt. D. Seaton. Had Seaton delayed his raid until the morning of March 25, he could have bagged the elusive Sarah Slater with her dispatches.

Howell's arrest created a problem for John Surratt: how would he convey Sarah to Port Tobacco and across the river? Fortunately, an old family friend, David Barry, came by the tavern that morning and agreed to help.

The three of them—Sarah, Barry, and John Surratt—drove down to Port Tobacco, and Barry then took charge of the carriage and horses and returned them to Howard's Livery in Washington with a note from Surratt to the livery manager: "As business will detain me for a few days in the country, I thought I would send your team back. Mr. Barry will deliver it safely and pay for the hire of it. If Mr. Booth, my friend, should want my horses let him have them, but no one else....I should like to have kept the team for several days, but it is too expensive—especially as I have a woman on the brain and may be away for a week or two." Apparently, John Surratt was developing a romantic interest in Sarah.

John and Sarah spent the night in Brawner's Hotel at Port Tobacco—a place that housed a nest of blockade-runners. They were put across the river and reached Richmond on March 29. They stayed at the Spottswood Hotel that night, where Surratt registered as John Sherman.

On April 1, two days before the fall of Richmond, Secretary of State Judah Benjamin promptly sent Sarah Slater and John Surratt back to Montreal. On the same day, a demolition team left Richmond for the purpose of blowing up the White House while Lincoln's cabinet was in session. This last desperate measure was foiled on April 10 by the 8th Illinois Cavalry a few miles outside of Washington. They spotted the Confederates and arrested them.

Benjamin gave Sarah and Surratt ten twenty-dollar gold pieces for expenses, along with dispatches dealing with money transactions. The Confederate secretary of state realized that the end of the Confederacy was near. Presumably, he wanted large cash balances in Montreal moved to England and France for use by any Confederate officials who might manage to get out of the South. Sarah also may have carried sizable sums of money out of Richmond that would be destined for England.

Sarah and Surratt arrived in Washington about 4:00 p.m. on April 3. He briefly visited his mother's boardinghouse, secured some clothing, and learned that a detective had been looking for him. He left the house quickly and took a room for the night at the Metropolitan Hotel. Sarah probably spent the night with Mary Surratt and delivered messages to Booth.

Early the next morning, April 4, Sarah Slater and John Surratt took the train to New York City. On the night of April 14, Booth shot Lincoln at Ford's Theatre.

Sarah Slater was never seen again. The attractive twenty-two-year-old spy vanished without a trace.

If John Surratt knew what had happened to her, he kept it a secret for the rest of his life. What is known is that he arrived in Montreal on April 6 and delivered his dispatches. Edwin G. Lee then sent him to Elmira, New York, to determine the feasibility of freeing Confederates from the notorious prison camp there. While in that area in mid-April, he picked up a newspaper and saw that he had been accused of attacking Secretary of State William H. Seward on the night that Lincoln had been shot. Surratt was further described as "a notorious secessionist of southern Maryland whose name, with that of John Wilkes Booth, will forever lead the infamous role of assassins."

Immediately, Surratt scrambled across the border into Canada. He found refuge with friends in Montreal, and then he was concealed by Catholic priests. He was with them when his mother was hanged, along with three other co-conspirators, on July 7, 1865.

With the help of the priests and Brig. Gen. Edwin Lee, Surratt escaped to Europe and enlisted in the papal guard at the Vatican. He expected to be safe. But after being recognized by a former friend from Maryland, he fled to Egypt, where he was finally apprehended and returned to the United States for trial in 1867. He was charged as an accomplice in Lincoln's murder. The jury deadlocked, and he was remanded to the Old Capitol Prison.

Some months later he was released on bail. Then the government again arraigned him for trial, this time charging him with treason. The charge was dismissed because it was made after the two-year statute of limitations on such crimes had passed. Surratt was permanently free.

Meanwhile, Sarah Slater's husband, Rowan, attempted to find her. In a letter to his brother James, then a clerk in a New York City retail store, he mentioned her: "You wrote me that you heard that Nettie (Sarah) was dead. I hope she is in a better world. If you have any of the particulars about her, let me know....I wish to know all." James, however, knew nothing.

Sarah vanished for a reason, but no one knows what it was. Were her contacts with Booth, Howell, the Surratts, and Atzerodt merely incidental to her work as a courier, or were they something more sinister? Or maybe Sarah finally became aware of the heinous plot these persons were part of and decided to disassociate herself from them promptly.

She may have reconnected with her two brothers, who also had mysteriously disappeared. And all of them may have escaped to Europe.

That, however, is just speculation. The real answers will probably never be known.

3

"Singing as Sweetly as Ever"

Olivia Floyd

Spinster Olivia Floyd lived in an imposing home, but neighbors reported that grave doings went on at night. The house was near a tiny village teeming with some of the Confederacy's most notorious spies, couriers, and smugglers. Most of them operated between the Confederate capital in Richmond and the covert Confederate operation headquartered in Montreal, Canada.

Olivia lived in Charles County in southern Maryland—a land of Secessionists and Confederate sympathizers in a state that remained with the Union. The town was Port Tobacco. It was built around an old canal close to the point where Tobacco Creek widens into a broad estuary that joins the Potomac River. Secluded creeks and inlets created a jagged shoreline and made the area an ideal haven for clandestine operatives.

It was through Port Tobacco that John Wilkes Booth had planned to row a captured president across the Potomac to Virginia. And it was through the village and across the river that Booth later planned to flee after assassinating Lincoln.

Port Tobacco was near one of three major axes of communication in the Secret Line of the Confederate Signal Corps. The village was also on the major travel route for couriers carrying messages from Richmond to Northern cities and to Montreal.

In colonial and early American times, Port Tobacco was once the second largest town in Maryland, with a proud history dating back to 1634. Around 1780 noted physician and scholar Dr. Gustavus Brown built a two-story Georgian-style dwelling house on a hill beside the old stage road that leads out of the town. He named it Rose Hill and entertained there on a lavish scale. One neighbor was John Hanson, who is often spoken of as the first president of the United States by virtue of his service as president of the Continental Congress in 1781 and 1782. Dr. Brown also was a lifelong friend of George Washington, and Rose Hill was one of two homes Washington visited in the Port Tobacco area.

This previously unpublished photograph shows Olivia Floyd when she was about twenty years old. She lived at Port Tobacco, Maryland, with her mother and a younger brother.

In the early 1800s, Dr. Brown sold the property to Ignatius Semmes, who passed it to Sarah Semmes Floyd, her husband, David, and their children, one of whom was Olivia Floyd. By 1848, the vivacious, dark-eyed Olivia, then twenty-two, lived at Rose Hill with a younger brother, Robert, and their mother. They managed the six-hundred-acre farm.

In 1861 the war came, and Robert enlisted in the Confederate army. While riding with Jeb Stuart's cavalry, he suffered severe wounds in 1863 and died on April 3.

Early in the war, Union officers were temporarily lodged at Rose Hill, and Olivia entertained them in the evenings with refreshments and music around a huge fireplace in the parlor. Her gracious hospitality led to lively conversation, and the constantly flowing champagne led to shared military secrets.

When her guests retired to their rooms upstairs, she would tiptoe outside, saddle her horse, and ride to Laider's Ferry on the Potomac, where she relayed the secrets to waiting Confederate parties who carried them across the river to Virginia.

Later, Union army officials realized that Olivia was not "one of them." Instead, she was a strong Southern sympathizer and a message carrier for the

Rose Hill at Port Tobacco was spinster Olivia Floyd's home for at least fifty-seven years. The mansion was built by Dr. Gustavus Brown, a lifelong friend of George Washington.

enemy. Thus Union soldiers encamped near Rose Hill kept her on their watch list. Sharp-tongued Miss 'Livia was ready for them. She always wore two pistols and threatened these "damn Yankees" when they set a menacing foot on her property.

"Leave my livestock and fences alone, you Yankees," she allegedly said in one instance, "or I'll put ten of you in hell in five minutes."

An article in the files of the Southern Maryland Studies Center reports that Olivia concealed her valuables from the Federal soldiers

Highway marker for Rose Hill.

"in the vault occupied by the crumbling bones of old Dr. Brown." She also hid secret documents in a wooden boat model made by her brother.

But even when the Union realized she was working for the enemy, Olivia observed the Yankees as closely as they watched her—perhaps even more so. Whatever she saw or heard she relayed to couriers at Laider's Ferry.

With Port Tobacco being the last stop on the great spy trail before crossing the Potomac into Confederate territory, couriers from Northern cities often left messages at Rose Hill for Olivia to forward. She sometimes placed them in the crotch of a tree on the bank of Port Tobacco Creek, where they were picked up and taken to Richmond. An alternate method was to place them in her bosom, ride her horse to the ferry, and hand-deliver the papers to the agents who carried them across the river to Virginia.

One letter from Olivia was intercepted by Federal officials. Consequently, on November 10, 1862, an associate judge advocate for the army, Col. L. C. Turner, reported to Secretary of War Edwin M. Stanton that Olivia Floyd was "engaged in all sorts of disloyal practices and is in frequent and intimate communication with an officer in our army who signs himself 'J.'" Turner said that the officer was a Confederate agent. Based in Alexandria, Virginia, the agent supposedly helped many Southern sympathizers escape to Richmond. Turner ordered Olivia's arrest and incarceration at the Old Capitol Prison in Washington. She apparently was to be held there until she revealed J.'s identity.

Surprisingly, the order was never carried out. Federal authorities probably discovered who J. was and no longer perceived Olivia as a threat. They were wrong about her.

By 1864 Olivia was the critical link in the spy chain between Richmond and Canada. Among the spies who worked with her were John H. Surratt (Booth's right-hand man in the plot to kidnap Lincoln); Josephine Lovett Brown (wife of Lt. Robert W. Brown of the Canadian office of the Confederacy); Augustus Spencer Howell, a Confederate agent in southern Maryland; and two Episcopalian clergymen.

Years later the *Richmond Times-Dispatch* wrote: "So sharp was [Olivia's] lookout and so careful her conduct and so many her resources that the Federal troops were never able to catch either her dispatches or convoys of merchandise. She conveyed clothes, money, and letters through the lines."

A clandestine force of Confederates based in Canada sought to cripple the Union by striking across the border in a series of raids, including this attack on St. Albans, Vermont. They robbed banks and attempted to burn the town. Olivia Floyd would later play a key role in saving the raiders' lives.

During the war, Confederate president Jefferson Davis became aware of her daring deeds, and he thanked her for "the great service to the Confederate cause."

Perhaps most memorable of her service was in November 1864 and/or January 1865, when Olivia assisted in the release of Confederate raiders, dressed in civilian clothes, who used Canada as a base from which to rob banks in St. Albans, Vermont. After the raiders had been captured by Canadian authorities, they faced hearings to determine if they should be extradited to the United States and tried there as civilians—with death by hanging a likely certainty if convicted. (See chapter 2 for related material.)

The raid had been planned and executed by twenty-two-year-old Lt. Bennett H. Young, the son of wealthy slave owners in Kentucky. While he was studying to become a Presbyterian clergyman, the Civil War erupted, and Young joined a Kentucky cavalry unit that later became part of the famous Morgan's Raiders. Although Young was captured during a raid, he escaped from a Union prison and made his way to Richmond. This so impressed Secretary of State James A. Seddon that he tapped Young for duty in the Secret Service and sent him to join

Several of the St. Albans raiders and co-conspirators appear in this photograph. Their leader, Lt. Bennett Young, is seated at the right.

the Confederate operation in Canada. Seddon then ordered Young to assemble approximately twenty other escaped Confederate soldiers and conduct raids on Yankee towns along the Canadian border.

"Bring home to them some of the horrors of war," Seddon wrote to Young.

Young's charm, swagger, and skills in subterfuge and swift incursions made him one of Seddon's pets. The Confederate official would take care of Young. After Young and other members of his raiding party were captured in Canada, Seddon used Sarah Slater and Olivia Floyd to help him. Young would later repay Olivia.

Two different accounts of Olivia's role in gaining the release of Young and his men have been reported. It is possible that both stories are accurate since they occurred at different times.

At the first extradition hearing on November 12, 1864, Lieutenant Young introduced two documents dated June 16, 1864, allegedly signed by Secretary Seddon. One of these was Young's commission as a Confederate lieutenant;

the other was Seddon's authorization "to organize a raiding party" for the attack on St. Albans. Historian James O. Hall in a 1975 article in the *Maryland Independent* wrote that confirmation copies of these documents may have been handled by Olivia Floyd on their way to Canada.

If true, the following scenario may have validity. In 1972, author Oscar Kinchen reported that in early November 1864 a Confederate spy, Episcopal priest Richard Stewart, came to Rose Hill with an urgent message. He explained the problem in Canada and told Olivia: "I can't do anything for they are watching me, but *you* can." He then took off his hat and removed a note from its inner band. The note was from Jefferson Davis, and it stated that the men on trial were commissioned officers in the Confederate army.

A few days later Stewart returned to Rose Hill. "You will have a visitor soon, and he will ask you in cryptic language: 'Have you any land for sale?' You must reply: 'I have.'"

Two days passed before the stranger arrived and asked the question. When she gave the proper answer, they went into the parlor. He unscrewed the ferrule from his walking cane and removed several sheets of fine tissue paper. They contained official transcripts from the War Department in Richmond that established the belligerent character of the St. Albans raiders and said that they acted under orders from the Confederate government.

Another messenger arrived a week later. He ripped open the lining of his vest and pulled out money and instructions. Shortly, Olivia retrieved the documents, hid them in her hair and bosom, and made contact with a courier to move the papers along the underground route to Canada.

In the second scenario, the hearing in Canada was recessed for a month—until February 11—so that the raiders would have more time to prove their military status. The judge added one requirement: the person delivering the papers to him must prove that he or she was the same person who received them from Secretary Seddon. The judge apparently doubted the authenticity of the documents presented by Young in November.

To assure that this information reached Richmond in a timely manner, the Canadian office of the Confederacy sent several couriers by different routes. One courier was captured in Ohio and sentenced to death as a spy, but Lincoln commuted his sentence. Two others successfully completed their journeys. One of them delivered his parcel to Olivia at Rose Hill. She was the last link in the chain of communications into Confederate territory.

Union scouts must have observed the courier. Within an hour of the delivery, soldiers raided the mansion. Olivia, however, was ready for them. She anticipated the danger and started a blazing fire in the dining room fireplace. She unscrewed the hollow top of one of the huge brass andirons and concealed the dispatch in it.

The commanding officer queried Olivia while sitting on a chair, with the heel of his boot on the andiron. His men ripped open hassocks, tore pictures from the wall, and thoroughly searched the house, but they found nothing.

The next day Olivia hid the message in one of her curls and traveled to a Confederate signal station on Pope's Creek. From there it was relayed to the Confederate White House in Richmond and to Secretary Seddon.

This probably was the first message to reach Richmond about the perilous situation in Canada. If so, it was the message that prompted Seddon to recruit the mysterious Sarah Slater to take the official documentation to Canada.

As mentioned in chapter 2, Sarah snaked through enemy lines via the Confederate underground and reached Montreal in time to save the St. Albans raiders.

Apparently, news of the outcome of the hearing was slow to reach Port Tobacco, and Olivia Floyd grew restless. She wrote to Reverend Stewart in a prearranged cryptic language: "Dear Cousin: The fairy lake on which you gaily rowed your fairy boat is now deep in ice. Nor can I procure Cousin John's picture, or any feed for the canary bird."

Just before Lincoln's assassination on April 14, Stewart reported to Olivia: "I have procured Cousin John's picture and the seed for the canary bird, and it is singing as sweetly as ever." He was telling her that the raiders had been released.

Earlier that spring, Olivia hid eighty thousand dollars in bank notes for one of her Confederate contacts. She placed the money in a thick cushion in the sofa near the fireplace. Union soldiers visiting or searching the house often sat on that cushion, not realizing they were sitting on a fortune. The rightful owner retrieved the money shortly after the war ended.

After the war and her mother's death, Olivia Floyd was alone in the big house with her servants and farm manager. But not for long. She changed from a devotee of dangerous clandestine missions to a connoisseur of social and psychic experiences—always ready for another party or séance. She told fortunes, demonstrated supernatural powers as a successful medium, and believed in ghosts—perhaps because Rose Hill had one.

It seems that a peddler drank too much at a local tavern and bragged about valuables he was carrying—a bag of gold and deeds to an estate inherited from his brother. When the peddler left the tavern, accompanied by his large black dog—a dog so black that it appeared to be blue—they were followed up a winding road leading to Rose Hill. In a dark area the thief robbed the peddler and killed him and his dog. To avoid being discovered, the murderer buried the loot on a hillside on the Rose Hill property. When he returned to recover the treasure, he was scared away by a ghostly dog that came running up the hill in a cloud of blue smoke. The murderer fell ill a few days later and died. According to local legend, the treasure is still buried along Rose Hill Road, and the ghost of the blue dog guards it.

In 1897 Olivia told the *Maryland Independent* she had seen the dog's ghost. Others who claim to have seen the ghost said they tried to follow the specter, but the blue dog vanished before they could find the treasure.

Each year upon the anniversary of the murder—February 3—the fearsome wraith of the huge blue dog supposedly shows up on the spot, his eyes shining big as saucers. Some folks say he also appears irregularly to warn of death or accident.

Olivia told of the night the blue dog "howled and came over the hill in a thundering cloud of blue smoke" just before three knocks sounded on her door bringing news that her brother, a Confederate soldier, had been killed in battle. While looking out the window, she said she saw the beast itself, "as large as a young heifer," making its way, "huge eyes blazing, across the hillside."

Even today the road is known widely as "the Blue Dog Road," and the howling beast still haunts the environs of Rose Hill.

Olivia's popularity as a fortune-teller and psychic spread across southern Maryland and enriched her coffers—that is, until her doctor and priest shut her down. Her doctor said that practicing occultism was bad for her health, and her Catholic priest ordered her to stop such "dangerous associations."

In her later years, Olivia was described as an extremely short, humpbacked woman with snow white hair and piercing black eyes. A local newspaper reported, "She always wore bizarre, gypsy-like earrings and combed her hair into tight, corkscrew curls at the side."

Because of her unfortunate humpbacked deformity—caused by a childhood accident—she was lame and walked with a cane. Her appearance, her high-pitched, croaking voice, and her unusual flair for the mystical and supernatural gained for her a description by those who knew her as "a rather nice, little old witch."

The high point of her declining years was an invitation from Lt. Bennet H. Young, the leader of the St. Albans raid. Remembering Olivia's role in handling the message that saved his life and the lives of other raiders, he proposed an expense-free visit to his home in Louisville, Kentucky, so she could be his guest at a reunion of Confederate veterans. Young, a noted Louisville attorney, was the national commander of the United Confederate Veterans. To her surprise, she was the reunion's guest of honor. Young presented her with a ribboned medal. She later gave him the wooden boat and the andiron in which she had hidden secret messages.

Olivia died at Rose Hill on December 10, 1905, at the age of eighty-one. She was buried beside her brother in the parish

Olivia Floyd is shown in her later years. She died in 1905 at the age of eighty-one.

cemetery on the hillside overlooking the Potomac. Bennett Young paid her funeral expenses and donated headstones for Olivia and her brother.

The *New York Times* published the news of Olivia's death on December 12. The newspaper described her as "the famous woman Confederate blockade runner" who had "once defied a whole company of Union soldiers."

GRANT'S MOST VALUABLE RICHMOND SPY

Elizabeth Van Lew

Young Elizabeth Van Lew was one of the Southern belles of Richmond, Virginia—wealthy, pretty, and well educated. Her soft Southern voice and gentle countenance complemented an almost unearthly brilliance in her blue eyes. So endowed, she had no shortage of beaus. But she would never marry, apparently because of a serious romance turned sour.

Her parents were Northerners, but they married and lived in Richmond. Wanting the best education for Elizabeth, they sent her to schools in Philadelphia, where abolitionists taught and influenced her. By 1836, at the age of eighteen, she was back in Richmond with strong antislavery views while enjoying the luxuries of her parents' newly acquired three-and-a-half-story mansion. Highly respected, the Van Lews hosted lavish balls and elaborate garden parties attended by the bluebloods of Richmond's high society. Among their well-known guests were John Marshall, chief justice of the United States, and past president John Adams. Edgar Allan Poe read his immortal poem, "The Raven," in the parlor. Swedish soprano Jenny Lind stopped at the mansion when she sang her way across America.

Elizabeth, known as Miss Lizzie, held parties of her own at the mansion and attended balls and garden parties at the homes of friends. She was driven to these gatherings in an exquisite carriage pulled by four snow-white horses.

Elizabeth Van Lew, a spinster, lacked the sexiness, flash, and high society glamour of Rose Greenhow.

To escape Richmond's hot, humid summers and to ease John Van Lew's respiratory ailment (he would die of it in 1843), the family spent leisure time in the western mountains of Virginia at top-rung resorts: White Sulfur Springs, Sweet Springs, and Hot Springs. At Hot Springs, Miss Lizzie palled around with the daughter of a slave trader. The girl chatted about her father's recent dealings. He had placed on the market a slave mother and her baby. When the mother realized she had been sold to one buyer and her baby to another, she fell dead. Miss Lizzie later wrote that she never forgot this dreadful story and that it had a lasting effect on her own life.

Years before the Civil War, Elizabeth Van Lew's parents hosted lavish balls in their mansion (shown here) on Richmond's prestigious Church Hill. Their guests included Chief Justice John Marshall, President John Adams, author and poet Edgar Allan Poe, and Swedish soprano Jenny Lind.

"Slave power," she wrote in her *Occasional Journal*, "is arrogant, is jealous and intrusive, is cruel, is despotic."

Miss Lizzie had always been a serious, introspective child. "From the time I knew right from wrong," she wrote, "it was my sad privilege to differ in many things from the...opinions and principles of my locality." She described herself as "uncompromising, ready to resent what seemed wrong."

As Miss Lizzie grew older, her sharp, large nose, thin lips, firm jaw, and high forehead gave her the appearance of a birdlike creature. Her dangling dark ringlets softened these sharp features but not her strong will or her self-reliance. She became even more outspoken and independent at a time when Southern women were expected to be quiet and dependent.

In 1859, when Miss Lizzie was forty-one and the war was just two years away, the hanging of abolitionist John Brown after his raid on Harpers Ferry spurred her own determination to fight slavery.

"Southern people thirsted" for war and "cried out for it," she wrote. "It was not enough that one old man should die. Mobs went to private houses to hang the true of heart [loyalists to the Union]. Loyalty now was called treason, and cursed. If you spoke in your parlor or chamber, to your next of heart, you whispered....People were, if anything, more morbid than ever on the subject of slavery, and I heard a member of the Virginia Legislature say that anyone speaking against it [slavery], or doubting its divinity, ought to be hung....Another gentleman, a state senator, told me that members of the senate did not dare to speak as they thought and felt, that they were afraid."

After the secession of the Southern states and the formation of the Confederate States of America, Northerners in Richmond lived in uncertainty about their own future, as did the Van Lews, even though Miss Lizzie was a Virginian by birth. War seemed certain.

In May 1861 the new Confederate government voted to move its capital from Montgomery, Alabama, to Richmond. The government would occupy the state's capitol building, which had been designed by Thomas Jefferson. Five railroads ran through the capital, and small boats navigated the James River to bring in goods from oceangoing ships. The city's population quickly tripled to about one hundred thousand.

A multitude of volunteers descended on Richmond, ready to serve the cause. Among the first were troops from South Carolina. Diarist Sallie Ann Brock wrote that "admiring crowds of ladies" met the volunteers at the railroad depot, eager to "get a sight of the heroes of Fort Sumter." Next, the ladies lovingly made uniforms, tents, and other supplies for the soldiers. That is, except for Miss Lizzie and her mother, who turned down their neighbors' requests to participate. The Van Lews' defiance resulted in "personal threats" and a warning that their refusal was "not acceptable."

The Van Lews quickly realized their mistake. To avoid deportation, imprisonment, and even possible execution, they had to lead a double life: pretend loyalty to the cause while praying and working for the Union. They took flowers and religious books to the South Carolinians mustered at the fairgrounds. This paid off. Threats against the Van Lews ceased…for a while.

On July 21, 1861, at Manassas in northern Virginia, the Confederates defeated the Federals. In the bloodiest battle America had witnessed up to that time, the dead and wounded totaled 1,584 for the Federals and 1,969 for the Confederates. The Southern wounded reached nearly 1,600, and those who weren't left on the battlefield were rushed to Richmond by wagons and trains. Significantly, more than 1,300 Federals were captured and taken to Richmond to be housed in makeshift prisons quickly converted from factories and tobacco warehouses.

When news of the victory reached Richmond, the city celebrated. Church bells rang. People danced. Soldiers fired pistols into the air.

Miss Lizzie, then forty-three, watched the celebration from her columned back porch. Distressed and angry, but never one to crumble, she stood straight as tears streamed down her face. In the city she loved, she had come to loathe its values. She was more determined than ever to help the Union survive and to do so without slavery.

Inexperience Trumped by Ingenuity

Ligon's Prison, a three-story brick structure with wooden beams, faced a church, slave shanties, and a stable. As churchgoers passed the building on the first Sunday after it had been transformed into a prison, men and children leaned from the windows of their horse-drawn carriages, hoping to catch a glimpse of a Yankee prisoner. Young Southern ladies didn't look, except for a quick peek from behind their handheld fans. It was considered poor taste for women to see "foreign devils."

But not for Miss Lizzie. To her, the prisoners were fellow loyalists in need of help, as well as sources of valuable information about the strength and disposition of Confederate troops they saw while being transported from the battlefields to the prison. She just had to figure out a way to acquire that intelligence and smuggle it out of Richmond to the Federal authorities.

That summer Miss Lizzie visited Lt. David H. Todd, overseer of the prison complex, and offered to serve as a hospital nurse for the wounded Union prisoners. Todd, a sour-faced, tall, thin man with large tattoos on his arms and chest, was a half brother of the first lady of the United States, Mary Todd Lincoln.

Todd looked at Elizabeth in surprise. "You are the first and only lady that has made any such application," he said. He told her that he knew people who would be glad to "shoot the lot of them." So Miss Lizzie asked if she could be allowed to visit the prisoners.

"We cannot permit you to see them," he asserted.

Undeterred, she went over Todd's head and called on Christopher Memminger, secretary of the Confederate treasury. Finding him alone in his office, she begged him for permission to visit the prisoners. But he would not hear of such a thing. "A class of men like that are not worthy or fit for a lady to visit," he explained.

Miss Lizzie changed her tactics. She reminded Memminger of the time he gave a beautiful discourse on religion. That changed his smirk to a smile. Miss Lizzie then said that "love was the fulfilling of the law, and if we wished 'our cause' to succeed, we must begin with charity to the thankless, the unworthy." She won her point. Memminger gave her a note to the provost marshal, Brig. Gen. John H. Winder.

Miss Lizzie once told a friend, "Oh, I can flatter almost anything out of old Winder; his personal vanity is so great."

She found him at his shanty office, seated at a table. She later wrote: "His silvery white hair waved in beautiful locks, and after sitting a moment, I said to him, 'Your hair would adorn the temple of James. It looks out of place here.' Then I told him I should be glad to visit the prisoners and would like to send them something. He raised no objections, and wrote, '[Miss Van Lew] has permission to visit the prisoners and to send them books, luxuries, delicacies and what she may please.'" She could not, however, enter the prisons or talk with the inmates.

A few days later she and her mother brought supplies and "a little chicken soup and cornmeal gruel" to the "helpless" men who had been captured at Manassas. And to win over the grouchy prison commandant, David Todd, they sweetened him up with ginger cakes and buttermilk while engaging him in pleasant—and informative—conversation.

Prisoners soon learned to communicate with their benefactors by underlining words in the books. These words, when strung together, constituted an impromptu code. Initially she posted these gleanings in letters to the Federal authorities. Later she became more sophisticated and used household servants as couriers delivering baskets of farm produce northward. One egg in each basket had been drained and then filled with tiny slips of paper bearing enciphered messages.

The Van Lews' daring contacts at the prison brought them under greater scrutiny and what Miss Lizzie described as "the threats, the scowls, the frowns of an infuriated community." She said, "I have had brave men shake their fingers in my face and say terrible things. We had threats of being driven away, threats of fire, threats of death....'You dare to show sympathy for any of those prisoners!' said a gentleman. 'I would shoot them down as I would blackbirds!' Surely madness was upon the people. Some wished all Union people could be driven into the street and slaughtered. Some proposed the hanging of all persons of Northern birth, no matter how long they had been in the South."

The *Richmond Examiner* chastised the Van Lews in the July 29, 1861, issue but did not name them:

Two ladies, a mother and a daughter, living on Church Hill, have lately attracted public notice by their assiduous attentions to the Yankee prisoners confined in this City. Whilst every true woman in this community has been busy making articles of comfort or necessity for our troops...these two women have been expending their opulent means in aiding and giving comfort to the miscreants who have invaded our sacred soil, bent on raping and murder, the desolation of our homes and sacred places, and the ruin and dishonor of our families. The largest human charity can find ample scope in kindness and attention to our own poor fellows....

The Yankee wounded have been put under charge of competent surgeons and provided with good nurses. This is more than they have any right to expect, and the course of these two females...cannot but be regarded as an evidence of sympathy amounting to an endorsement of the cause and conduct of these Northern Vandals.

Not to be outdone, the *Richmond Dispatch* issued a stinging warning. If these "Yankee offshoots" weren't careful, opined the editor, they would be "exposed and dealt with as alien enemies."

To legally expose and punish women traitors to the South, the Confederate Congress passed a sequestration act in late August. It enabled Confederate officials to seize property belonging to alien enemies, especially women. Before the war's end, the government would seize more than five hundred thousand dollars' worth of property.

Under these circumstances, Miss Lizzie and her mother felt compelled to show their Southern colors by offering a refuge for hungry and wounded Rebels. At the same time, they had their servants deliver items to the Union prisoners. A Manassas amputee, Pvt. Lewis Francis, said he would have perished had it not been for the food and clothing they provided.

Richmonders resented any act of kindness and compassion to "damn Yankees," and they let the Van Lews know it. Miss Lizzie went directly to Jefferson Davis's office and asked for protection. Allowed to confer with Davis's private secretary, she argued that her actions were entirely appropriate for a Christian lady. She was told to "apply to the Mayor." She did, but to no avail.

Believing that if a plan doesn't work, try a different one, Miss Lizzie seized an opportunity when prison overseer David Todd was reassigned to another duty. Miss Lizzie, in a shrewd move, inveigled his successor, Capt. George C. Gibbs, to board at the Van Lew mansion with his family. If his presence there wouldn't prove their loyalty, it would certainly make it difficult to disprove it.

Mobilizing a Network of Spies

In March 1862 Richmonders shuddered as Maj. Gen. George B. McClellan landed the Union Army of the Potomac, one hundred thousand strong, at Fort Monroe on the tip of the Virginia Peninsula. Moving slowly and cautiously, he pushed the Rebels up the Peninsula past the historic areas of Yorktown, Williamsburg, and Jamestown to within six miles of Richmond. Then came the famous Seven Days' battles from June 25 to July 1.

Even though Gen. Robert E. Lee lost a fourth of his army and won only one battle, he succeeded in knocking the Yankees from the gates of the Confederate capital, thanks primarily to McClellan's failure to advance when he had the opportunity.

During this period Richmond was under martial law. With widespread fear throughout the city, diarist Sallie Ann Brock wrote, "Spies...were ready at any moment to deliver the city into the hands of our enemies." Jefferson Davis instructed General Winder to expose and imprison the "treasonable machinations of the Unionists in our midst."

Altogether Winder's agents imprisoned some twenty-eight individuals, but most were released in a matter of days, thanks to friends in high places. President Davis was premature in thinking that a treasonable band existed in Richmond, but the scare tactics he implemented actually brought about such a band. The Van Lews and other Unionists were so frightened by the president's actions that they mobilized their resources to conspire and fight back.

On June 26, while battles were raging nearby, Miss Lizzie and her friend Eliza G. Carrington rode in the Van Lews' carriage to former U.S. Congressman John Minor Botts's farm in Hanover County, northeast of Richmond. Botts, a native Virginian who had strongly opposed secession, was one of Miss Lizzie's political idols. What they discussed is unknown, but Botts, then sixty years of age, was fired up after being confined for several weeks at Castle Thunder prison. Botts and Charles Palmer, a shipping merchant, would later connect Miss Lizzie with other Unionists, and they would become key members of her network. Among them were grocer Frederick William Ernest Lohmann, aged thirty-six, and Amish-looking farmer William S. Rowley, aged forty-six, described by Miss Lizzie as "the bravest of the brave, the truest of the true, and a man of rare perception and wonderful intuition."

Throughout the stifling summer months, Miss Lizzie's shrewd and resourceful mind schemed and improvised, and she conferred secretly with the handful of Richmond Unionists. As she stole about in the night on secret missions, she disguised herself as a farmhand, wearing buckskin leggings, a one-piece skirt and waist of cotton, and a huge calico sunbonnet.

Meanwhile, McClellan's battles on the edge of Richmond forced

Former Congressman John Minor Botts was among the powerful Unionists arrested and imprisoned for treasonable acts. He became a key member of Miss Lizzie's network of spies.

Confederate officials to tighten security in the jails. Giving aid to prisoners was no longer tolerated. Unable to help the prisoners legally, the Van Lews and their friends focused on illegal, devious methods and on ways to facilitate their escape.

Miss Lizzie influenced surgeons to place prisoners in hospitals, where she or her servants could visit them and give them food. For a while she conveyed messages through a secret space inside a custard dish, and she received messages from the prisoners when she retrieved the dish. One container she used was a curious French contrivance: a metal platter with a double bottom, one section of which was ideal for concealing messages. The upper portion was intended to hold hot water beneath the plate to keep the contents warm. Advised that a suspicious guard planned to inspect the container, Miss Lizzie was prepared for him. When he asked to see it, she deftly slipped her shawl from around it and placed the plate suddenly in his hands. That day the double bottom contained no messages but was filled with blistering hot water, and he dropped it with a roar of pain. He never again asked to inspect it.

When commandants banned her from bringing food, she and some wealthy friends bribed the guards to pass food, clothing, and even furniture to the prisoners. These same guards were inclined to look the other way when inmates attempted to escape.

At Miss Lizzie's urging, Erasmus Ross, a nephew of Union sympathizer Franklin Stearns, obtained the position of clerk of Libby Prison—which made him a valuable contact between the prisoners and the Richmond underground.

One escapee, Lt. Col. William H. Lounsbury, recounted his experience with Ross in a 1912 book. Noting that Ross was a clever Confederate pretender, Lounsbury said: "He never called the rolls without swearing at us and abusing us." Then one evening Ross struck him in the stomach and gruffly said, "You blue-bellied Yankee, come down to my office. I have a matter to settle with you." When they were in the office, Ross pointed to a Confederate uniform behind a counter. Lounsbury put it on and ran across the street, where "a colored man stepped out and said, 'Come with me, sah, I know who you is,' and he took me to Miss Van Lew's house on Church Hill."

Another escapee later recalled: "Miss Van Lew kept two or three bright, sharp colored men on the watch near Libby Prison, who were always ready to conduct an escaped prisoner to a place of safety. Not all of them were secreted at her house—for there were several safe places of refuge in Richmond supported by her means."

Lounsbury, however, was taken to the Van Lew mansion and concealed in a secret chamber in the attic. With its slanted floor and sloping ceiling, the chamber was not a five-star accommodation, but it served its purpose well. It had a door that could only be opened by pressing a spring hidden behind an antique chest of drawers.

Miss Lizzie's underground

Through Miss Lizzie's Richmond underground network, she helped many prisoners to escape. She hid some of them in a secret chamber in this attic of her mansion. The opening, seen here, was accessed by pressing a spring hidden behind an antique chest of drawers.

was the escape route to Northern lines, and during the war she hid many soldiers in her home's secret chambers. Lounsbury noted that she told him "the roads to take and where to go to the woods to escape the pickets and where to go down the James River."

One night, when Miss Lizzie's young niece, Annie, was visiting her, the niece noticed her aunt climbing the stairs with a plate of food and tiptoed after her. Annie stopped at the top of the stairs to the attic. She was frightened by dark shadows that made the furniture look like ghosts. She watched as her aunt leaned over and touched something. Then she saw a panel in the wall swing open and a man with a shaggy beard peer out of the chamber and reach out and take the food. From the corner of his eyes he saw the girl put her finger to her lips to persuade him not to reveal her presence. Then she fled.

An hour later Annie snuck upstairs and pushed the hidden spring. The soldier grinned and talked to her. She remembers that he laughed as he said, "My, what a spanking you would have got if your aunt had turned around!" Presently she closed the panel and crept off to bed. She never dared to go to the attic after that, nor tell her aunt what she had done.

Miss Lizzie's circle of sources widened and included even clerks in the War and Navy departments. From them she received intelligence about strengths of

In Richmond, some twenty-eight Unionists were imprisoned in Castle Thunder, a converted tobacco warehouse notorious as a hellhole. Prisoners were hanged by their thumbs and flogged.

Rebel units, their movements, and where they were stationed. Escaped prisoners, fugitive civilians, and slaves also were sources of intelligence.

Lincoln's Emancipation Proclamation of January 1, 1863, made life much more difficult for the Van Lews and the Richmond underground. Responding to Lincoln's declaration, Jefferson Davis decreed that captured black soldiers would be enslaved and that captured white officers who had led black troops would be executed. The Virginia legislature toughened its position on anti-slavery Unionists. It allowed any person to kill anyone who was helping runaway slaves.

The Union Secretary of War Edwin M. Stanton joined the fray by ending the official exchanges of captured commissioned officers. That, in turn, substantially increased Richmond's prison population. At Libby, for example, rooms that previously held a hundred prisoners now bulged with seven hundred. Food was scarce, and supplies sent to Richmond's prisons by Northern civilians and agencies were withheld from the inmates. Starvation became the leading cause of death. The living gnawed on bones. The Confederate capital's Castle Thunder was equally hellish.

Life for Richmonders in 1863 was no picnic either. With the Confederate army desperately needing horses, officials confiscated them from civilians. Miss Lizzie wasn't about to give up her horse. So she led the horse into the mansion and up the stairs to the library. She wrote in her journal: "[We] spread straw upon the study floor, and [our horse] accepted at once his position and behaved as though he thoroughly understood matters, never stamping or neighing loud enough to be heard."

A Union General Discovers Miss Lizzie

Undaunted by Richmond's nightmarish atmosphere, but ever more cautious, the Van Lews and other Union loyalists intensified their work. But it was not until the third year of the war, in December 1863, that the Union government finally made contact with Miss Lizzie.

That contact came from Maj. Gen. Benjamin F. Butler, commander of the Union Department of Virginia and North Carolina, with his headquarters at Fort Monroe on the Virginia Peninsula. Concerned with the operations of the Army of the James against Richmond, he needed strategic information from Richmond insiders.

The process developed through the efforts of fifteen-year-old Josephine Holmes, acting on behalf of Miss Lizzie's Richmond underground.

To help prisoners to escape from Richmond's hellholes, Miss Lizzie sent Josephine to Libby's hospital, where Union Capt. Harry S. Howard and assistant surgeon John R. McCullough were being treated for minor illnesses. Josephine visited Dr. McCullough and gave him a bag of fine Virginia tobacco. After she left, Dr. McCullough found a note at the bottom of the bag: "Would you be free? Then be prepared to act. Meet me tomorrow."

Josephine returned the next day, whispered a plan of escape, and told him he could bring one comrade with him.

Following her instructions, McCullough pretended to be dead on the specified day. Captain Howard covered him with a blanket, and with the help of three other inmates, he carried him to a makeshift morgue on the hospital grounds. There he lay from midday until dusk. Then, as other inmates distracted guards with a fake fight, McCullough and Howard casually walked out of the hospital to a place where they made contact with Josephine.

"Follow me at a distance," she advised, "and keep me in sight by observing my white handkerchief." She took them to her father's house.

Around midnight another member of the underground, Burnham Wardwell, conveyed them to the home of William S. Rowley, where they stayed in hiding for ten days while Unionist women made disguises for them. Then, Rowley and Unionist railroad superintendent Samuel Ruth paid three thousand dollars in Confederate money for passes out of the city. Finally, Rowley guided them through Confederate lines to the Potomac River. After crossing the river they had a clear path to Washington.

The Washington press reported the dramatic escape, and the story was picked up by the Richmond papers. The escape shocked prison authorities. They now understood why so many deceased Yankee officers had disappeared. A new position was created: dead-house keeper. His job was to guard the dead.

Meanwhile, Dr. McCullough met with General Butler at Fort Monroe, described Richmond's underground operations, and gave him a letter from Miss Lizzie that Josephine had passed to him.

On December 19, 1863, Butler wrote a top-secret letter to Charles O. Boutelle, a topographical engineer in the U.S. Coast Survey Office. Boutelle knew Miss Lizzie. Butler's letter said in part:

> *You will find enclosed a letter from a dear friend of yours in Richmond. I am informed by the bearer that Miss Van Lew is a true Union woman as true as steel. She sent me a bouquet, so says the letter carrier [Dr. McCullough]. Now, I much want a correspondent in Richmond, one who will write me... without name or description of the writer, and she need only incur the risk of dropping an ordinary letter by Flag of Truce in the Post Office, directed to a name in the North. Her messenger thinks Miss Van Lew will be glad to do it.*

The "flag of truce" arrangement between the Union and Confederacy enabled civilians and correspondents to send mail back and forth between the North and the South.

Boutelle reassured Butler, and Butler sent Captain Howard back to Richmond to see Miss Lizzie. Howard, a scout for Butler, then made his base at Rowley's home, recruiting Rowley as a Federal agent. Howard also sent to Miss Lizzie a letter purported to be from "James Ap. Jones" to his "Dear Aunt." Actually, a second message, written in invisible ink, appeared when acid and heat were applied. That letter read as follows:

> *The doctor [McCullough] who came through and spoke to me of the bouquet said that you would be willing to aid the Union cause by furnishing me with information if I could devise a means. You can write through the Flag of Truce, directed to James Ap. Jones, Norfolk, the letter being written as this is, and with the means furnished by the messenger who brings this. I cannot refrain from saying to you, although personally unknown, how much I am rejoiced to hear of the strong feeling for the Union which exists in your own breast and among some of the ladies of Richmond.*

The letter was from Butler. For her own protection, Miss Lizzie tossed it onto flaming logs in her fireplace.

Miss Lizzie then rode to Rowley's house to meet with Captain Howard. She eagerly accepted his offers, not only to be a Federal agent, but also the head of Butler's spy network and Butler's chief correspondent in Richmond. Rowley would be part of that network, reporting directly to Miss Lizzie.

Howard advised Miss Lizzie on how to use a "peculiar kind of ink and writing materials" and a secret cipher for encrypting her messages. Miss Lizzie's niece Annie later said that her aunt "always carried [the cipher key] in the case of her watch" and that dispatches "were written with a colorless liquid which… with the application of milk came out perfectly black." She said that her aunt would sometimes tear cipher messages into two or three pieces and roll them into tiny balls, to be handed over in that shape. The cipher key was a thirty-six-box grid. It contained the letters of the alphabet and the numbers zero through nine. Each letter or number was represented in ciphered messages by its coordinates. Howard provided an example on another small piece of paper: "36 63 55 52 63 = Union."

Miss Lizzie's first dispatch, from "Eliza A. Jones" to her "Uncle," was hand delivered to Butler on February 4 by a messenger with the help of a guide paid for by Arnold Holmes, whose fifteen-year-old daughter had bravely set up the linkage. Here's the transcribed dispatch:

It is intended to remove to Georgia [Andersonville Prison] very soon all the Federal prisoners; butchers and bakers to go at once. They are already notified and selected. Quaker knows this to be true. [Quaker was probably Rowley's code name.] [Confederates] are building batteries on the Danville road.

This from Quaker. Beware of new and rash council. Beware! This I send to you by direction of all your friends. No attempt should

Miss Lizzie always carried this cipher key in the case of her watch. She wrote dispatches with a colorless liquid. Recipients applied milk to make the messages visible.

be made with less than 30,000 cavalry, from 10,000 to 15,000 infantry to support them, amounting in all to 40,000 or 45,000 troops. Do not underrate their strength and desperation. Forces could probably be called into action in five to ten days…25,000, mostly artillery. [Robert F.] Hoke's and [James L.] Kemper's brigades have gone to North Carolina. [George E.] Pickett's are in or about Petersburg. Three regiments of cavalry [were] disbanded by General Lee for want of horses. Morgan is applying for 1,000 choice men for a raid."

The messenger, a boy who had been staying at the Van Lew home, revealed that Charles Palmer (a pro-Union shipping merchant) was the primary source of Miss Lizzie's troop estimates and that Palmer believed that "Richmond could be taken easier now than at any other time since the war began." The messenger also said that Quaker advised attacking Richmond from the west.

Butler promptly forwarded the messages to Secretary of War Stanton with an urgent appeal: "Now, or never, is the time to strike." He proposed making a "dash" with six thousand men and achieving two objectives: "to release the large number of prisoners in Richmond [before they were transferred to Andersonville] and "to capture the Confederate Cabinet and Mr. Jefferson Davis."

Stanton endorsed the plan, and Butler assigned Brig. Gen. Isaac J. Wistar to execute the mission.

It turned into a fiasco, partly because a Yankee deserter warned the Confederates. But the failure was equally Butler's. He ignored Miss Lizzie's estimate of the need for forty-five thousand troops as well as Quaker's recommendation to mount the attack from the west.

Planning the Great Escape

Meanwhile, Miss Lizzie and her colleagues were engaged in preparations for the remarkable escape of a hundred Union officers from Libby Prison. Two house-builders by trade—Col. Thomas E. Rose of the 77th Pennsylvania Infantry and Maj. Andrew G. Hamilton of the 12th Kentucky Cavalry—conceived a plan to escape by digging a tunnel from the Libby cellar, known as "Rat Hell," to the outside world.

They started by cutting a hole in the back of the kitchen fireplace on the ground floor and chiseling through the fireplace diagonally to the cellar below. Fifteen men worked in shifts. Trying to find the right route out of the cellar nearly broke their spirits and their backs. To avoid detection, the men worked at night, using large chisels, candles, and wooden spittoons to convey dirt out of the tunnel.

They made three attempts, taking up thirty-nine nights of digging. The first ran into a canal that flooded the tunnel and nearly drowned Rose. The second passed under a brick furnace and partially collapsed under the weight. The third ran into immovable oak planks. One of the officers later wrote: "Most of the party were now really ill from the foul stench in which they had lived so long." But they kept trying. And the fourth attempt—tunneling sixty feet under a vacant lot to a yard between two buildings—succeeded.

Details of the plan reached Miss Lizzie via Robert Ford, an African American Unionist who took care of horses and mules at the prison. Ford was a free black from the North who had been captured in the Shenandoah Valley while serving as a teamster in the Union army. He was taken to Libby Prison.

Preparing to receive some of the escapees in her home, Lizzie nailed up dark blankets at the windows of an end room, set up beds, and kept gas burning in the room.

"The ninth of February was a long day, and long to be remembered; never was my anxiety so great as for the setting of that day's sun," wrote prisoner I. N. Johnston on the day of the great escape. It started at 7:00 p.m.

Lt. Col. Harrison C. Hobart remembered the scenario. "In order to distract the attention of the guards a dancing party with music was extemporized in the cook room. As the guards were under orders to fire upon a prisoner escaping, without even calling him to halt, the first men who descended into the tunnel wore that quiet gloom so often seen in the army before going into battle."

On the following morning, Commandant Turner was horrified to learn that the "number of prisoners fell alarmingly short." A total of 109 were missing. Libby officials scoured the building, finally finding the tunnel. Turner suspected Lizzie's contact, Robert Ford, of complicity and meted out five hundred lashes, nearly killing him. Turner dispatched couriers in all directions and doubled pickets on roads and bridges. Within days, 48 of the 109 escapees were recaptured, including Colonel Rose. Two others drowned while trying to escape.

But the man they really wanted got away. He was Col. Abel D. Streight of the 51st Indiana Infantry. In prison he angered prison officials by taunting the guards and threatening to report their actions to higher authorities. Streight and the fifty-eight others who had evaded capture sought refuge in the safe houses of Union loyalists in Richmond.

Several found their way to the Van Lew mansion on the night of February 9 and knocked on the door to the servants' rooms. Miss Lizzie's driver opened the door and heard their plea, but he refused to allow them in. He thought they might be Confederates posing as escapees in an attempt to expose the Van Lews.

Unfortunately for the prisoners, Miss Lizzie was not at home and was unaware of the timing of the escape. On that night she had donned a disguise (old clothes and cotton stuffed in her cheeks) and had ridden to another safe house where her brother, John Newton, was hiding. He had deserted the Confederate army and was determined to flee to Union lines. Miss Lizzie spent the night. She did not learn of the Libby escape until the following morning, when her driver appeared with supplies for John and his hosts.

The news of the escape exasperated Miss Lizzie. After all of her preparations to help the Libby prisoners, she had missed the big moment. Now, after the breakout, security would be tightened around Richmond. It would be extremely difficult for her brother to reach Union lines.

"As desperate situations sometimes require despicable remedies," Miss Lizzie wrote in her journal, she gallantly strode into General Winder's office and sought a medical exemption for John, claiming he had a debilitating injury and was not fit for military service. Amazingly, Winder was sympathetic. He met with John and suggested he choose a different company—Winder's company, the 18th Virginia Regiment. "That is mine and I can protect you," he said. He did, indeed. John never saw a day of active service.

Miss Lizzie and Winder were close. In her dealings with him, she always presented herself as a pro-Confederate with Christian compassion for the wounded and sick men of both sides. She even invited the Winders and their daughter to dinner and wrote in her journal that Winder's wife "had a strong feeling for the U.S. government."

Gen. Ulysses S. Grant engaged Gen. Robert E. Lee in a bloody campaign in northern and central Virginia during the dreadful spring and summer of 1864. Grant was relentless, despite severe losses.

At the battle of the Wilderness, he lost 17,000 to Lee's 11,000. At Spotsylvania, 11,000 fell, compared to 4,000 Southern casualties. At Cold Harbor, a crossroads ten miles northeast of Richmond, Grant sustained one of his worst defeats of the war, losing 7,000 men in the first thirty minutes of a poorly planned assault.

Just after the battle, Lizzie's brother, John Newton, visited Grant's headquarters and conferred with Federal army scout Judson Knight. Although Winder had promised John no battlefield duty, other officials were determined to force him to fight. To avoid it, John fled Richmond and reached Union lines. Knight attempted to recruit John as a Union scout. John declined, saying he wanted to go to Philadelphia. He then added: "If you can ever get into communication with my mother or sister, they are in a position where they might furnish you with valuable information."

Six days after the breakout Lizzie made contact with Streight and three of his comrades. Their escape path had been arranged through communications between Streight and Unionist Abby Green, with Robert Ford relaying messages to and from the prison. First, Streight and his party went to the home of a loyal black woman, where Abby Green met them and took them to property owned by John Quarles on the outskirts of town. Lucy A. Rice, who boarded at the Quarles's home, gave up her rooms to them and provided them with clothing and provisions. Like Abby Green, Lucy had long been in contact with Libby's inmates. This safe house, and others, were "supported by Van Lew's means," according to Union Col. David B. Parker, a colleague of Miss Lizzie after the war.

Knowing this, the fugitives asked to meet Elizabeth Van Lew. Lucy Rice picked her up and took her to the modest house. Miss Lizzie recalled the experience: "I followed Mrs. Rice into the house...and found myself in [their] presence. I was so overcome with terror for them that I quite lost my voice for some time....I was particularly delighted with [one of the men] who made the tunnel—Maj. Bedan McDonald—broad shouldered and kind hearted, an honest, true, genial looking man. It was a pleasure to take the hand [of one who] had worked so faithfully, so hard, to deliver himself and other prisoners. He put in my hand the chisel [he used] to [break through the cellar wall]."

Shortly afterward, Streight, McDonald, and their fellow fugitives started on what would be a thirteen-day trip to Union lines. They kept moving and succeeded primarily through the heroism of sharp, shrewd black Unionists who fed and guided them.

"Their safe arrival, after many days of suffering and wandering, gladdened our hearts," Miss Lizzie wrote. The *New York Herald* noted: "The perils and sufferings through which [all of the fugitives] passed, form one of those exciting episodes which war only can produce."

While Miss Lizzie's contribution to their escape seems small, it actually was significant. Her money and connections kept the lines of communication open from inside the prison to the outside world. And, in the words of Union Col. David B. Parker, she was the "guiding spirit" of the brave men and women, white and black, who made it possible for some Union soldiers to escape the horrors of prison life in Richmond.

Still, thousands remained and suffered, and many died. On February 27, 1864, the authorities permitted Miss Lizzie to visit the perimeter of Belle Isle Prison, located on an island in the James River. With no barracks, prisoners only had tents to sleep in, but there were ten thousand prisoners and only three thousand tents. The continuous exposure to the weather played a large role in the rising death toll on the island. Miss Lizzie, who was under constant surveillance, was sickened by what she saw.

"It surpassed in wretchedness and squalid filth my most vivid imagination," she wrote. "The long lines of forsaken, despairing, hopeless-looking beings, who, within this hollow square, looked upon us, gaunt hunger staring from their sunken eyes....Oh weary, longing, dying eyes—day of deliverance, will you never come?"

Well, the Federal government indeed would try, and very soon.

The Kilpatrick-Dahlgren Debacle

Shortly after returning from Gettysburg in November 1863, Abraham Lincoln reviewed a troubling report from seven surgeons who recently had been released from Libby and Belle Island prisons. "No prison or penitentiary [we've] ever seen in a Northern state equaled in cheerlessness, unhealthiness, and paucity of rations these two military prisons in Richmond," they asserted. Prisoners, they said, were sometimes shot just for looking out of the windows. Letters and statements from others, including Elizabeth Van Lew, supported these allegations.

While the Union and Confederate armies were generally dormant during the winter months of 1863–64, Lincoln was approached by swashbuckling twenty-eight-year-old Brig. Gen. H. Judson Kilpatrick. He bragged that he could execute a successful raid on Richmond, destroy railroads, and liberate Union prisoners of war at Libby and Belle Isle. With Robert E. Lee's army in winter camp, Kilpatrick reasoned that Richmond was not only accessible but conquerable. Union intelligence from Miss Lizzie reported weak defenses for the Confederate capital—about three thousand Virginia militia.

Lincoln authorized the raid. Kilpatrick would lead some three thousand cavalrymen to Richmond, free thousands of prisoners, and distribute broadly an amnesty proclamation offering full pardons to Southerners who wished to come back into the Union.

Col. Ulric Dahlgren was made second in command. Dahlgren, just twenty-one years old, had a spotless military and personal record, although he tended to be rash and bloodthirsty. He was short and thin, with red hair and a red goatee. Dahlgren had lost a leg at Gettysburg, but he was still eager to "smell hell."

Reports by Miss Lizzie and others on the brutal treatment of Union prisoners of war resulted in a cavalry raid in February 1864 to liberate them. Leading the raid was Brig. Gen. H. Judson Kilpatrick, shown above on the way to Richmond.

Nearly five hundred men under Dahlgren moved out first, on February 28. They were followed an hour later by thirty-five hundred men under Kilpatrick. Dahlgren's force was to assail the city from the south while Kilpatrick attacked from the northwest.

Within a mile of Richmond, Kilpatrick encountered artillery fire, lost his nerve, and fell back to Mechanicsville to rethink the plan. There he was set upon by the cavalry of Confederate Maj. Gen. Wade Hampton, who had learned about the raid from two men captured from Dahlgren's cavalry. The engagement was enough for Kilpatrick. He retreated to Union lines on the Peninsula.

Dahlgren, meanwhile, ran into complications eastward, above the James River. On the city's outskirts his force clashed with the Confederate home guard. Dahlgren retreated, with the Rebels in pursuit. During the night Dahlgren and ninety of his men were trapped and ambushed. Dahlgren was killed, and most of his troops were captured. On the following morning the Confederates buried Dahlgren where he fell, in a sloshy, muddy hole. Four days later, on March 6, the body was disinterred and taken to a railroad depot in Richmond, where,

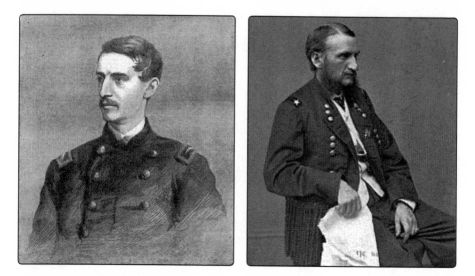

Col. Ulric Dahlgren (left) and Brig. Gen. Judson Kilpatrick (right) led a cavalry raid to free Union prisoners of war in Richmond. Near Richmond, Dahlgren's force was ambushed, and he was killed. Confederate officials claimed they found papers on his body with instructions to kill Jefferson Davis and his cabinet.

according to the *Richmond Whig*, "large numbers of persons went to see it." Then, around 2:00 p.m., the body was buried in a secret location.

Earlier, just after the ambush, William Littlepage, a thirteen-year-old member of Richmond's home guard, had searched the dead Yankees for valuables and found on Dahlgren's corpse some loose papers, which he passed to his superiors. The papers revealed startling information. One document was the draft of an address Dahlgren apparently planned to read to his men. A portion of it read: "We hope to release the prisoners from Belle Island first....We will cross the James River into Richmond, destroying the bridges after us and exhorting the released prisoners to destroy and burn the hateful city." A special order added: "The men must keep together and well in hand, and, once in the city, it must be destroyed and Jeff. Davis and Cabinet killed."

These papers, along with Dahlgren's artificial leg, were sent to Richmond and shown to Davis and members of his cabinet. Robert E. Lee, outraged by the notes, urged publication in the press so "that our people & the world may know the character of the war our enemies wage against us, & the unchristian & atrocious acts they plot & perpetuate."

The notes were published, further fanning the flames of hatred against Lincoln and the Union. To add to the furor, Dahlgren's artificial leg was displayed in a store window, and one of his fingers was cut off by someone who admired a ring he wore.

For Miss Lizzie this barbarous treatment of Dahlgren's body was not only shameful but outrageous. Further, she believed the papers to be forgeries. She wrote in her journal: "The forged papers said to have been found on Colonel Dahlgren's body had maddened the people, [and] Southern people when maddened, who have been used to giving way to wrath with violence on Negroes, stop not at trifles."

She vowed "to discover the hidden grave and remove [Dahlgren's] honored dust to friendly care."

The body would not have been discovered had not a black man been out in the Oakwood burying ground at midnight and watched them bringing Dahlgren. He revealed the location to Miss Lizzie's agents, and during a thunderstorm on the night of April 6, they disinterred the coffin and brought it to William Rowley's residence.

Before moving the body to a more secure place, seven members of the underground, including Miss Lizzie and her mother, conducted a brief ceremony. They paid their last respects and then transferred the body from its roughhewn pine box into a metallic one. The coffin was placed in Rowley's wagon, carefully concealed by "young peach trees, packed as the nursery men pack them." With two men walking as guides, Rowley drove the wagon toward the farm of Unionist Robert Orrock Jr. Rowley had one seemingly insurmountable obstacle—getting through Confederate picket posts.

Miss Lizzie wrote: "If one [of the pickets] had run his bayonet into this wagon only a few inches, death would certainly have been the award of this brave man [Rowley], and

Farmer William S. Rowley was one of Miss Lizzie's best agents. He guided many escaped prisoners out of the city, as well as the body of Col. Ulric Dahlgren, which he concealed in his wagon.

not only death, but torture to make him reveal those connected with him—his accomplices."

Rowley, of course, was aware of the danger, but he was a consummate actor and a man of iron nerve. Approaching the pickets, he saw that they were examining everyone and everything. His anxiety intensified until he recognized the guard who strolled over to inspect his wagon. Rowley reminded him of their previous contact. The guard seemed indifferent at first.

"Whose trees are those?" the guard asked.

Rowley calmly replied, "They belong to a German in the country."

The guard talked about the stupidity of planting peach trees at this season.

"Ah, well, that was the German's worry," said Rowley.

The guard sighed, "It would be a pity to disturb those trees, when you've packed them so nice."

Rowley answered nonchalantly: "I did not expect them to be disturbed. But I know a soldier's duty."

Other wagons were lining up behind Rowley, waiting to be inspected, and the lieutenant in charge yelled at the guard, "Search the man so that he can go."

"Your face is guarantee enough," the guard said to Rowley in a low voice. "Go on!"

And so the body of Col. Ulric Dahlgren resumed its journey. The rest of the trip was uneventful. At Orrock's the body was reburied, and a peach tree was planted over the grave. The ghoulish mission had been accomplished.

Miss Lizzie and her compatriots then sent a cipher report through the network to General Butler, who notified the grieving father—Adm. John A. Dahlgren, commander of the Federal fleet lying off Charleston, South Carolina. The admiral later noted that "a stranger called and hinted at some information, which he said had reached him, to the effect that the remains of Colonel Dahlgren had been found and removed by some friends to a place of safety, but that great secrecy was necessary to avoid the search of the rebel authorities."

Confederate leaders did not realize that Ulric Dahlgren's body had been stolen until April 14, 1864, when, in compliance with Union requests, they opened the grave to obtain the body and ship it north. The *Richmond Examiner* reported: "Dahlgren had risen, or been resurrected; the corpse was not found." The Confederate officer who had been in charge of the Oakwood burial called it the "great resurrection." The government now realized it had a dedicated loyalist resistance to contend with.

Grant Indebted to Miss Lizzie

Ulysses S. Grant, whom Lincoln named as general in chief of the Union armies in 1864, established contact with Miss Lizzie in June 1864. According to his chief of secret service, George H. Sharpe, Grant demanded "specific information," and Miss Lizzie "steadily conveyed it to him."

Her intelligence gatherers and couriers consisted of men and women of both races who were willing to take orders without questioning them. Many of them were simple folks—farmers, storekeepers, and factory workers. The intelligence chief later said: "The Van Lews' position, character, and charities gave them a commanding influence, and many families of plain people were encouraged by them to remain true to the flag, and were subsequently able to receive our agents. For a long, long time, she represented all that was left of the power of the United States government in the city of Richmond."

Miss Lizzie set up five relay stations between Richmond and City Point, Grant's headquarters. One of them was her own vegetable farm on the edge of the city. A courier would pick up messages from Lizzie and take them to one of the rendezvous points, where another courier would carry them on. The system worked so speedily that, in addition to the military information she transmitted, she was able to provide Grant's table with flowers still fresh from her garden.

Miss Lizzie transmitted to Colonel Sharpe an average of three intelligence reports a week about Richmond's defenses and the movement of troops between the Richmond area and the Shenandoah Valley. The latter enabled Grant to know whether Lee was reinforcing Jubal A. Early in the Valley or whether Early was reinforcing Lee. Equally important, or perhaps of greater importance, Miss Lizzie informed Sharpe and Grant that no supplies were being sent to Early's army. "It is understood that Early must subsist himself or starve," she reported.

With that information in hand, Union Maj. Gen. Philip H. Sheridan launched a series of attacks in the Valley that crippled Early and forced Lee to send reinforcements to him.

Only days earlier Lee had recalled Maj. Gen. Joseph B. Kershaw's division from the Valley to join the Richmond-Petersburg front. But before Kershaw could reach Richmond, Lee ordered him back to the Valley. And with Kershaw isolated between the two theaters and useless militarily, Grant and Sheridan could make critical moves, and they did.

Grant pounced on battered Confederate lines north and south of the James and captured Fort Harrison, a formidable redoubt outside Richmond. Sheridan defeated Early at Cedar Creek and gained firm control of the Valley. Those successes were due in no small part to the military intelligence provided by Miss Lizzie's agents and Union agents in the Valley.

Grant also learned much about Richmond's defenses and the condition and size of Lee's forces from Miss Lizzie. Reports noted that "there was a camp of seven regiments of infantry in the neighborhood of Deep Bottom," that fortifications were being strengthened on the north side of Richmond, that the manufacture of heavy ammunition had ceased due to the lack of soft iron, that food and other resources were hard to come by, and that Lee had ordered Richmond's fire brigade to round up able-bodied men to be sent to Petersburg. The brigade worked so swiftly and carelessly that one blind man was forwarded with the others.

Blacks were essential to the Union spy operation, both free and enslaved. Miss Lizzie noted in her journal, "Reliable information is gathered from Negroes, and they certainly show wisdom, discretion, and prudence." One of the best of the free black agents was Sylvanus J. Brown, who, having a pass to sell goods at markets in Richmond, often left the city with white and black persons concealed in his cart, and then assisted them in escaping to Union lines. Perhaps his most dangerous reconnaissance mission was the task of taking a Union army scout "across the Chickahominy Swamp and by the Rebel camps close up to Richmond to see the position of the Confederates."

Rebel authorities soon suspected Brown of treachery. They offered a reward to anyone who would capture him "dead or alive."

Miss Lizzie's male servants ran innocent-looking errands that were actually death-defying missions to convey to Grant dispatches sewn in their clothes. After the war the *New York Tribune* described part of the operation: "Every day two of [Van Lew's] trusty servants drove into Richmond [from her Henrico vegetable farm] with something to sell—milk, chickens, etc. These Negroes wore great, strong brogans [heavy work shoes reaching to the ankle] with soles of immense thickness, made by a Richmond shoemaker. [When they left the city] they never wore the same shoes they wore into the city. The soles of these shoes were double and hollow, and in them were carried through the lines, letters, maps, plans, etc. which were regularly delivered to General Grant at City Point."

Female servants of the Van Lew family also carried secret messages to Grant. On several occasions Confederate guards stopped and searched the family's seamstress. They examined her assorted patterns, unwittingly holding in their hands a Federal dispatch. But they never discovered the messages.

On one occasion Miss Lizzie came close to being exposed as a spy. As she walked along the street to meet an agent, a man approached her and murmured, "I'm going through the lines tonight." Since he had not identified himself, Miss Lizzie frowned, made no acknowledgment, and kept walking. She was afraid to trust him. The next day she watched a Confederate regiment march by her house, and she recognized the man, a junior officer now in his gray uniform. By such hairs as these did the sword hang over her day after day.

Lizzie's Spy in Jeff Davis's House

Mary Elizabeth Bowser's name appears in numerous articles and books as an educated servant whom Miss Lizzie had planted as a spy in the Confederate White House, the official residence of President Jefferson Davis. While Davis conducted business there, he did not regard his slaves as a security threat. Official papers did not have to be given special protection when slaves were around because, by law, slaves were illiterate.

Miss Lizzie certainly was aware of this law and of the espionage value of a slave who was secretly able to read and write. To carry out such a masquerade would require a bold, dangerous plan that placed everyone involved at high risk.

The Van Lews had twenty-one slaves in 1850 but only two by 1860—both of them elderly women. But the Van Lews had not gone through the legal procedures required to free slaves. Freedom meant exile. Under Virginia law, freed slaves had to leave the state within a year after winning their freedom. Only by ignoring that law could Miss Lizzie carry out the daring placement of an agent in the Confederate White House.

Miss Lizzie and her mother raised the eyebrows of their elitist friends in 1846 by having a slave baptized as Mary Jane Richards. Later Miss Lizzie sent Mary Jane to Philadelphia for an education. In 1855, Mary Jane sailed to Liberia, the African nation founded by Americans as a colony for former slaves.

On March 5, 1860, a ship bearing Mary Jane Richards arrived in Baltimore from Liberia. She went on to Richmond—which was an illegal act for a freed slave. Five months later she was arrested for "claiming to be a free person of color." She was briefly jailed and released after Miss Lizzie paid a ten-dollar fine and claimed that Mary was still a slave. This declaration would give her perfect cover as an agent—unless authorities discovered that the woman was educated.

To create two identities for Mary, Miss Lizzie gave the name Mary Jones for the 1860 census record as the only free black servant of the Van Lew family. A third identity emerged in 1861: marriage records of St. John's Church list the wedding of the Van Lews' servant "Mary" (no last name was used) to Wilson Bowser in April 1861. Was this a real wedding or part of a plan to perfect a cover identity for Mary Ann Richards with the help of a priest? Even if the wedding actually occurred, it was a short marriage. She had no children. And after the war she married a man named Garvin.

But during the war, Mary Elizabeth Bowser came into existence. In her slave identity, she had to pretend to be ignorant and illiterate. Doing so enabled her to make espionage history.

If Bowser actually obtained a position as a dining room servant in the Confederate White House and spied on Jefferson Davis—and the evidence supports this contention—the arrangement could only have been safely carried out through extensive coaching and training, the careful manipulation of multiple aliases, and Miss Lizzie's clandestine, razor-sharp abilities.

As a well-educated domestic servant in the Davis mansion, Bowser/Richards certainly could have picked up valuable information in her role as a waitress and by observing official papers left unguarded on tables. The Davises and their guests, believing she was dumb and illiterate, would have spoken freely in her presence. One report indicates that Bowser/Richards had a photographic memory and could repeat word for word everything she saw on Davis's desk.

Many decades after the war, Varina Davis, Jefferson Davis's widow, denied the possibility of a spy in her house. In a 1905 letter to the regent of the Confederate White House Museum, Mrs. Davis wrote that she never "had in

Miss Lizzie's literate African American agent, Mary Bowser, obtained a position as a servant in this dining room at the Confederate White House and spied on Jefferson Davis. He held councils of war in this room, and the table was usually covered with maps and confidential papers. Mary had a photographic mind and could repeat word for word everything she saw, read, and heard.

her employ an educated negro 'given or hired' by Miss Van Lew as a spy" during the war.

However, author William Gilmore Beymer came to a different conclusion in 1910 after Miss Lizzie's niece told Beymer's aide that a Van Lew servant, Mary Elizabeth Bowser, did work for Jefferson Davis and that she was one of her aunt's favorite servants. The niece added that sometime before the war, her Aunt Lizzie had freed Mary and sent her north for an education. "Then she came back," and during the war, she "sort of disappeared from Miss Van Lew's house." And it was during this period that she was "working for the Jefferson Davises." In the June 1911 issue of *Harper's Monthly*, Beymer noted that no record existed of what happened to Bowser after the war.

In all likelihood, Bowser reverted to her real name—Mary Ann Richards. She would later join forces with the Christian Commission to promote the education of the freed people and then accept a position with the Baptist Home Missionary Society to teach nearly two hundred African American children at a newly established school.

Lizzie's Spy on the Rebel Rails

Miss Lizzie recruited Samuel Ruth in October to establish another channel of communication: the railroad. Ruth, as mentioned earlier, was a staunch Unionist who ran the Richmond, Fredericksburg, and Potomac Railroad, a vital supply line for Lee's army. Ruth, like Miss Lizzie, masqueraded as an ardent Confederate while slowing down the trains and reducing the railroad's efficiency.

General Grant's chief of secret service, George H. Sharpe, viewed the railroad as a means of moving information quickly, and Ruth was the man to make that happen. Ruth and farmer Charles Carter passed information back and forth while Carter was delivering produce to Richmond from a nearby county. When this arrangement appeared to attract the scrutiny of Confederate agents, Carter gave his information to a black courier, who then met with Ruth. Ruth also recruited his own agents, many of them railroad employees.

Ruth's intelligence reports pertained almost exclusively to Confederate supplies and troop movements—information a railroad executive would see in the course of a day's work. One of his reports to Miss Lizzie enabled Grant to raid a railroad depot, take four hundred prisoners, and destroy four railroad bridges and twenty-eight freight cars.

A Snitch in the Family

Meanwhile, back at the Van Lew mansion, Miss Lizzie anticipated increased surveillance by Confederate authorities and possibly even searches of the house. "Visitors apparently friendly were treacherous," she wrote. "I have turned to speak to a friend and found a detective at my elbow. Strange faces could sometimes be seen peeping around the columns and pillars of the back portico."

To conceal secrets and other incriminating communications, she hid her letters for Union generals inside small, hollow bronze

Col. George H. Sharpe (left), who became Gen. Ulysses S. Grant's secret service chief, worked closely with Miss Lizzie and obtained frequent intelligence from her. Seated next to Sharpe is John C. Babcock, one of his agents.

figures of animals put together in halves. The letters were placed in the crack where the halves came together.

She soon discovered that she and her mother were being formally investigated. Provost Marshal Thomas Doswell called in neighbors and family friends and applied tough tactics to get them to speak against the Van Lews. But no one could think of anything to betray the Van Lews, even after they were admonished to "refresh your memory."

One person didn't need her memory refreshed. She spoke out boldly against the Van Lews. Surprisingly, this snitch was none other than Miss Lizzie's sister-in-law, Mary C. Van Lew. Mary swore in her deposition, "They are strong abolitionists...that [her own husband] John Van Lew had gone North on account of his preference for that Government...that she had frequently visited the Van Lews and often heard them express ardent desire for the success of Federal arms and the failure of the Confederate States to establish its independence."

Investigator Doswell gave Mary's deposition to the Adjutant and Inspector General's Office and asked: "Shall other evidence be taken with a view to the removal of these parties from the Confederacy?" Charles M. Blackford's response sheds light on Miss Lizzie's ability to avoid arrest, prison, or removal from Virginia: "Miss Elizabeth Van Lew of this city is very unfriendly in her sentiments toward the Government....But it does not appear that she has ever done anything to infirm the cause. Like most of her sex she seems to have talked freely—and in the presence of female friends, who have informed on her. The question is whether she shall be sent beyond the lines because of her opinion."

The ultimate decision in her case was "no action to be taken." Interestingly, political opinion was the key to the arrest of many Richmonders, but Miss Lizzie's wealth and position, as well as her habit of talking too much, saved her. The authorities refused to believe that this frail spinster lady would commit acts of disloyalty.

The government continued its counterintelligence efforts, however, and on a tip from a wealthy Southern lady, the Confederate authorities arrested eight members of the Unionist network on January 20, 1865. The group included F. W. E. Lohmann, John Hancock, James Duke and his sons, John Timberlake, and Isaac Silver. Then a Confederate counterspy, claiming to be a Union man, infiltrated the network in February.

Although the Van Lews' ranks were shrinking, their efforts were not. Miss Lizzie, Samuel Ruth, and Charles Carter continued to send information to Grant's headquarters. Ruth, seeking to further cripple Lee's supply line—the railroad—asked Northern newspapers to promise payments of large premiums to "engine-runners, machinists, blacksmiths, molders, and other mechanics" who deserted Confederate service to work for the Union. Many newspapers did so. Ruth noted after the war that the announcements were "distributed to the Army and passed over by the pickets." Large numbers deserted, and Confederate railroad services nearly came to a halt.

Short-Lived Glory

On March 14, 1865, Grant took note of "a letter from a lady in Richmond," probably Miss Lizzie, revealing that Confederate troops had been ordered down the Danville road. Grant correctly inferred from this message that the enemy planned to fall back in a southwesterly direction toward Lynchburg.

Grant then struck with fierce blows at Lee's right flank, and on the night of April 1–2, he hit Lee with the heaviest bombardment of the war. That led to the immediate evacuation of Richmond. Federal troops entered the city on

THE FALL OF RICHMOND VA ON THE NIGHT OF APRIL 2ⁿᵈ 1865.

When the Confederates evacuated Richmond on the night of April 1–2, 1865, they torched the bridges and tobacco warehouses. Winds spread the flames and consumed numerous homes.

April 3. To celebrate, Miss Lizzie raised atop her mansion the first Union flag to fly over Richmond in four years.

A howling mob of Richmonders gathered nearby and stared angrily at the flag. Quickly, the mob shoved its way to the mansion, trampling the gardens and shrubs. "Burn the place down!" they shouted.

Miss Lizzie confronted them: "I know you, and you, and you," she cried out, pointing to individuals and calling them by name. "General Grant will be in this city within the hour; if this house is harmed, your houses shall be burned by noon." The mob backed away.

To protect the Van Lew mansion from the wrath of angry Richmonders, the Federal army placed an armed guard around the house, and two of Grant's staff officers called on the family to pay their respects. Grant even handed down an order that "all of Miss Van Lew's wants [be] supplied."

Grant himself visited Miss Lizzie and drank tea on the columned porch with his special spy. Julia Grant remembered his insistence on calling on her, for "she had rendered valuable service to the Union." Later, Grant wrote to Miss

Lizzie, saying: "You have sent me the most valuable information received from Richmond during the war."

A week or so later, Gen. Benjamin Butler issued directives that enabled John Van Lew to return to Richmond. In a letter to the War Department, Butler praised Miss Lizzie, calling her his "secret correspondent who furnished valuable information during the whole campaign." Later, Colonel Sharpe declared that "the greatest portion" of the information passed to the general's army in 1864–65 was "owed to the intelligence and devotion of Miss Van Lew."

Miss Lizzie requested and received official recognition for her friends and associates, and many of them were appointed as Federal detectives.

In July 1866, *Harper's Weekly* featured a long story on Miss Lizzie and her mother. The article began: "The late war called forth many heroic characters, whose deeds have been proclaimed through the civilized world; but there are many whose works, although unobtrusive, and hitherto unheralded, have been such as to do honor to the American name—indeed, to the human race; and we know of none more deserving of a nation's gratitude and applause than the estimable lady and her daughter who form the subject of these remarks."

When Grant became president in 1869, one of his first official acts was to nominate Miss Lizzie as postmaster of Richmond. The Senate confirmed her two days later. The lucrative post was one of the highest Federal offices a woman could hold in the nineteenth century. The *Richmond Enquirer* and *Richmond Examiner* condemned the appointment "of a Federal spy" as a "deliberate insult to our people." She held the position until 1877, when President Rutherford B. Hayes ousted her for political reasons.

During her term in office, she contributed much of her salary to charities benefiting African Americans. And during the war years she had expended much of her wealth in spy work. Now, she was broke. She still had her mansion and her unproductive farm, but no one would buy them.

"I tell you truly and solemnly," she wrote, "that I have suffered for necessary food. I have not one cent in the world....I honestly think that the government should see that I was sustained."

In 1883, she passed a civil service examination "with the highest rating" and moved to Washington, D.C., where she became a post office clerk. Two years later she was demoted by a vindictive supervisor to "a clerkship of the lowest salary and grade." At about the same time a Northern newspaper called her "a troublesome relic." That was enough. She resigned.

Heartbroken, she returned to the lonely house on Church Hill. She and an invalid niece were all that were left of the family. She wrote to Northern friends for help. Her letters brought a response that was quick and generous. Boston men—mostly friends and relatives of Col. Paul Revere, whom she had helped in Libby Prison—gave an ample annuity. It met her basic needs for the rest of her life. But her quality of life descended to its lowest level.

"We live here in isolation," she wrote. "No one will walk with us on the street; no one will go with us anywhere, and it grows worse and worse as the years roll on and those I love go to their long rest."

And so, in the old mansion with its haunting memories, Miss Lizzie lived out her remaining days, nursed by a former female slave to whom she had given freedom long years before.

Elizabeth Van Lew died on September 25, 1900. She was buried in Richmond's Shockoe Hill Cemetery. Longtime friends Otis H. Russell (a former collector for the port of Richmond) and John P. Reynolds Jr. (a Boston benefactor) collaborated to obtain a giant memorial stone from Massachusetts for her grave. Reynolds designed the bronze tablet on the face of the stone. The inscription reads:

Elizabeth L. Van Lew

1818–1900

She risked everything that is dear to man—friends—
fortune—comfort—health—life itself—all for the
one absorbing desire of her heart—that slavery
might be abolished and the Union preserved. This boulder
from the Capitol Hill in Boston is a tribute
from Massachusetts friends

THE CRAZY BET MYTH

Elizabeth Van Lew became known as "Crazy Bet" after her death. That image unfairly lingers to this day.

Blame John P. Reynolds Jr., a Bostonian who first met her when she was sixty-five and broke. Reynolds represented a small group of prominent Bostonians who established a subscription fund for her as thanks for her wartime assistance to Massachusetts soldiers. Reynolds personally delivered payments to her each year from 1883 to 1900, the year of her death. They became close friends, and she left him all her personal papers—several hundred pages of tattered and out-of-order documents—a treasure trove of information about a true American heroine.

Reynolds took on the responsibility of perpetuating Miss Lizzie's memory, and on September 26, 1900, he wrote a narrative of her life for the Boston *Evening Transcript*. His main point—a false one—was that she succeeded as a spy by acting crazy. "For a long time, if not continuously," Reynolds wrote, "she pretended to be a little lightheaded and would go singing through the streets, perhaps a basket of fruit on her arm, as if she were a peddler, and so she soon was known as 'Crazy Van Lew.'" Thus, said Reynolds, this supposedly harmless woman "was allowed to pass the guard and go into Libby Prison."

Reynolds wrote this article before he had read any of the papers willed to him. He based his article, not on research, but on the Miss Lizzie he knew—the one he met in 1883, after Reconstruction. During this time, her wartime loyalty, her gender, and her assertiveness resulted in scathing and mean-spirited attacks from Richmond newspapers and politicians—attacks that prompted President Rutherford B. Hayes to replace her as postmaster, a position she had held for eight years. Richmonders ridiculed and reviled her. One leading citizen told her, "We can never forgive you." It was also a period during which illnesses took the lives of her beloved brother, John, and her deeply cherished niece, Eliza.

She "shrank from everything," she wrote to a friend in Boston, adding, "The fearful effect upon my life and health you cannot conceive." Thus, when Reynolds first saw her, Miss Van Lew appeared disheveled, nervous, frightened, and paranoid. Reynolds projected this same image into the past.

Writer William Gilmore Beymer came under Reynolds's influence and began writing a biographical piece on Miss Lizzie for *Harper's Monthly*. He showed Reynolds a draft, and Reynolds complained that he hadn't adequately emphasized her affected eccentricity and craziness.

Beymer seized the suggestion, and "Crazy Bet" became the theme of his article. In the years that followed, other writers further embellished the story. Before long the public believed that she was an eccentric woman who hoodwinked Confederate authorities by dressing in odd clothes and acting silly or hysterical. Even the respected magazine *Civil War Times Illustrated* called her "a strange little woman."

In reality, she never acted crazy in order to carry out spy activities. She did, at times, resort to disguises to conceal her identity, but never for the purpose of being presumed insane.

It was only after her bitter battle to retain her position as postmaster—twelve years after the war—that she was charged with being mentally unstable or crazy. And these were politically motivated, slanderous attacks about her behavior in office, not her wartime demeanor.

During the war, her challenge was to appear to be a loyal Confederate who could not possibly engage in espionage. This she did very well while serving as an imaginative, brilliant, and efficient spy and spymaster.

THE SPY WHO SAVED SHIPS

Elizabeth Baker

The need was urgent and the reward was huge. The Confederate government had a problem and would pay big money for a quick solution.

The problem: the Federal blockade of Southern seaports, effectively isolating the Confederacy from the outside world.

The challenge: invent a device to destroy Federal ships so that vessels could go back and forth between Southern and European ports.

The immediate concern was to break the blockade at the mouth of the James River so that commercial trade could leave or enter Richmond. Without that trade, the city would suffer from a lack of supplies and food.

In the fall of 1861 naval authorities in Washington heard rumors that the Confederacy had found a solution: a new kind of ship that could float under water and detonate huge torpedoes its crew attached to enemy ships. Reports indicated that an experimental model was in production at the Tredegar Iron Works in Richmond. If true, these "infernal machines" might be able to destroy the Union fleet and turn the tide of war in the South's favor.

The Federal government called on Allan Pinkerton, head of the Union Intelligence Service, to send a spy to Richmond. The spy's mission was to find out if such devices were being built, and if so, to get inside the factory where they were being made (areas never before penetrated by Federal agents) and

Allan Pinkerton (left), chief of the Union's Intelligence Service, selected one of his agents, Elizabeth Baker, to get into Richmond, confirm the existence of submarine construction, and draw a sketch of it.

make a sketch of it. Pinkerton chose a young well-to-do widow, Elizabeth H. Baker, for the delicate mission.

Navy officials shook their heads in disbelief. Tongues wagged over conference tables. Some men reportedly exclaimed: "He's sending a woman!" "What do they know about these things!"

Pinkerton had his flaws, but he was a good judge of people. He owned the National Detective Agency in Chicago that had solved a series of train robberies during the 1850s, and Elizabeth Baker was one of his best agents. Equally important, she was a native of Richmond and knew her way around the city. Her Virginia accent and Southern charm would serve her well.

From Chicago, Elizabeth wrote to two close friends in the Confederate capital, Captain and Mrs. Atwater, saying that she missed Richmond and would like to visit them. "Please do come," they wrote back, "and stay with us as long as you are in the city."

In November 1861, after a roundabout trip to avert suspicion, Elizabeth arrived in Richmond. The Atwaters were an upscale couple. They arranged a full social calendar for Elizabeth, including parties and receptions at the homes of high-society families—people who shared secrets willingly after a few glasses of champagne or bourbon.

Although Captain Atwater held a commission in the Confederate navy, he was really a Union sympathizer. He stood ready to enlist in the Union navy if the right opportunity presented itself. Elizabeth discussed her own loyalty to the North with Atwater. They both agreed that ambitious politicians were responsible for the war and that the common people of the South had nothing to gain from it.

As would be the case with any good spy, Elizabeth did not reveal the real purpose of her visit. With Atwater as her tour guide around the city, she closely observed the earthworks and other fortifications and made copious notes about them.

Conveniently, one day Atwater mentioned to Elizabeth that he was to observe tests of a new device, a prototype of an underwater boat that could sink ships.

Elizabeth asked if she could watch the tests, and Atwater responded affirmatively. He assured her that there was no danger, and she could be his guest.

Later that week, on a beautiful September day, the Atwaters and Elizabeth traveled by carriage to the site of the demonstration. A large crowd of politicians and military brass and their wives gathered there as well.

An admiral began the program by talking about the strange underwater vessel that would transport an equally strange torpedo. He said that the submarine had been designed by underwater explosives engineer William Cheeney and that the vessel was powered by only two men, who operated a mechanical propulsion device. A flotation collar on the surface of the water supported air hoses that trailed down to the submerged ship so that the crew could breathe. The collar was painted a dark green to simulate the color of seawater.

The speaker pointed to a large scow in the river. "That is the target," he said.

The observers saw the green flotation collar move closer to the barge and then stop. The third member of the crew, a diver, exited the boat and placed a giant torpedo on the hull of the barge. The torpedo would be fired with a fuse connected by a long wire coiled on board the submarine. The diver returned, and the vessel backed away from its target.

A few minutes later, a mighty roar threw the barge high into the air, ripping it to pieces and sending the remains to the bottom of the river. The crowd cheered. Elizabeth cringed. She realized that the device was lethal and could destroy Union ships anywhere. Its potential seemed unlimited.

The speaker then emphasized: "What you have seen is only a small working model of a far greater device nearing completion at Tredegar. The real thing will decimate Union gunboats blocking the mouth of the James River. It will allow Confederate steamers to carry cotton and tobacco to distant markets and return with the materials we need."

After returning to the Atwater home, Elizabeth made extensive notes and sketches in the privacy of her room.

Early the next morning, Atwater and Elizabeth visited the Tredegar Iron Works, a massive munitions factory. As they walked into a warehouse, the noise was deafening from the din of mallet upon iron and the screech of iron sheeting. Workers labored across the outer shell of the underwater ship. The vessel resembled a large dark bumblebee set on a framework of heavy timbers.

They were told that the Confederacy expected to have two of these ships in the James River within two months.

Atwater turned to Elizabeth and said, "Imagine that thing floating below the sterns of ships, with divers attaching explosives to them."

She nodded and pondered the destruction of the Federal navy.

Later, Elizabeth made more sketches and concealed them with her other notes in the crown of her embroidered bonnet. Anxious to get this information to Federal officials, she asked Atwater to obtain a pass for her through Confederate lines.

With the expedited pass in hand two days later, she left for Fredericksburg on her way to Washington. There, she met with Allan Pinkerton and gave him her notes and sketches. Pinkerton then raced to the office of Secretary of the Navy Gideon Welles, who brought in George B. McClellan, general in chief of the Union army.

They wired blockade commanders about these developments. They advised them to keep a sharp lookout for the green-colored floats and to destroy the air tubes connecting the floats to the submarines.

In response, Federal navy officials in the Hampton Roads area of Virginia also devised and rigged antisubmarine nets around their ships. These were arrangements of spars (thick, strong poles) encircling each vessel, from which either heavy nets or chains were suspended to a depth of fourteen feet. The commanders believed that a diver attempting to attach a torpedo would become entangled and caught in the nets.

In October 1861 the new Confederate submarine was transported to the mouth of the James River for an attack upon the USS *Minnesota*. As anticipated by navy commanders, the submarine ran afoul of the antisubmarine net and barely escaped. The boat was beached and later taken back to Richmond.

Three weeks later Welles received a telegram from the captain of one of his gunboats. After seeing a green float, he had snagged the air hoses and pulled them up. The Confederate crew, trapped inside, drowned.

No further mention of this first submarine appears in Confederate records, and no drawings or financial records of it survive, except for a receipt from Tredegar for construction of a forty-six-inch propeller.

These incidents and the background provided by Pinkerton's female spy received extensive newspaper coverage in the North. Confederate leaders, having lost the element of surprise, went back to the drawing board.

Elizabeth Baker's other missions for the Federal Secret Service are not recorded, but she accomplished more in this one mission than did many other agents in years of work. Her covert activity, acted upon by Federal authorities, saved many Union ships from destruction and kept intact the Northern blockade of Southern ports.

DOUBLE TROUBLE
SISTER ACT

Ginnie and Lottie Moon

The Moon sisters should have worn a sign that read "Approach with Caution." They were always in control and were not girls to be messed with. Yet they also were compassionate and kind, always doing small favors for friends and even strangers.

When the war started, Ginnie was seventeen and devastatingly gorgeous. Lottie was thirty-two, married, and while not beautiful, she was described by her husband as "the damnedest, smartest woman in the world." Both were petite, high-strung, and charming. And both could laugh at themselves and at the Yankees, whom they despised with a passion. They were not quintessential Southern ladies. They could be perfect ladies when they wanted to be and merry pranksters and hell-raisers the rest of the time. They were spies in the making.

Lottie and Ginnie were born into an old Virginia family but reared in Oxford, Ohio, near Cincinnati. The girls' parents raised them unconventionally, encouraging them to read controversial books, such as works on the origin of the species and Thomas Paine's *The Age of Reason*. The girls developed scintillating minds, personalities laced with wit, and the ability to find quick fixes to seemingly insurmountable obstacles.

Lottie grew up shooting guns, acting in amateur plays, and riding horses at breakneck speed. She mastered an unusual trick that would prove useful for

Ginnie Moon

Lottie Moon

her as a spy. She could throw her jaw out of place with a cracking sound and pretend to grimace as if she were in insufferable pain.

Both Lottie and Ginnie redefined the word *betrothal*. It was said that lovely Ginnie boosted the South's war morale by getting herself engaged to sixteen boys at one time. When asked why, she explained: "If they'd died in battle, they'd have died happy, wouldn't they? And if they lived, I didn't give a damn."

Lottie attracted men too and was engaged to twelve simultaneously. The first one to get her to the altar was Ambrose E. Burnside, a stout, kindly young lieutenant. They planned a large wedding with all the trimmings. As they stood before the minister during the ceremony, Burnside promised to love and cherish Lottie so long as they both should live. Then the minister turned to Lottie and asked if she would take Ambrose as her lawfully wedded husband. She said nothing for several seconds as everyone grew restless. Finally she blurted out, "No sirree, Bob, I won't." Then she stalked out of the church. When this news reached her hometown, a close friend remarked, "That's just like Lottie."

Ambrose, a West Point graduate, advanced to attain the rank of major general and became commander of Lincoln's Army of the Potomac in the Civil

War. It was probably to his advantage that he was not married to a Confederate spy.

Lottie's next planned marriage—a few months later—was to James Clark, an attorney destined to be a justice of the Supreme Court of Ohio. Clark, who was aware of Burnside's experience with Lottie, prepared for just such a contingency. On the evening of January 30, 1849, the wedding guests gathered at the Moon house in Oxford. Upstairs, two doors opened. Lottie and James met in the hall. Before they descended the stairs to the parlor, James pulled a

Union Major General Ambrose E. Burnside

small pistol from his pocket. He pressed it to her back and whispered in her ear: "Lottie, there will be a wedding here tonight or a funeral tomorrow." This time, at the ceremony she said "I do" and "I will." The Clarks settled in Hamilton, Ohio, fourteen miles from Oxford, and later moved closer to Cincinnati at Jones's Station.

Both Lottie and James were high-spirited, brilliant, and Southern-oriented. He assembled one of the state's best private libraries, and the couple gathered at their home the best minds in the region to discuss political issues. Judge Clark became a Copperhead (a peace Democrat) and a VIP in the Knights of the Golden Circle, a secret society of antiwar Dixie partisans in the North. The society had a sizable membership in Cincinnati—a city with deeply divided loyalties.

James Clark

The Oxford Female Institute in Ohio.

Fiery Ginnie Moon, fifteen years younger than Lottie, was a student at the Oxford Female Institute in 1861, the year the war began. By then, the girls' father had died and their mother had moved to Memphis, Tennessee. Living in a Yankee state and attending a Yankee college were not on Ginnie's list of things she wanted to do. She hated it so much that she begged the principal, John Scott, to send her home. When he refused, she rebelled by pointing her pearl-handled pistol at the Stars and Stripes on the institute's flagpole and shooting out all the stars, one by one. The principal had had enough of Ginnie. He expelled her and packed her off to her sister and brother-in-law in their nearby Ohio home. Ginnie's brief stay with them became a learning experience—an education on how a girl can serve the Confederacy.

Lottie's First Clandestine Mission

In the late summer of 1862, Walker Taylor, a Confederate spy from across the Ohio River in Kentucky, arrived at the Clarks' home in a frenzied state of mind. He was on a covert mission, and his cover was that he was buying mules for his farm. What he really needed was a courier to deliver dispatches from Mississippi to Confederate Maj. Gen. Edmund Kirby Smith in Kentucky.

Taylor was afraid to try to get through Cincinnati because he was too well known. Eager to serve the Confederacy, Lottie enthusiastically volunteered. Wearing a floppy sunbonnet and shabby shawl, she disguised herself as an old

Irish washerwoman and safely crossed the Ohio by ferry. She then planned to take a train to Lexington, but lacking a pass, she was not allowed to board.

Seeing several Irishmen, she went to them. With tears and gestures she poured out a doleful tale about her "poor darlin' husband a-dyin' in a hospital in Lexington." She asked them: "Wasn't it little enough to let a poor woman see her darlin' once more?" She aroused their sympathy, and they smuggled her aboard.

At Lexington she slipped away and followed the Lexington Pike until she saw a Confederate officer riding into town. As luck would have it, she knew the man, Col. Thomas Scott. She motioned for him to come to her. He dismounted, but her disguise was so good that he did not recognize her. What he saw was an old lady who looked like she had crawled out from under a rock.

"Colonel Scott," she said, "I have some very important papers for you to deliver." She thrust them into his hands. "Promise on your life that you will give these to General Smith, and nobody else."

"Who are you?" he asked.

"That doesn't matter," she said. "What does matter is getting these documents to him at once!"

Then she turned and walked away, and he stood there scratching his head in bewilderment.

Back at the railway station Lottie boarded a coach. Soon she heard men talking about a warning just issued—a warning to watch for a female spy on the train. Lottie began to cry and caught the attention of the sixty-nine-year-old gentleman seated in front of her. He was Gen. Leslie Coombs, a veteran of the War of 1812, during which he had been a captain of spies in a Kentucky regiment. He was a strong Union man.

Concerned about the sobbing woman behind him, Coombs turned around to see what was wrong. Lottie repeated and embellished her story of a stricken husband and hungry children waiting for her.

"And I'm terribly frightened," she said, "that somebody will mistake me for one of those dangerous spies they are talking about."

"Now don't you worry, ma'am," he said. "I'll look out for you."

At Covington he slipped her off the rear platform of the car and watched as she headed toward the ferry. From Cincinnati she walked nineteen miles through woods and fields to her home at Jones's Station, arriving early in the morning. She recounted her experience to her husband and eighteen-year-old Ginnie. The story would shape Ginnie's life.

Lottie's success brought about more adventures. The next was to the Canadian office of the Confederacy in Toronto—an office created to raise havoc in Northern cities, make life miserable for Northern civilians, and help Rebel prisoners of war to escape. This mission for Lottie involved delivering dispatches and letters to agents in Toronto and carrying papers from them to Richmond.

Crossing the Canadian border to get to Toronto was no problem. Crossing the Southern border to Richmond required ingenuity. But for "the damnedest, smartest woman in the world" it wasn't much of a challenge. Lottie pretended to be a British lady suffering from rheumatism and hoping to gain relief at a mineral spring in Virginia. She traveled by train from Toronto to Washington, D.C., where she convinced government officials of her story.

Soon she scurried south, but not to a mineral spring. She went straight to Richmond and delivered the secret messages she carried. Then she had to get back home. The shortest route took her across the Shenandoah Valley, not far from those curative mineral waters.

Near Winchester, at the upper end of the great valley, she ran into a difficult obstacle—Union Brig. Gen. Robert Huston Milroy. "I've gone to the wrong place," she moaned. "I really wanted to visit Hot Springs, Arkansas, not Hot Springs, Virginia. Won't you please give me a pass through the lines?"

Milroy suspected chicanery and sent for his surgeon to examine her. When the doctor questioned Lottie about her health, she told him she had a severe case of rheumatism. As he examined her, she cried out at every touch. "It hurts so much," she sobbed.

She also played her old trick of dislocating her jaw with a grinding, cracking sound, causing her face to take on an expression of extreme agony.

They carried her downstairs. The doctor made his report, saying that Lottie was a sad case. General Milroy gave Lottie a pass to Cincinnati, and her journey continued without interruption.

Ginnie's Clever and Brazen Spirit

Ginnie Moon was sent home to Memphis about the same time Lottie left for Toronto. In Memphis she began her service to the Confederacy by helping her

Double Trouble Sister Act | 101

mother roll bandages and nurse wounded soldiers. That service was short-lived, however, with the Union takeover of Memphis in the summer of 1862.

What was she to do? Well, why not inveigle military secrets from young Union officers and sneak the information to Confederate posts? She decided to use her good looks for a good cause. And she succeeded beyond her expectations. Acting on her own initiative, she snagged information about troop movements and fortifications from a high-ranking officer during a midnight tryst, boldly passed through Union lines on the pretext of meeting a beau, and even smuggled medical supplies to Confederates in a casket, claiming she was accompanying a deceased relative.

"She needed no pass to get through Union lines," wrote the *Memphis Commercial Appeal*. "Her eyes and her way won her permission."

With her boldness bolstered by her success, Ginnie continued her jaw-dropping adventures during the winter of 1862–63. At that time, Confederate Brig. Gen. Nathan Bedford Forrest was on a mission in West Tennessee to disrupt the communication of Union forces under Ulysses Grant that were threatening Vicksburg, Mississippi. The innovative cavalry leader needed intelligence, and night after night the imaginative eighteen-year-old girl rode out to deliver information to the man known as the "Wizard of the Saddle." Forrest subsequently made lightning blows at the Yankees and led thousands of Union soldiers on a wild-goose chase trying to locate his fast-moving cavalry. Forrest's brilliant maneuvers forced Grant to revise and delay his strategies for the Vicksburg campaign.

Later that winter, in December 1862, Ginnie was visiting Jackson, Mississippi, when she learned that Maj. Gen. Sterling Price needed a messenger to deliver vital intelligence to Ohio's antiwar Dixie partisans in the Knights of the Golden Circle. Ginnie knew that her brother-in-law, Judge Clark, Lottie's husband, was a VIP in the Knights. Ginnie went to the general and asked if she and her mother could be the couriers. "We have relatives in Ohio," she said, "and that's a good excuse for a trip." She added: "I won't be caught. Let me go." Price agreed and gave her an escort of eight soldiers back to Memphis to pick up her mother. The remainder of the trip to Ohio and her sister's house was uneventful.

Judge Clark read the message, which sought to induce antiwar midwesterners in the Knights of the Golden Circle to revolt against the Union government and push for a negotiated peace with the South. Clark conferred with fellow Knights and prepared an affirmative answer.

Union agents in the Cincinnati area, however, had been watching Judge Clark and his family for some time. While Ginnie and her mother were visiting the Clarks, the Union assigned a counterspy to take a closer look. He was a charming and popular young Ohioan—the kind of man who would be welcomed into most any home. In fact, he made himself so agreeable that the Clarks invited him to spend several days with them. What this agent used as a cover is unknown, but it worked well.

Lottie was absent at this time, on her mission to Canada and Richmond. But the young man and Ginnie made eye contact quickly, and she added him to the list of admirers smitten with her. However, the agent did not gain any information as easily as he might have hoped. Ginnie's mother was tight-lipped, as usual, and Ginnie's brother-in-law, the judge, said nothing incriminating. The only thing that puzzled the agent was why the ladies worked so hard from dawn to dusk at making quilts.

The agent extended every possible kindness. He even helped Ginnie and her mother get passes for their return trip to the South. But he also sent a confidential note to the captain of the steamboat they would board in Cincinnati. It said simply, "Do not depart without special orders."

On April 3, 1863, Judge Clark accompanied his mother-in-law and Ginnie to catch the steamboat, the *Alice Dean*, and he then returned home.

After they had boarded with their two heavy trunks, they were told that the ship's departure would be delayed. That sounded like trouble. Ginnie had in her possession a dispatch from the secret society. It was wrapped in fine oiled silk and tucked in her bosom.

While her mother remained in their stateroom with the trunks, Ginnie waited in the ladies' cabin. "I saw a Yankee officer coming through the cabin," she later recalled, "and he looked at the numbers on the doors." Then he talked briefly with the captain, who pointed at Ginnie. He approached her and asked her to accompany him to her stateroom. She complied, and he entered and locked the door.

"I am Captain Harrison Rose of the custom house," he said, "and I have a note to show you."

Ginny read it while gritting her teeth: "Arrest Miss Virginia Moon. She is an active and dangerous rebel in the employ of the Confederate government. Has contraband goods and rebel mail and is the bearer of dispatches."

"Now," said Rose, "I must search you."

"Ridiculous," Ginnie replied. "You, a man, ordered to search me? I will never endure it."

"Well," said he, "how can you help it?"

Ginnie later explained the situation in her memoir: "There was a slit in my skirt, and in my petticoat I had a Colt revolver. I put my hand in and took it out, backed to the door and leveled it at him across the washstand [which was between them]. 'If you make a move to touch me, I'll kill you, so help me God!'"

She had the upper hand, but she realized she was creating problems for herself in the long run. So she took a different tack. "Does General Burnside know of this? I don't think he does. He has been a friend of mine since I was five. He would not permit such an indignity to be put upon me. You had better be careful what you do or I will report you to him."

Her threat got his attention.

"All right," he said. "But you *will* be searched at my office."

He took her gun and baggage and left the stateroom to call a carriage and an orderly. Ginnie locked the door and pulled the treacherous dispatch from her bosom. She dipped it into a pitcher of water, rolled it into three balls, and swallowed each of them. The dispatches contained the acceptance of the terms upon which the Confederacy would unite with the Knights of the Golden Circle. Had it been discovered, the three signers would have faced the gallows.

When the captain returned, the door was unlocked. He escorted the two women off the boat and through the crowd on the dock to his office.

On the way he mumbled to Ginnie, "I suppose you feel like hurrahing for Jeff Davis."

Well, why not, she thought to herself. As she later wrote in her memoir: "I raised my hand over my head and said in a loud voice, *'Hurrah for Jeff Davis!'*"

When officials opened the trunks at the office, they found fifty letters to Southerners and a ball of opium. The officer in charge, Capt. Andrew Kemper, asked: "What are you doing with that?"

"My mother requires it," she replied.

Kemper chuckled. Mrs. Moon sat up straight in her chair but didn't speak.

Ginnie observed, "She might be under the influence of opium right now."

Kemper then picked up a heavy quilt and ripped it open. Inside he found opium, quinine, and morphine—drugs badly needed in the South.

Another officer entered the room. As he was closing the door, Ginnie's hoopskirts got in the way. As he pushed them aside he heard a rattle and noted that they were quilted. He took her to another room, called for a housekeeper, and told her to examine Ginnie's clothes.

The housekeeper found some fifty letters addressed to Confederate officers and, fastened to her in a huge bustle or sack, forty bottles of morphine, seven pounds of opium, and a quantity of camphor. The housekeeper gave her other clothes to wear and then called for Kemper, who confiscated the goods.

Kemper arrested Ginnie and her mother, but he was not sure where to take them. Ginnie asked where General Burnside stayed.

Kemper replied, "The Burnet House."

"We'll go there or nowhere," Ginny exclaimed.

Kemper handed them paroles, and Ginnie signed for both of them.

After dinner she immediately dispatched her card to Ambrose Burnside's office. He responded promptly. He would be happy to see her.

Ginnie did not know what to expect from her sister's old beau—the man Lottie had jilted at the altar some fourteen years earlier. Burnside had brought candy to Ginnie each time he had called on her sister. Ginnie, then nearly five years old, had called him "Buttons" because she liked his military uniform. In Burnside's current assignment in Ohio he had a reputation for treating Southerners harshly. In fact, he was about to issue an order providing treason trials for all who showed Southern leanings, including the death penalty for anyone convicted of helping the Confederacy.

Burnside held out both hands to welcome Ginnie, and then, speaking softly, asked, "My child, what have you done this for?"

"Done what?" inquired Ginnie, as if she didn't know.

"Why did you try to go South without coming to me for a pass?" he said. "They wouldn't have dared stop you."

"General, I have a little honor. I couldn't have asked you for a pass and carried what I did."

"Well," he said with a smile, "I will take this matter out of the hands of the customhouse officials and try you myself."

Relieved, Ginnie thanked him.

Officers on Burnside's staff all noticed his sympathetic concern for the eighteen-year-old girl. To keep in his good graces, they, too, showed an interest in Ginnie.

"I was asked down to the parlors every evening to meet some of the staff officers," she recalled. "The Yankee women in the parlor looked indignant to see these officers being so polite to a Secesh woman."

Ginnie apparently received proposals of marriage from some of these Union officers.

A few days later a distressed and flustered lady burst into Burnside's office and demanded to see him. He invited her in. Speaking with a British accent she said: "I am an Englishwoman traveling from Virginia's springs to the Arkansas waters. Only a few hours ago I learned that two other women had been arrested. I hasten to ask protection from such a possible misfortune to myself, and also for a pass to proceed." She added that she wanted to spend a few days in Cincinnati to relax, but "this continued excitement is worse than the fatigue of travel."

Burnside, like most men, never forgot his first love, especially the one who walked away from him at the altar. He knew he was talking to Ginnie's sister, Lottie Moon Clark.

"I still remember with pleasure the hours I used to spend with you in Oxford," he said quietly.

Lottie's fake accent and disguise had failed her. Burnside told her to stop her clandestine activities and everything would be all right.

Three weeks after becoming a prisoner at the Burnet House, Ginnie asked Burnside for a parole to Jones's Station, where Lottie and her husband resided. The general issued the parole for both Ginnie and her mother, returned Ginnie's revolver, and granted them passes to return to their home in Memphis. He told them they would have to report regularly to Maj. Gen. Stephen A. Hurlbut, whose 16th Corps of the Army of the Tennessee was based in Memphis to defend against enemy attacks. No action was ever taken against Lottie or Ginnie.

———

Back in Memphis, Ginnie flirted with countless Union officers and collected enough military secrets to change the outcome of battles. When General Hurlbut learned of her conquests, he ordered her to get out of the Union lines and "stay out!"

Off she went to Confederate strongholds in the South, eventually winding up in Danville, Virginia, with a sister-in-law. Ginnie's brother had served in the Confederate army until illness and defeat discouraged him. He escaped to France and asked his wife, two children, and Ginnie to join him and sit out the war overseas. The two women obtained passes in July 1864 and traveled to Newport News on Virginia's eastern shore. Just days before their departure to Europe, Maj. Gen. Benjamin F. Butler discovered their presence and detained them.

Union Major General Stephen A. Hurlbut

"You can't leave the country," Butler told them, "unless you take the Union oath."

Ginnie's sister-in-law put her husband first and took the oath.

"I didn't hear a word of it," she later told Ginnie. "I kept saying the multiplication table as hard as I could."

Ginnie, of course, refused to take the oath, and Butler locked her up at Fort Monroe for several months. Her successful wooing of prison guards and her penchant for troublemaking led prison officials to regard her as a Federal liability. Eager to get rid of her, they shipped her under a flag of truce to City Point on the James River, and she was once more within Confederate lines.

Ginnie Moon: Postwar Charity Worker and Actress

The war ended in 1865, but Ginnie never accepted defeat. She returned to Memphis and lived there for the next sixty years.

She usually wore black silk dresses and always carried a parasol, with her pearl-handled revolver tucked inside of it. Showing compassion for the downtrodden, she raised money for the poor, sick, and crippled. Some called her "a one-woman charity fund."

Around 1919 Ginnie moved to California with one of her former foster children who had become a Broadway star—Viva Warren Jones—and her husband. Determined to seek work in the fledgling movie industry, Ginnie secured an interview with producer Jesse Lasky at his Famous Players-Lasky Studio in Hollywood.

Lasky asked her only one question: "What makes you think you can act?"

Ginnie replied, "I am seventy-five years old, and I have acted all the parts."

The producer nodded. "You'll do."

Indeed, almost six decades earlier she had acted throughout the war, risking her life and fooling Yankee soldiers and officers.

In Hollywood she played character parts. She was in Douglas Fairbanks's classic, *Robin Hood*, and in films with other famous stars of the silent screen.

Five years later, when the Joneses moved back to New York City, Ginnie went with them. She chose to live alone in an apartment in Greenwich Village—a section of the city renowned for its unorthodox ways of life. It was the perfect place for this self-described "unreconstructed Rebel." There, Ginnie could do whatever she wanted and still fit in. She adopted an alley cat, chain-smoked, wore her black silk antebellum dresses, and immersed herself in the religious cults of Asia. On a ride with friends up Riverside Drive, she once glanced at Grant's Tomb.

"Damn him," she shouted.

On September 11, 1925, a new resident—a girl from Texas—came downstairs to meet the old lady that everybody talked about. When there was no response to her knock on the door, she turned the knob and walked in. She found the eighty-one-year-old Miss Ginnie on the floor, dead. She was clad in black silk, with her arm stretched toward the door. Her tomcat sat beside her.

Ginnie has been honored appropriately with a large plaque in Confederate Park in Memphis. She undoubtedly would be pleased with its location—a few yards from a statue of Jefferson Davis. He lived in Memphis following his two-year imprisonment after the Civil War. Davis resided at the city's famous Peabody Hotel and served as president of the Carolina Life Insurance Company.

Visitors listening carefully while walking through Confederate Park late at night might well hear Ginnie's voice proclaiming, "Hurrah for Jeff Davis!"

Lottie Moon: Postwar Writer, Poet, and Lecturer

After Lottie Moon Clark's encounter with Ambrose Burnside in Cincinnati, she was under the strict surveillance of his agents for three months. Although no action was ever taken against her, Lottie's work as a spy was finished. She and her husband settled their affairs in Ohio and moved to New York City. Judge Clark practiced law and wrote a column for the Sunday editions of the *New York Ledger*. Lottie honed her journalistic skills, contributed articles to the pro-South *New York World*, and eventually became a correspondent in Paris covering the Franco-Prussian War.

She claimed she was presented to the court of Emperor Napoleon Bonaparte III and Empress Eugenia by the American minister to France, Elihu Washburne.

In London, Lottie attended a party at the home of novelist Edward Bulwer-Lytton. He challenged her to write a novel in which the wielder of power would be a woman. Lord Lytton said to her: "It is a gallant battle cry, *Place aux Dames.* You will succeed."

Lottie replied, "In such a combat and with such a cause, there is no such word as *fail.*"

After returning to America, Lottie wrote poetry and widely read novels about life on the western plains. A poem she wrote at the end of the Civil War, "Peace," was included in an anthology of Southern poetry. Its first stanza reflected her personal feelings:

> They are singing peace on this heavy ear,
> No peace to this heavy heart;
> They are singing peace, I hear, I hear,
> Oh, God, how my hopes depart.

She eventually wrote the book Lord Lytton suggested to her: *How She Came into Her Kingdom*, published under the nom de plume Charles M. Clay.

Lottie also lectured throughout the North and Midwest, advocating women's rights, help for the poor, and a strict justice for everyone, except African Americans. She maintained that they were inferior to whites.

After Lottie's husband died in 1881, she earned her living by translating French novels. She was working on a novel based on her experiences in France when she died of cancer on November 20, 1895.

Lottie has been memorialized in ways she probably would not have approved. Two bars in Oxford, Ohio, used her name. One was Lottie Moon's Underground (named because the owner mistakenly connected Lottie to the Underground Railroad). The second bar was called Lottie Moon's. Its advertising sign was a scantily clad woman reclining on a crescent moon. Both bars have gone out of business.

The Lottie Moon House in Oxford, at 220 E. High Street across from Miami University, was the home of the parents of Lottie and Ginnie Moon in the 1840s and 1850s. It was the site of Lottie's wedding in 1849.

THE PERILS OF PAULINE

Pauline Cushman*

It took actress Pauline Cushman ten years to become an overnight sensation. Her monumental moment occurred in April 1863, midway through the Civil War.

At the time, she was at Wood's Theatre in Louisville, Kentucky. The state was under Union control, but Louisville had a large, emboldened body of Rebel sympathizers.

Pauline acted the part of Plutella in the popular comedy *The Seven Sisters*. Plutella (one of the sisters) assumes many characters, including a dashing Zouave officer and a fashionable gentleman who drinks wine with a friend. In other roles, Pauline took off a few of her clothes—just a few, but enough to make men remember her. She was "a man's woman."

Among Pauline's friends in Louisville were two paroled Rebel officers, a Colonel Spear and Capt. J. H. Blincoe. They proposed that Pauline offer a Southern toast in the wine scene and see what effect it had on the audience. Giving a Southern toast in a Union state sounded like a career-ending action to Pauline.

*Note: The dialogue in this chapter comes from Pauline Cushman's notes as recorded by her biographer, Ferdinand L. Sarmiento, in *Life of Pauline Cushman, The Celebrated Union Spy and Scout*, published in 1865.

"I would be locked up in jail if I were to do any thing of the kind," she exclaimed.

"Would three hundred dollars convince you to do it?" one of the men asked her.

"Let me think it over," she responded.

Pauline, although born in New Orleans, was pro-Union. She proceeded to the office of Colonel Moore, the U.S. provost marshal, and reported the proposal.

"Go ahead," he advised. "Drink the Rebel toast. To further our cause we are often compelled to do things that are repulsive to us. Fear nothing. It is for a deeper reason than you know, that I beg of you to do this thing. Your country will benefit from it, as you will discover later."

Moore promised he would be at the theater and would protect her if necessary. Pauline agreed, wondering how an apparently treasonable act might help her country.

Meanwhile, her Rebel friends distributed flyers to secesh circles announcing that something special was to occur at the theater that night. Stirred by the flyers and rumors of impending excitement, they packed the theater.

Finally, the critical moment arrived. Pauline, in the role of a gentleman, advanced to the footlights, showing off her well-curved figure in a tight-fitting man's costume, with a painted moustache curled across her cheeks. With a goblet in hand, she raised it, and in a clear, ringing voice offered the following toast: *"Here's to Jeff Davis and the Southern Confederacy. May the South always maintain her honor and her rights!"*

The pro-Union segment of the audience gazed openmouthed in shock. The Southerners erupted with applause, cheers, and shouts. Yankees yelled back. It was a seemingly endless melee.

Stage managers usually relish showstopping scenes, but not one like this. The manager stormed onto the stage and, in a rage of his own, demanded, "What the hell do you think you are doing? You have just ended your career!"

She replied: "I am not afraid of the whole Yankee crew, and I would do it again."

In her toast of two short sentences she made herself the sweetheart of local Confederates. She also had convinced the South that she was a most virulent Secessionist. She didn't realize until later that this action would make her a valuable spy for the Union.

Guards arrived to arrest her, but with the probable interference of the provost marshal, they did not. Instead, she was ordered to report to Union headquarters at ten o'clock the next morning.

Colonel Moore met and escorted her into the office of Brig. Gen. Jeremiah Boyle, a prewar lawyer who commanded Union forces in Kentucky. Boyle, a zealous administrator, didn't beat around the bush.

"You deserve our thanks, Miss Cushman," Boyle said. "There are, however, many things to be done yet," he emphasized. "You have sowed the seed; you must now prepare to reap the harvest. You must enter the Secret Service. Colonel Moore will explain what is involved, and what we want you to do."

The colonel advised her to moderate her secesh pronouncements in public as a fitting consequence of her arrest.

"You can say that you had a severe reprimand from General Boyle and myself," Moore instructed her. "In private, of course, you can abuse the government, and say all the mean things you can about it. This will inspire confidence among the Rebels and make you of incalculable value to your country....I will be in touch with you soon about all of this."

Pauline promised to comply with these directives. But, by doing so, she knew she would be shunned by her friends for being disloyal and supported by Rebel sympathizers whose very nature revolted her.

She also realized that her acting career was in jeopardy. On that same day, she received a note at her boardinghouse from the theater's manager: "By order of the management, I am requested to inform you that your services are no longer required in this establishment. You will be unable to continue your present role for some time to come."

But now she had a more exciting role—the role of a spy. Her first assignment was to root out treasonable plots in Louisville and identify everyone connected with them. To do this, she frequented small saloons, where she observed respectably dressed men discussing their secret plans with shabbily clothed countrymen. Pauline, of course, reported these activities, and the perpetrators were summoned to the provost marshal's office to account for their actions. At other times Pauline collected useful information by dressing as a young, wealthy Southern gentleman and playing billiards at fashionable billiard saloons.

Her most dangerous service in the Louisville area was tracking down the haunts of guerrillas—clusters of civilians organized to harass Union forces behind the lines. This task often compelled her to don male attire and remain in the saddle all night. When she came upon their hideouts, she would conceal herself in the bushes and observe their various methods of communicating through the lines. She saw them fold letters lengthwise and stuff them in the craw of a chicken, mix documents in bags of flour, hide them in the handles of farmers' butter knives, and place them in the false soles and hollowed-out heels of shoes.

Her reports on their hideouts, methods, and activities enabled Federal authorities to take action against them.

From Tomboy to Temptress to Actress

Pauline's childhood and teen years prepared her for this life of adventure. The only girl in a family of seven, her real name was Harriet Wood. Born in New Orleans, she was the daughter of a Spanish merchant and a French lady of excellent social position and attainments. Her father prospered for a while in the Queen City of the Mississippi, but then he speculated badly and suffered a series of financial losses. When Pauline was a baby, he abandoned his enterprises in New Orleans and moved to a frontier trading post named Grand Rapids, Michigan. There, he established a trading business with the Indians and again prospered.

In Pauline's early teens she was a tomboy. The young Indians who came through her father's store taught her to ride, paddle a canoe, hunt and shoot, and find her way through woods and swamps. One biographer declared: "She could converse upon all manly sports and habits with the ease and polish of a highborn gentleman, [and she had] the dash and daring of a headlong, headstrong boy."

As Pauline grew in beauty and intelligence, she became less of a tomboy and more of a temptress. She had long, straight hair with a blue-black sheen, and wide, full lips. Determined to become an actress, she set her sights on New York City. When she was eighteen, she took to the road to the big city in the east. Pauline went straight to the stage managers of New York theaters. But lacking theatrical training and experience, she learned what so many midwesterners had learned before—it's a long row to hoe to find an acting job in New York. One person, however, saw something special in Pauline. He was Thomas Placide, manager of the famed New Orleans Varieties. He offered her a season in her hometown. She changed her name to Pauline Cushman, and her career as an actress began.

New Orleans liked her. Posing in a loose shawl, she displayed dimpled shoulders over which the city went wild. One man, beholding her, "seemed to lose all restraint over himself," according to one newspaper. Another newspaper later wrote, "Her form is perfect—so perfect that the sculptor's imagination would fail to add a single point, or banish a single blemish."

She played in other cities, nearly always receiving good reviews, and fell in love with Charles Dickinson, a music teacher and theater musician. They married in New Orleans, moved in with his family in Cleveland, Ohio, and had two children, Charles and Ida, neither of whom reached adulthood. When the war began in 1861, Pauline's husband joined the Union army as a musician in the 41st Ohio Infantry's band. Within a year he died of dysentery.

Pauline, although never becoming a star, continued to perform in the theater until that special dramatic moment in Louisville in March 1863.

Foiling a Plot to Poison Soldiers

One of her most important successes as a spy in Louisville was the detection of a plot to poison sick and wounded Union soldiers. Several of these soldiers had been assigned to the care of the manager of the boardinghouse where Pauline resided. The manager was a middle-aged woman who secretly professed strong Southern sympathies. One day Pauline saw the woman conversing with a "suspicious-looking" character. Around midnight she became even more curious when she saw a light in the manager's room. The door was partially open, and Pauline noticed her mixing white powder with coffee. Pauline pretended to be ill and gently tapped on the door. The manager hastily put the powdered coffee in a cabinet before responding. Seeing that it was only the brave Southern heroine, she became more composed.

"Oh, it is only you," she said in a relieved tone. "What do you want at this late hour?"

"I came down to get some medicine," Pauline answered, "for I feel quite ill. But what has kept you up so late? And what mysterious brew were you making that kept me waiting before you came to the door? Something wicked, I bet!"

Believing Pauline to be a fellow Confederate supporter, the manager took Pauline into her confidence.

"Nothing of that sort, my dear, unless you call killin' off a few Yankees wicked. And I reckon you are too good a Confederate for that," replied the manager.

"Killing off a few Yankees?" asked Pauline, showing surprise.

"Yes, only a few, unfortunately. Drat me if I wouldn't like to kill off the whole lot."

"But how are you going to accomplish it without being detected?"

"Easy enough." She showed Pauline the package of white powder, a deadly poison. "Them Federals will be quarterin' some sick and wounded soldiers here, and I'll give them each a dose of this stuff regularly."

For a few moments Pauline stood paralyzed by this fiendish plan. Then she left the room and returned to her own, where she waited until the woman had retired. Pauline then walked to the provost marshal's home, pounded on the door until he awakened, and disclosed the plot to him.

They didn't arrest the Rebel lady immediately for fear of exposing Pauline's cover. Instead they chose a different place to house the soldiers, sent Pauline on a new mission, and then made the arrest.

A Sterling Sting Operation

This lady stood out among the throng of people seeking passes and other favors at the Union headquarters of Brig. Gen. Jeremiah Boyle in Louisville. She was elegantly dressed, poised, and attractive. Her name was Mrs. Ford. She moved in the highest circles of Louisville's aristocratic society. So did her husband, before the war. But now he was a representative in the Confederate Congress. Kentucky, however, was a Union state. That made Ford a fugitive from his home. Thus Mrs. Ford came to the general's office to obtain a pass to proceed through the lines and join her husband in exile.

Also present at the headquarters was a quiet man who seemed to be doing nothing more than watching everyone else, as if he were looking for someone in particular. Soon, he noticed Mrs. Ford. Presently, when she moved away from the crowd, he approached her. As they talked, they looked very serious and at times quite animated. The subject must have been of great interest to both of them.

During this conversation the stranger informed Mrs. Ford that he was not what he seemed, but was in reality Captain Denver of the Confederate army, visiting Louisville to spy upon movements of the Federal army. With this information, Mrs. Ford invited him to visit her house. Denver hesitated, which Mrs. Ford thought strange, but then he accepted.

Denver called soon afterward at her residence and was cordially received by the family. Their conversation focused on the war, and Denver, of course, warmly espoused the Confederate cause. To show his confidence in the Fords, he revealed his intention to escape through the Federal lines and take with him all the quinine, morphine, and other medicines he could carry and deliver them to the nearest Confederate command. Mrs. Ford was skeptical about his chances of getting those supplies through the lines without getting caught.

"It is not safe; it is not wise," she said, "but it is a noble task for so true and firm a Southerner as you are."

She said that she, too, wanted to smuggle large quantities of medicines through the lines, as well as information about Federal movements and plans. And since her husband was in the South, she expected to receive a pass from General Boyle as soon as the matter was brought to his attention.

Captain Denver remarked that he lacked the funds to make extensive purchases and needed the assistance of Secessionists in Louisville.

"This need not trouble you," noted Mrs. Ford. "I can arrange it to your satisfaction. Come back around noon tomorrow, and I should have good news for you."

That same evening the captain ran into an old friend, Dr. Rogers, a Confederate surgeon and paroled prisoner. He was en route to Cairo, Illinois, by Federal order to report for transportation to Vicksburg, Mississippi.

When Captain Denver met with Mrs. Ford the next day, he mentioned the doctor to her. "He is on his way South, and it would be greatly to our advantage to go thither under his protection."

She replied: "That sounds very advantageous, but first I would like to meet him. Can that be arranged?"

Dr. Rogers came by her home that evening. After the expected conversational pleasantries, the doctor expressed his concern about carrying contraband goods. "It would be a violation of my parole," he said, "and might lead to my arrest and imprisonment."

With apparent but false sincerity, Mrs. Ford said she would not engage in any enterprise that the military authorities did not sanction.

Dr. Rogers seemed satisfied and changed the subject. "I must tell you in strict confidence," he said, "a secret of the utmost importance."

"It will be safe with me," she said.

Dr. Rogers continued: "Several months ago George Nicholas Sanders, a powerful member of our Canada office, made his way to England to negotiate a Confederate loan. His mission was completely successful. The loan was taken by the Rothschilds. His return has been anxiously awaited by Jefferson Davis. Now, you had better sit down before I go any further....Our friend, Captain Denver, is this same George Nicholas Sanders, and he is now on his return to the Confederate capital. You must not hint a word of it to anybody, or even intimate to Sanders that you know him in any other character than as Captain Denver."

Mrs. Ford sat repeating to herself, "Oh, my God! This is great news for the South!"

Dr. Rogers had more to say: "He will accompany us to Vicksburg in his present disguise. Until that point is reached, no one, however friendly to the South, must know who he really is. The interests at stake are too vast to be hazarded by exposure to a mischance, which a single careless word might bring upon him. But if he is suspected or discovered, we must assist him in securing the papers so that they cannot be found."

Mrs. Ford asked many questions about Sanders and how he had managed to escape the vigilance of the Federals. Dr. Rogers answered as best he could. He then took his leave to make final preparations to start the next evening.

Everything proceeded without a hitch. They obtained passes, purchased tickets, and secured berths in the sleeping car. They arrived in Cairo, Illinois, on schedule.

Then their luck changed. They were arrested. Captain Denver, alias George Sanders, and Dr. Rogers were indignant. Mrs. Ford trembled. She was led away in silence. Federal agents examined all of her trunks and clothes. They found a large amount of quinine, other contraband goods, numerous letters, and documents containing much information that would have been valuable to the Rebels.

After an extensive investigation, Mrs. Ford was sent South to join her husband. She later wrote a book about her experience and treatment under Federal rule.

This episode perhaps was the best sting operation pulled off by any spy in the Civil War. Captain Denver, alias George Sanders, was none other than Pauline

Cushman. And Dr. Rogers, the purported Confederate surgeon, was a member of the detective police of the Army of the Cumberland.

An Undercover Mission of Great Peril

Shortly after the capture of Mrs. Ford, the proprietor of a new theater in Nashville, Tennessee, arrived in Louisville looking for a good company of actors. The manager of the Louisville theater recommended Pauline Cushman.

"She is a good looking woman," he said, "and an accomplished actress, but she will talk 'secesh.' If you can keep her out of the provost-marshal's hands, she will be a good draw."

The Nashville proprietor offered a position to Pauline, and after checking with her military authorities, she accepted it. They explained to her that, in order to protect her identity as a Secessionist, they had to refuse to give her a pass, and that the only way to get out of Louisville was to run the blockade.

She proceeded to the train station and asked a secesh gentleman to attend to her trunk. Then she told a guard at the door of a car that she needed to speak to a friend inside "only for a minute." He let her pass, and she stayed within the car. When the guard came through the car to inspect the passes, she showed her order from the manager of the Nashville theater to report immediately to him. The guard hesitated, but she shed a few tears. He acquiesced, and she was soon on her way to Nashville.

At the theater she became popular with the secesh crowd, but her stay was a short one. Returning from rehearsal one day, she found a summons from Col. William Truesdail, the local chief of police for the Army of the Cumberland commanded by Maj. Gen. William S. Rosecrans. On entering Truesdail's private office, she was received warmly and complimented for her previous important services to the country. Then he told her he had selected her for an undercover mission "of extraordinary peril—an undertaking which might end in glory, or in an ignominious death by the bullet or by the rope."

Pauline shrank back but answered in a firm tone: "Thousands of our noble soldiers have gladly given up their lives for their country. Should I hesitate to do as much? No; I will do all that a woman should do, and all that a man dare do, for my country and the Union."

Truesdail thanked her and then briefed her. Rosecrans was preparing a campaign (which would come to be known as the Tullahoma campaign) to drive

Braxton Bragg's Army of Tennessee out of Middle Tennessee. He needed intelligence about the placement, fortifications, and abilities of Bragg's army. To get it, he wanted Pauline to visit five known Confederate camps at Columbia, Shelbyville, Wartrace, Tullahoma, and Manchester.

"Your allure, beauty and reputation as a Southern supporter will get you into the camps," Truesdail said. "Once in, you are to request a meeting with the commanding officer and tell him about your desire to find your brother [A. A. Cushman]who is in the Confederate army somewhere. Your anxiety to find him will establish a believable reason for your traveling from place to place. You will ask the officer for assistance and a letter to get you safely to the next camp."

She was to make no direct inquiries about the strength, positions, and movements of Confederate forces, but in her interactions with Rebel officers, which she could surely arrange by using her feminine wiles, she was to keep her eyes open and note everything of importance.

"They will undoubtedly invite you to ride with them through the camps, and this will enable you to notice details of defenses and weaponry. At the hospitals ask to visit the sick and wounded and inquire about the adequacy of medical supplies. But, and this is very important, do not make any memoranda or tracings of any kind. Use your acting skills to memorize everything of importance."

He also told her to "make no confidants, say as little as you can, give the same answer to all parties, and never deviate from your story, when once framed."

To protect her cover and deceive the secession sympathizers in Nashville, Federal officials spread the word that Pauline was being sent across the lines for having uttered treasonable sentiments and given countenance to the rebellion. While protecting Pauline, the information served as a warning to the Rebel residents of the fate they faced if they aided the Confederacy. Showing sympathy for poor Pauline, a crowd of these gentry gathered in front of her residence on the announced day of her removal from Nashville.

It was a glorious May morning in 1863, just before her thirtieth birthday. She was to be conveyed in a closed carriage, first to the office of the chief of police, and next beyond the limits of the Federal lines. At Colonel Truesdail's office he reminded her of the dangerous mission and gave her one last chance to change her mind.

"No sir," she replied. "The worst can come—heaven forbid that it should! Yet, I say it can come, and find me prepared to meet it without one regret."

Three miles from Nashville, out of sight of any human habitation, the carriage stopped, and she and her military escort alighted. They found there the colonel's servant holding a fine bay horse. Pauline shook the hand of her escort, and they parted. She mounted her horse, and galloped toward the Confederate camp at Columbia.

At Columbia she made friends with Confederate officers, especially with a Captain Blackman and a Major Boone. Boone was a lady's man, and Pauline was a lady he wanted to snare. She took full advantage of their time together and acquired substantial intelligence about military plans, as well as a letter to introduce her to the officer at the next camp. Blackman was equally enchanted by the lovely lady. And being a Rebel quartermaster just back from Vicksburg, he had information she wanted, and he unconsciously provided it.

Pauline then proceeded to Shelbyville, where she expected to make contact with General Bragg. She had been instructed to watch his movements more closely than those of anyone else. But much to her annoyance, Bragg's headquarters was no longer there.

At the table d'hôte at which she dined in Shelbyville, she noticed a young captain—an engineer—and found out that he was working day and night to finish drawings for important new fortifications in the area. She decided to ignore her instructions about securing enemy papers and, at whatever risk, obtain them. She would then return expeditiously to Federal lines and to Nashville. If questioned she would say that she needed to retrieve her theatrical wardrobe.

To ingratiate herself to the young engineer, she presented her "letter of safeguard," and he began to show some interest in her. Shortly, he smiled and seemed to make a mental inventory of her charms. She won his admiration and confidence so completely that he offered to give her his own letter of introduction to General Bragg.

The next day the engineer heard a tap at his door. Pauline stood there and apologized for bothering him. She told him she had to leave earlier than she had intended and hoped he could let her have the letter to General Bragg.

"I'm sorry you are leaving us so soon," he said as he surveyed her beautiful figure. "I'll have to go downstairs to my desk to write the note."

When he left, Pauline tiptoed to a table covered with drawings. She couldn't resist the temptation. She picked up what looked interesting and slipped the papers into her dress. In a few moments the engineer returned and gave her the letter of introduction. She left, hoping he wouldn't notice that some of his papers were missing.

On her way back to Nashville she stopped at Wartrace, a small town just seven miles from Shelbyville. Numerous skirmishes between Union and Rebel cavalry were fought in and around the village. If she could reach one of the roving bands of Union cavalry, she could transmit valuable information to them. Pauline thought she could best accomplish this by wearing a man's suit of clothes. But having none, she decided to appropriate one by "midnight requisition."

Fortunately, a young man about her size was staying at the same boarding-house she was in. Knowing that he slept in the upper story of the house, she scouted around late at night, found the room, grabbed the clothes while he was sleeping, and returned to her own room. Then she dressed herself in the stolen suit, saddled the best horse she could find, and rode out of town and into the woods.

She had ridden about three miles when she saw a large watch fire with several armed men around it. Dismounting, she tied her horse to a tree. She crept closer to the fire, until she got within earshot of the party. From what she heard—bloodthirsty and wicked language against the Union—she flinched, realizing they were Rebel guerrillas. They began singing a mongrel song. The words she heard were: *"The Yankees run, ha! ha! / The niggers stay, ho! ho! / It must be now the Rebs are going / To have a jubalow!"*

Having heard enough, Pauline moved away as hastily as she dared. As she reached the spot where her horse was tied, she stepped incautiously upon a branch of a tree. It snapped with a loud noise.

"What's that?" cried one of the Rebel gang. He jumped up and seized his gun. The captain ordered: "Grab your muskets, men. We'll scour the woods!"

By this time Pauline was on her horse and galloping away. The guerrillas followed, and the chase was on.

The Rebels were gaining on her when she approached what appeared in the moonlight to be a cliff. A large rocky promontory lay straight ahead. Shutting her eyes, she spurred the horse, and the steed jumped from the rock into the unknown. The promontory itself was about ten feet perpendicular. Below it

Chased by Rebel guerrillas, Pauline gambled and spurred her horse and jumped from a rocky promontory.

was a gently sloping grassy hill about a hundred feet above a small stream. The horse and its rider made a perfect landing on the hill and continued toward the stream. The guerrillas chose not to make the jump.

At the stream Pauline pushed into the adjoining woods. She thought she had made her escape, but one of the Rebel guerrillas had discovered a bridle path leading down to the creek, and the chase was on again.

Pauline seemed to be gaining ground on her pursuers. Each moment their voices and the tramp of their horses became more indistinct. Then, out of nowhere, mounted on a horse directly in her path, she saw an armed cavalryman. Fearing he was a Rebel, she yelled out, "Stand aside, or I will send a pistol ball through your head!"

"All right, comrade," he answered back in a weak voice. "I don't want to stop you. It is all I can do to stay on my horse. I am badly wounded. Warm blood is trickling through my clothes."

"Wounded?" asked Pauline. "What are you doing here, away from your comrades?" She assumed he was a Rebel.

He replied, "We had a skirmish with you 'Rebs' near here about five or six hours ago, and I was wounded and got left behind."

"Then you are a Federal soldier!" she joyfully exclaimed.

"I am."

With that knowledge, a plan of escape flashed through her mind.

"You can aid me," she told him. "Aid me and our country."

"Our country?" queried the soldier. "Ain't you a Rebel?"

"No, indeed, I am a Yankee, a Yankee spy and scout—and a woman."

"What? You are a woman?"

"I am. My name is Pauline Cushman. Now, will you help me?"

"I've heard of you, and, yes, I will help you."

Pauline told him she had a plan to save both of their lives and that he should not be frightened by what she was about to do. Then she fired her pistol into the air.

"Now," she said, "I have fired that shot to pretend that I am a Rebel and that I just shot you. You must, therefore, swear that I shot you. Whether you do this or not, you will soon have to give yourself up as a prisoner. Your wounds make it impossible for you to ride long enough to reach your comrades. Surrendering will save your life. Do what I ask, and you will save me as well, and do a service to our country. I have information invaluable to our generals. If I am captured, it will be lost to them."

He replied: "I will do anything to save you. There is not a soldier in the Army of the Cumberland but would do as much."

Drawn by the sound of the pistol, the Rebel horsemen galloped up to find the Union soldier lying at the foot of a tree, bleeding freely. Pauline was bent over him, with a gun in her hand.

"Who are you?" asked one of the guerrillas.

"I am a farmer's son over near Wartrace," replied Pauline, "and I surrender to you. I have shot one of your fellows here, and only wish I had shot more of ye." By this statement, Pauline, pretending to be a man, was telling the pursuers that she thought they were Yankees.

They looked puzzled.

Pauline continued: "I mean just what I say. I am only sorry I didn't kill more of you damned Yankees that come down here and run off all our Negroes!"

The Rebels now concluded that they had mistaken Pauline for a Yankee and that she had mistaken them for Yankees.

One of the Rebels, however, still wasn't convinced. He shook the dazed, wounded soldier and said: "I say, Yank, who was it that shot you?"

Raising himself slightly, he pointed at Pauline.

"There!" yelled one of the Rebels. "He says the boy [Pauline] shot him. What do you want better than that?"

So far, Pauline's game had gone her way. The Rebels placed the wounded soldier on a horse and were going to take him to Wartrace to get medical aid. Then the game took a new twist. They commanded Pauline to follow them. She hadn't planned on that. Thinking quickly, she decided to create a scare tactic to cause confusion and help her to get away from them.

As they passed through a narrow gorge in the forest, Pauline distanced herself from the others and fired five shots in rapid succession. The Rebels assumed they were being ambushed by Federal cavalry. They galloped away as fast as their horses could take them, and Pauline turned her horse toward Wartrace, determined to get there first. She did. And she returned the horse and the man's clothes undetected.

Returning to Columbia, she renewed her intimacy with Major Boone and Captain Blackman. These men were fascinated by her. Blackman even urged her to join the Confederate army as his aide-de-camp, with the rank of lieutenant. She accepted his proposition, expecting to gain much information of value to the Union. He obtained a complete Rebel officer's uniform for her, and he promised that as soon as she returned from her proposed trip to Nashville, she would accompany him as his aide.

Meanwhile, they took long rides over the neighboring countryside. These rides enabled her to pinpoint the location of camps and fortifications and to learn the plans and projects of Rebel leaders. She made careful drawings of the Rebel works and indicated the exact positions of their guns. She concealed the drawings between the inner and outer soles of her boots.

No Way Out

On her route back to Nashville, everything fell apart. By stealing drawings from the engineer and concealing them on her person along with her own notes and sketches, she had ignored the orders of her spymaster, Colonel Truesdail. Her imagined heroics would soon burnish her reputation as a spy and put her life in great danger.

Her next mistake was stopping at Benjamin Milam's house, where she had spent her first night out of Nashville. Milam carried on a large business in smuggling supplies from Nashville to Rebel friends. At first he thought that Pauline was a Rebel, but then he had his doubts. Perhaps, he pondered, she might be a Yankee spy, and in Nashville she might reveal his treasonable acts to Federal officials. So he left the house to alert one of his partners in crime.

As Milam and his colleague returned, a man of rough exterior appeared at the back door. He demanded to see Pauline.

"Have you a pass from Tullahoma to get beyond our lines?" he said boldly, as if he knew the answer.

"By what authority do you ask?" she inquired. "I didn't know a pass was needed."

"My name is Fall, and I am a Confederate scout. I am afraid you will have to go with me to our station at Anderson's Mills. General Bragg has ordered the arrest of anyone going out of the lines without a pass."

Pauline knew at once Milam was responsible for her arrest. Glaring at him she snapped, "You have violated your duty as a host. You have betrayed me. And, mark you: as sure as my name is Pauline Cushman, I will get even with you yet!"

The officer in charge at Anderson's Mill held her as a prisoner of war and ordered her to be taken to Spring Hill, where the famous cavalry commander Maj. Gen. Nathan Bedford Forrest was headquartered.

Midway they stopped at the home of a well-known secesh physician for lunch. Shortly, Confederate cavalry under Brig. Gen. John Hunt Morgan rode up to escort Pauline closer to Spring Hill.

Morgan, a celebrated general, would later lead 2,460 troops past Union lines into Kentucky, Indiana, and Ohio—the farthest north any uniformed Confederate troops would penetrate during the war.

Pauline was pleased with the new arrangement. Morgan was gallant and charming and a delightful companion. He called her Pauline, and she called him Johnny. Her only regret was that the trip with him was too short. He took leave of her at Hillsboro and turned her over to a group of scouts. They were to convey her to Forrest's headquarters.

During their journey a fierce thunderstorm ensued, and the roads became impassable. Having no other choice, they stopped at a shack by the wayside and asked for shelter. This turned out to be the home of a wounded Rebel soldier who had lost both legs in a recent skirmish. He lay on a wretched pallet, groaning and cursing. His wife hovered at his side, crying. Crouched close to a fireplace, Pauline noticed an elderly black man. Believing she could trust him, Pauline determined to make him the instrument to carry out a plan of escape.

She approached him, talked about her plight, and asked for his assistance. He said he would do what she asked. She knew that the Rebels feared an attack by General Rosecrans. Her plan was to make them believe that a Union force was actually attacking them. She gave the man a ten-dollar greenback to run up the road a piece and then back again, shouting as loud as he could, "The Yankees are coming!"

Around midnight on this dark and stormy night, the entire black population in the area ran into the house where the guards and their prisoners were sleeping and yelled those frightening words, "The Yankees am a-comin'!"

The plan worked. The guards fled, and Pauline grabbed a pistol that belonged to the wounded soldier. She mounted her horse and headed toward Union lines at Franklin. Soon, however, the heavy rain and strong wind made the ride unbearable, and Pauline stopped at a house to seek shelter from the storm and plan her next move.

Early the next morning she was awakened by four of the Rebel scouts from whom she had escaped the night before. She could not get out of this predicament. They detained her. Then, about ten o'clock, she again found herself in the presence of John Hunt Morgan. He was polite but resolute. Discharging the scouts, he took control of the prisoner and rode with her to General Forrest's headquarters.

Crude and fierce-tempered, Forrest was physically imposing and intimidating at 210 pounds and six foot two inches tall.

"Well, Miss Cushman," said the famous cavalry leader, "I am glad, indeed to see you. I've been looking for you a long time. You are pretty sharp at turning a card, but I think we've got you on this last shuffle. Let's get to the point," he said bluntly. "You have certain documents about you, and should their evidence show you to be, as I suspect, a spy, nothing under heaven can save you from a hanging!"

"Well, sir," she retorted, "suppose you proceed now and root up the whole thing. I am ready!"

"I have no time now," he said, "to investigate your case. I am going to send you to General Bragg's headquarters at Shelbyville. In the highly unlikely event that you should prove your loyalty to the South, you may always depend upon me for protection. But this, I am sorry to say, I do not believe possible, so prepare for the worst."

Bragg was a small man with iron-gray hair and whiskers. He was stern but gentlemanly. After reviewing the papers handed to him, he began the interview. He asked carefully about Pauline's parentage, loyalties, and business in the South. He queried her about the plans and operations of Federal commanders. She pleaded ignorance of such matters and emphasized her love of the South.

Finally, the general ended the interview, saying: "Miss Cushman, I have to tell you plainly that there are very serious charges against you, and I must give you into the custody of our provost-marshal, Col. Alexander McKinstry. He is a very just and humane man and will treat you kindly. Your subsequent fate will depend entirely upon the result of our investigation."

"And if I am found guilty?" asked Pauline.

"You know the penalty inflicted upon convicted spies. If found guilty, you will be hanged," replied Bragg coldly.

Pauline then was escorted to McKinstry's office. He asked how she obtained the Confederate uniform they found among her effects. She answered truthfully about the intent of the Rebel quartermaster at Columbia to make her his aide-de-camp, that he had procured the uniform for her. McKinstry turned to a member of his staff and immediately issued an order for the quartermaster's arrest.

"All right, Miss Cushman," McKinstry said, "would you like to explain these materials we found concealed in your boots and in your satchel?" He placed on the table in front of her the plans, maps, and documents she had stolen from the engineer at Columbia, as well as the sketches and memoranda she had made of various fortifications at Tullahoma, Shelbyville, and Spring Hill.

As she realized that they were the only tangible evidence against her, she regretted deeply that she had not followed her instructions. McKinstry submitted his evidence to a military court and remanded her to custody. She was carefully guarded in a room in a private house on the edge of Shelbyville with barred windows and doubly fastened doors. This would be her prison from June 22 through June 26.

As Pauline waited for the verdict, she became feverish and was confined to bed. Her illness was never defined—but it was probably typhoid fever—and she also suffered from both depression and high anxiety. On the fifth day of her incarceration, Capt. Charles Pedden, the assistant provost marshal, entered her room with a solemn expression on his face.

"Tell me the worst," she entreated him. "Remove this dread uncertainty. I cannot bear it any longer."

"Prepare yourself, then, Pauline, for the worst!" A man of feeling and refinement, he knelt by her side and held her hand.

"Tell me at once. Has the court found me guilty?"

"It has," was his answer.

"And have they condemned me to—" She could not finish the question.

"To death!" replied Pedden. "You have been condemned to be hanged as a spy." Tears of agony rolled down his cheeks. Through his contacts with Pauline he had become infatuated with her.

Pauline sank back on her pillow, overcome by the terrible emotions she had long endured. "It is as I feared."

If the execution were to be carried out, she would be the first and only female spy hanged during the Civil War. The Rebels, however, were not going to carry a sick woman to the gallows. They would wait for her to get well. She also had the slim hope that Union forces might yet save her. They had frequently tried to take Shelbyville, but they had been repulsed each time. Pauline believed they would try again.

Meanwhile, as a substantial Union force advanced toward Shelbyville, the Confederates prepared to retreat. When told that Pauline was too weak to be moved, they chose to leave her behind. On June 27 they placed her in the comfortable home of a physician, Dr. Blackman, who was a Unionist at heart.

Later that day, Brig. Gen. Gordon Granger's command from the Army of the Cumberland marched into Shelbyville. According to the *Nashville Daily Press*, the army "met with a grand reception." Union flags were hung from homes and businesses "and men, women, and children welcomed him with tears and shouts of joy."

Pauline wrote that "the roar of artillery and small arms gave me great strength, and as the stars and stripes floated by my window, I got up from my sick bed and, wrapped in a blanket, I went to the porch to watch the Union troops pass by."

That night, two generals—Granger and Robert Mitchell—met with Pauline. She gave them all the information she had acquired and made only one request: "Please get me deep inside the Federal lines as soon as possible." Granger begged

Federal troops under Major General Gordon Granger arrive in Shelbyville in the nick of time to save Pauline's life.

her to remain in Shelbyville until she regained her strength, but in the end he ordered his ambulance brought to the house and furnished with cushions, pillows, blankets, and a mattress. The two generals propped her up in a chair and carried her to the ambulance.

In Nashville, Pauline rested for several months at hotels and boardinghouses. The Federal government paid much of the cost, authorized by Maj. Gen. James A. Garfield. The general, a future president, showed his interest in Pauline in other ways too. He ordered the arrest and imprisonment of the man who had betrayed her, Benjamin Milam, and he visited Pauline's sick room almost daily.

One evening, while Garfield was sitting near her bedside, a lady, closely veiled, entered the room. She said to Pauline, "Although you don't know me, your deeds of patriotism and daring have given you a certain claim upon the sympathies even of strangers. Hearing that you were sick, then, I have taken the liberty of bringing you a nice pound cake, which I made myself. I hope you enjoy it."

The general placed the cake on a side table along with some fruit he had brought for Pauline. But she was not hungry, so she did not taste the treats. Shortly, the general left, and a neighbor's child came by to visit "the sick lady." Pauline gave her a piece of the cake and some of the fruit. The child preferred the fruit, and ate it. She gave the cake to her little dog. Moments later, the child came crying to Pauline, exclaiming that her dog was acting crazy. Pauline found the dog writhing in convulsions, and soon afterward the dog died in great agony.

Garfield and others attempted to find the culprit who had put arsenic in the cake, but they were not successful. They concluded that it must have been a proud secesh woman determined to rid the Confederacy of a dangerous enemy at any price.

Feted as a Heroine

Pauline recovered slowly but fully from her illness. And Generals Granger and Garfield proclaimed her an honorary "Major of Cavalry" in appreciation for her services as a Union scout and spy. Pauline's biographer claims they also issued her a "special permit" to procure the uniform of a major. From then on she chose to be called Miss "Major" Pauline Cushman.

Following up on the honorary major recognition, the Union ladies of Nashville presented her with a shining blue riding habit, trimmed in military style, with dainty shoulder straps. An article in the *Nashville Daily Press* on December 1, 1863, noted that the dress was "made of the most costly material and is beautifully but modestly ornamented with national emblems." The newspaper described Pauline as "the daring heroine who has done so much service to the United States—a lady who occupies the warmest niche in the patriotic heart of almost every American soldier."

An 1893 newspaper article states that Garfield wrote to President

Pauline was honored for her services as scout and spy. From 1864 to 1870 she lectured and performed throughout the East wearing this uniform. Showman P.T. Barnum billed her as "the greatest heroine of the age."

Lincoln about the spy the troops had dubbed "the Major," and that Lincoln had responded, "Let her keep this title." Pauline affirmed this in her 1890 pension affidavit when she stated that she "received the commendation of President Lincoln and the war department for my service." Whether or not Lincoln was involved in conferring the honorary title is subject to debate. What can be stated with certainty is that Pauline was feted as a heroine throughout the North. She was the darling of the nation.

For the next six years she performed in major Eastern cities as Miss "Major" Pauline Cushman, drawing large crowds and complimentary reviews. She even sang at the opening of the Great Western Sanitary Fair in Cincinnati. Living her role, she frequently wore a military jacket, skirt, and plumed hat and rode in an open carriage with armfuls of roses. People often stopped her on the street to get her autograph.

When she arrived in New York on May 31, 1864, the *New York Herald Tribune* called her "one of the celebrities of the war." That night she was serenaded outside the Astor House hotel before a huge crowd.

For five weeks she was under contract with P. T. Barnum, the famous showman, businessman, and entertainer who may have been the first show-business millionaire. He boosted Pauline's popularity and recognition by promoting her as "The Spy of the Cumberland" and "the greatest heroine of the age."

Her popularity waned in the early 1870s, and she moved west, first to San Francisco, then to Los Angeles County, Arizona Territory, Texas, and back to the "City by the Bay." After two failed marriages to younger men, and with no surviving children, she was basically alone, except for a dozen female friends. Her intimate Civil War friend, General Garfield, was elected president in 1880 but was shot a scant four months after his inauguration. He died two months later from his wounds.

Pauline's health deteriorated rapidly. She endured severe rheumatic pain in her hips and knees and other physical ailments probably related to alcohol addiction. Also hooked on pain medication, she took a lethal overdose of opium on the night of December 1, 1893. The coroner ruled that the cause of death was "from morphine taken, not with suicidal intent, but to relieve pain." She was sixty years old.

The Women's Relief Corps of the San Francisco Grand Army of the Republic gave her a grand military funeral on December 6. Her white coffin was covered with a floral design of violets. She was buried with full military honors—flags, an honor guard, and a rifle salute. Her remains rest in the officers' circle at the national cemetery at the Presidio in San Francisco. The gravestone uses her married name and is inscribed simply: "Pauline C. Fryer, Union Spy."

On May 28, 1864, the *New York Times* carried the following item: "Among the women of America who have made themselves famous since the opening of the rebellion, few have suffered more or rendered more service to the Federal cause than Pauline Cushman, the female scout and spy."

Her biographer wrote: "The deeds of the Scout of the Cumberland will live as long as American hearts beat."

Mrs. Addie Ballou, a Civil War nurse, read an original poem at Pauline's funeral. Its final four lines are:

She has gone! and among them on history's pages,
When ours are forgotten, our children will tell
Of her deeds. And her name will live on through the ages.
Pass on, O freed spirit, pass on, and farewell.

THE HEROINE
OF WINCHESTER

Rebecca Wright

In 1864, a thirty-three-year-old Union general and a twenty-something young woman would make an irascible Confederate general hightail it out of a city long held by the graycoats. Their actions would also help reelect President Lincoln to a second term.

Lt. Gen. Jubal A. Early, affectionately called my "bad old man" by Robert E. Lee, had been a bright and shining star in the disintegrating Confederate galaxy during the summer of '64. In Maryland Heights (above Harpers Ferry) from July 4 through July 6—a time when the capital city was largely undefended—Early's army of twenty thousand men damaged railroads, destroyed telegraph lines, and stripped the countryside of food and military equipment. In Washington, panic set in. Lincoln, his wife, Mary, and son Tad were hustled back to the White House from their summer residence at the Soldiers' Home.

Early continued to Fort Stevens, on the outskirts of Washington, on July 11. As the battle progressed on the second day, the people and the government were as nervous as cats in a room full of rocking chairs. But by the end of the day, the reinforced Federals prevailed, and Early's army retreated. He concluded he didn't have enough strength to capture the city. Nevertheless, Washingtonians, including Lincoln, feared he might return at any time with a greater force.

Early withdrew to the Shenandoah Valley to undertake his second mission: get the damn Yankees out of there. On July 24, Early defeated the Union army at Kernstown, and on July 30, he ordered his cavalry to burn Chambersburg, Pennsylvania. Then, in August, he attacked the Baltimore and Ohio Railroad, which carried supplies to Union troops.

Rebecca Wright

Lincoln grew irritated over Early's successes and the constant threat he posed to Washington. To stop him, the president pressured Ulysses S. Grant to send Maj. Gen. Philip H. Sheridan's cavalry corps to the Shenandoah in August 1864.

"Give the enemy no rest," Grant told Sheridan. "Do all the damage you can to railroads and crops. Carry off stock of all descriptions, and Negroes, so as to prevent further planting. If the war is to last another year, we want the Shenandoah Valley to remain a barren waste." Grant impatiently urged the general to move immediately. The 1864 election was fast approaching, and Union victories were necessary to restore the public's confidence in Lincoln.

Sheridan had put together a collection of 120 spy-caliber soldiers known as Sheridan's Scouts. These risk-takers carried forged passes and wore either Confederate uniforms or civilian attire. They purchased information, intercepted enemy dispatches, hunted down notorious enemy guerrillas, and established networks of Union sympathizers. Seven of them would earn the Medal of Honor.

With intelligence they provided, Sheridan advanced into the valley, occupied ground four miles east of Winchester, and prepared to attack his adversary. He was disturbed, however, by conflicting estimates of the strength of Early's troops as well as contradictory reports of whether or not reinforcements sent to Early in August had been recalled to Richmond. He needed specifics from a reliable insider and a courier who could cross enemy lines.

His scouts recommended Tom Laws, a black produce vendor, as the courier. They said he was loyal, shrewd, and dependable. Furthermore, Laws possessed a pass from General Early that enabled him to travel to and from Winchester to sell his vegetables and eggs three times a week. Sheridan then asked Maj. Gen. George H. Crook, who commanded the 8th Army Corps, to single out someone in Winchester who could be counted upon to relay reliable information.

He suggested Rebecca Wright, a young Quaker schoolteacher who conducted a small private school in her home. Before the war she had taught in a large school in the region, but she was fired because of her well-known Northern sympathies and her denunciation of slavery. Single, she resided with her mother and pro-South sister.

Crook advised Sheridan that Rebecca might be willing to help, but her reputation as a Union loyalist would make the mission extremely dangerous for her. Sheridan hesitated, but then he decided to proceed.

Two scouts brought Tom Laws to Sheridan's headquarters on September 15. When the general was convinced of the man's fidelity, Sheridan asked him if he knew of Rebecca Wright. After Laws stated that he knew who she was, Sheridan told him the plan and, after a bit of persuasion, Laws agreed to carry a letter to Rebecca the next day.

Sheridan wrote the message on tissue paper, compressed it into a small pellet, and wrapped it in tinfoil. "Carry it in your mouth," he advised the courier, "and, if searched by Confederates, swallow it."

Around noon on September 16, a black man knocked at the door of the Wright home and asked for Miss Becky. When Rebecca appeared, she invited him inside. He then closed the door and drew from his mouth the roll of tinfoil and said: "Ma'am, there's a letter of importance inside the tinfoil. It requires an answer. Be careful, and preserve the wrapping for your response. I can pick it up at three o'clock on my way out of town."

Disturbed by the strange procedure, Rebecca unwrapped the pellet with trembling hands. She was afraid it might be a threat on her life. But when she opened it, the message read: "I learn from Major-General Crook that you are a loyal lady, and still love the old flag. Can you inform me of the position of Early's forces, the number of divisions in his army, and the strength of any or all of them, and his probable or reported intentions? Have any more troops arrived from Richmond, or are any more coming, or reported to be coming? You can trust the bearer." The message was signed by General Sheridan.

Startled by the risks of communicating with Sheridan, Rebecca consulted her mother. Could this be a hoax? Could it be a trap set by their enemies? If so, they could be hanged! Their devoted loyalty soon silenced other considerations, and the brave girl resolved to comply with the request, knowing it might jeopardize her life.

Just two evenings before, Rebecca had been gathering flowers in her yard when a Confederate officer wandered by and asked if he might call on her. He was boarding at a house nearby while recovering from a wound. She graciously consented for him to visit her after school was dismissed the following day.

"We were strangers," she later recalled, "with nothing to talk about. So the conversation turned upon the war. He described the situation from his viewpoint—how many troops they had and what they must rely upon. I asked questions without any purpose except to keep up the conversation, and he answered freely. I had no idea of what importance all this was, or what use it would ever be to me; but when I read General Sheridan's letter, it occurred to me that I could tell him what the Confederate had told me."

The key point that she remembered was that a division of infantry and a battalion of artillery had departed from Winchester to join Lee at Petersburg.

She penned the following message to Sheridan: "I...will tell you what I know. The division of General Kershaw, and Cutshaw's artillery, twelve guns and men, General Anderson commanding, have been sent away, and no more are expected, as they cannot be spared from Richmond. I do not know how the troops are situated, but the force is much smaller than represented. I will take pleasure hereafter in learning all I can of their strength and position, and the bearer may call again."

The black messenger rewrapped the note in the tinfoil and carried the message back to Union lines. It was more than Sheridan could have hoped for. Rebecca's message not only quieted the conflicting reports concerning Anderson's corps, but it was most important in showing positively that Kershaw was gone. Acting on these reports, Sheridan planned to attack Early's forces three days later.

The assault began as scheduled, but troop movements were slowed by a line of march through narrow canyons and roads clogged with supply wagons. Meanwhile, Early's scouts warned him of the approaching Union force, and he quickly gathered his army together at Winchester just in time to meet the attack. The assault continued for several hours. Finally, all Confederate lines began to give away, and later, two Union cavalry divisions thundered into the

General Sheridan rode swiftly the dozen miles from Winchester to Cedar Creek to rally Federal troops who had been surprised by Jubal Early and were in disarray. Sheridan's counterstroke reversed the situation and routed Early, ending the Valley campaigns.

Confederate left flank. Shortly after that, Early's broken and confused columns were rapidly retreating.

Casualties were heavy: 5,020 for the Union; 3,610 for the Confederates. Both armies lost key commanders—the Union, four generals; the Rebels, three generals and three colonels, including Col. George S. Patton Sr., whose grandson and namesake was a famous U.S. general during World War II.

The battle, because of its size, intensity, and number of casualties, is generally regarded as the most important conflict of the Shenandoah Valley. It marked a turning point in the Valley in the North's favor.

During the battle, Rebecca wondered if her note had anything to do with the sound of rifles and cannon. Her mother envisioned the town's destruction and perhaps the loss of their own lives.

"I had thought of that all day," Rebecca said years later. "I hid my face in my hands. I didn't think he had gotten the note. It was the most terrible day of my experience. Houses about us were on fire, our own fence was burning, and shells fell so near that my mother and I went into the cellar for safety."

When the noise receded, they came upstairs and looked out of their first- and second-floor windows. They saw "the old American flag coming into town."

Hearing knocking and sabers rattling, Rebecca rushed downstairs and met two Union generals at the door—Philip Sheridan and George Crook. Sheridan was looking for a place to wire Secretary of War Edwin M. Stanton and had been directed to Rebecca's home.

Sheridan warmly shook the hand of "the woman who had contributed so much to our success." He told her, she recalled, "that it was entirely from the information I had sent him that he had fought the battle. He thanked me earnestly, saying that he could never forget my courage and patriotism."

She begged him never to mention the incident, because she feared for her life should the Union forces leave Winchester, but he assured her that the Confederates were gone for good. Then, on a desk in her schoolroom, he wrote to Stanton: "We have just sent the rebels whirling through Winchester, and are after them tomorrow."

The wire relieved Lincoln from further anxiety over the safety of the Maryland and Pennsylvania borders, and Washington, D.C., itself. The president wired back: "Have just heard of your great victory. God bless you all, officers and men."

Rebecca continued to teach a small group of children in Winchester, and for the next three years no one in the city suspected her contribution to the battle. That changed in 1867 after she received the following letter from General Sheridan:

You are probably not aware of the service you rendered the Union cause by the information you sent me by the colored man a few days before the Opequon [Battle of Winchester] on September 19, 1864. It was on this information the battle was fought and probably won....By your note I became aware of the true conditions of affairs, inside of the enemy's lines, and gave directions for the attack. I will always remember this courageous and patriotic action of yours with gratitude, and beg you to accept the watch and chain which I send you by General J. Forsythe as a memento of September 19, 1864.

On the back of the letter was an endorsement by Ulysses S. Grant, recommending her for a position in the Treasury Department. But President Andrew Johnson failed to act upon it.

The letter somehow reached the Valley newspapers, perhaps by way of Rebecca's Rebel sister. And Winchester's predominately Southern population "went wild" with indignation. To them, Rebecca was a traitor.

Her mother's boardinghouse was boycotted to the point that the women became impoverished. Neighbors stripped her of her teaching position and ostracized her family and friends. Boys spit on her and heckled her on the street.

Rebecca endured this persecution for two years until Grant became president and made the appointment he had recommended in 1867. Rebecca then moved with her mother and younger brother to Washington to begin her work as a clerk in the Treasury Department. A few months later, she met and fell in love with William C. Bonsall, who had served in the Union army. They married. Years later they purchased a farm in Kansas, apparently for their retirement years, but he spent time there during the growing season. Unfortunately, crop failures for two years resulted in foreclosure, and he returned to Washington and worked at various jobs.

She remained in the Treasury Department for forty-seven years. Her job was in jeopardy only once—in 1882 when a man with political influence wanted it. Rebecca wrote to Sheridan about the situation, and he reminded Treasury Secretary James Folger that she had made possible the victory at Winchester, which had helped to reelect Lincoln. He told Folger she should have been pensioned, but since Congress opposed that, the Administration and the Republican Party could not afford to dismiss her.

Rebecca retired in 1914. Nothing is known about her life after that. There are no monuments in her honor, and no streets or schools are named after her. Few history books mention her name. But she was of immense value to the Union and to Lincoln. This heroine of Winchester affected the course of history.

Tom Laws, the African American courier, seemed to disappear for twenty-seven years. Then, in 1891, during a reunion of the 6th Corps at Winchester, the veterans searched the city and found him. He was living with his grandchildren. He was offered a position in Washington but turned it down. By then he was seventy-eight and content.

A Glorious Consummation

Harriet Tubman

Harriet Tubman is renowned for her work as a conductor of the Underground Railroad, but her espionage work, like that of many black spies, is far less known. The CIA recognized it in its publication "Black Dispatches," labeling her as "one of the Civil War's most daring and effective spies." Her clandestine exploits, centered along the South Carolina coast, are well documented, mostly because they were connected with important military operations.

Her success as a spy is remarkable, considering her background and the searing drama in which she played a key role.

Born into slavery in Maryland, she endured brutal beatings as a child and lashes that left lifelong scars on her back and neck. She once hid in a neighbor's pigpen and ate slop for five days to avoid more beatings. On another occasion she suffered a traumatic head wound when she was hit by a heavy metal weight thrown by an irate overseer who intended to strike another slave. The injury caused disabling seizures and powerful visionary and dream activity. During this period Harriet acquired a passionate faith in God and found guidance in the Old Testament tales of deliverance. Her visions from the brain trauma increased, and she regarded them as premonitions from God.

In 1849, to avoid being sold, she escaped to Philadelphia, using safe houses in the covert antislavery network known as the Underground Railroad. To notify her mother of her plans, she sang a coded song of farewell: "I'm Bound for the Promised Land." Soon she became active in the antislavery movement and advanced to the role of conductor on the Underground Railroad—a position that gave her knowledge of all the routes to free territory.

She had a close call when she was on a real train and seated in the same car with a former master. She grabbed a newspaper and pretended to read it. Since she was known to be illiterate, the man ignored her.

In 1850 she made the first of what would be thirteen clandestine trips to Maryland to rescue relatives and other slaves, and she guided more than seventy slaves to freedom. One acquaintance said, "She always came in the winter, when the nights are long and dark, and people who have homes stay in them." And she always left with the slaves on Saturday evenings, since newspapers did not print runaway notices until Monday morning. She traveled by night and in secrecy, telling time by the stars, and finding her way "by natural signs as well as any hunter," she said later. Frequently she used songs as a coded communication with fugitives she had hidden in the woods. "Go Down, Moses" meant "stay hidden." Another song, "Hail, Oh Hail, Ye Happy Saints," meant "all clear." She sang "Go Down, Moses" so often that she became known as "Moses," after

Harriet Tubman

THREE HUNDRED DOLLARS REWARD.

RANAWAY from the subscriber on Monday the 17th ult., three negroes, named as follows: HARRY, aged about 19 years, has on one side of his neck a won, just under the ear, he is of a dark chestnut color, about 5 feet 8 or 9 inches hight; BEN, aged aged about 25 years, is very quick to speak when spoken to, he is of a chestnut color, about six feet high; MINTY, aged about 27 years, is of a chestnut color, fine looking, and about 5 feet high. One hundred dollars reward will be given for each of the above named negroes, if taken out of the State, and $50 each if taken in the State. They must be lodged in Baltimore, Easton or Cambridge Jail, in Maryland.

ELIZA ANN BRODESS.
Near Bucktown, Dorchester county, Md.
Oct. 3d, 1849.

In 1849, following Harriet's escape, her owner ran this reward notice in Maryland newspapers for the return of Harriet and her two brothers.

the prophet in the Bible who led his people out of slavery in Egypt. She had often sung with other slaves:

Go down, Moses
Way down in Egypt land
Tell old Pharaoh
Let my people go

Always at risk, Harriet used disguises to avoid detection. She once disguised herself with a bonnet and carried two live chickens to give the appearance that she was running an errand. When she suddenly realized she was walking toward one of her former owners, she yanked the strings holding the birds' legs, and their agitation distracted him.

On all of her rescue missions she carried a loaded pistol to help rouse timid slaves and for protection from slave catchers and their vicious dogs. She also carried pictures of her friends. When she met strangers in safe houses or others who claimed to be covert operators, she showed them the photographs. If they recognized one of the likenesses, all was well.

On one trip a passenger panicked and wanted to turn back. Knowing he would be tortured until he revealed secrets about the Underground Railroad, she pointed her revolver at his head and said, "You go on or you die!"

Harriet was once asked if she really would shoot anyone who wanted to turn back. She replied, "Yes, if he was weak enough to give out, he'd be weak enough to betray us all, and all who helped us; and do you think I'd let so many die just for one cowardly man?"

Bostonian Ednah Dow Cheney, an activist in the Freedman's Aid Society, wrote in the *Freedmen's Record* in 1865: "She has needed disguises so often, that she seems to have command over her face, and can banish all expression from her features, and look so stupid that nobody would suspect her of knowing enough to be dangerous; but her eye flashes with intelligence and power when she is roused."

Harriet was never captured, and neither were the fugitives she guided. Years later she told an audience that she could say what most conductors could not say: "I nebber run my train off de track, and I nebber lost a passenger." Clearly, she was sharp, savvy, and focused.

Radical abolitionist John Brown met with Harriet on two occasions. The first occurred in April 1858 in the Canadian city of St. Catharines, Ontario, where a community of former slaves (including Tubman's relatives) had gathered. The second meeting was in Boston in May 1859. Both meetings were arranged by the black statesman and reformer Frederick Douglass and a group known as the Secret Six, Brown's wealthy supporters.

Brown had been engaged in guerrilla warfare against proslavery forces to prevent Kansas from becoming a slave state. After proslavers wrecked homes and stores in Lawrence (a town founded by abolitionists), Brown and seven men went to Pottawatomie, where they dragged a proslaver and his two sons from their home and hacked them to death.

Brown's second visit to Harriet followed his rapid exit from Missouri, where he had just completed a spectacular rescue of a slave party of eleven persons and taken them to Canada. It was an eighty-two-day wintertime journey of a thousand miles.

Harriet regarded Brown as an instrument of God for ending slavery. Both Brown and Harriet spoke of being called by God, and they trusted Him to protect them. Brown regarded her as "one of the best and bravest persons on the continent." He called her "General Tubman." And because she had the strength and courage of a man, Brown always referred to her as "he," not "she."

Although Brown advocated the use of violence to destroy slavery, Harriet did not, but she supported his goals. Brown had two strategies: to build a stronghold for runaway slaves in the Allegheny Mountains, where they could unite and initiate a crusade to end slavery, or to take over Kansas and make it a sanctuary for former slaves. Harriet supported these goals. Frederick Douglass did not. Brown asked Harriet if she would gather former slaves who might be willing to join him. She agreed to do so and began recruiting ex-slaves for his army. He, in turn, donated money to help ex-slaves in New York and Canada.

Brown's strategies morphed into a grand plan in 1859. He would start an armed slave revolt by seizing one hundred thousand rifles and muskets stored at the U.S. Arsenal at Harpers Ferry, Virginia (now West Virginia).

On the night of Sunday, October 16, Brown and eighteen heavily armed men, including several free blacks, entered Virginia from their training camp in Maryland. They attacked and seized the Federal arsenal, captured watchmen, and cut telegraph lines. Brown expected hundreds of local slaves to rise up against their owners and join him. Then, well armed, they would make a rapid movement southward—a movement that thousands of slaves were expected to join along the way.

But the slaves didn't show up at Harpers Ferry. Meanwhile, townspeople began shooting at the raiders, and local militia companies surrounded the armory, cutting off Brown's escape route. Then U.S. Marines arrived, commanded by Col. Robert E. Lee.

Within thirty-six hours, Brown's men had fled or been killed or captured.

Brown was tried and convicted of inciting a slave insurrection, the murder of five proslavery Southerners, and treason against the state of Virginia. He and six of his followers were hanged on December 6.

Harriet later told a friend, "He done more in dying than a hundred men would in living."

Indeed, his action had enormous repercussions. It terrorized Southerners with the fear of massive slave rebellions and aroused many Northerners who opposed violent confrontations over slavery. Further, the raid fragmented the Democratic Party and produced the conditions that enabled Abraham Lincoln to win the presidential election of 1860. That, of course, led to secession and the Civil War.

Until meeting with Brown, Harriet had worked primarily with Quakers. Brown called them "milk and water" abolitionists. Now, Harriet seemed more receptive to bolder tactics and to armed rebellion by slaves and former slaves.

On April 27, 1860, something happened in the river town of Troy, New York, that either represented new boldness on her part or a remarkable coincidence. She was there, she said, to visit a cousin while on her way to Boston. Gerrit Smith, one of John Brown's Secret Six financiers, had invited her to speak at a conference in the "Cradle of Liberty."

The timing was interesting. On the same day, a runaway slave, Charles Nalle, was captured in Troy, taken to the U.S. Commissioner's office, and was about to be returned to his master in Virginia. Newspaper accounts reported the exploits of "an old colored woman" who first appeared at the window of a second-floor room in the commissioner's building.

The "old woman" was thirty-eight-year-old Harriet Tubman in disguise. A crowd had gathered below, and Harriet apparently gave them a signal that produced "great excitement." The *Troy Daily Times* reported that "the old colored woman" was yelling in the street, "Give us liberty or give us death" and "with vehement gesticulations urging on a vigorous attempt to rescue the prisoner. Here the scene became intensely exciting. Revolvers were drawn, knives brandished, colored women rushed into the thickest of the fray...and the friends of Nalle closed upon the officers, fearless and unterrified."

The mob pulled Nalle away from the police and ran with him to the waterfront, where a skiff awaited him. He was put on board and rowed across the river. Some four hundred supporters, including Harriet, followed by storming a Hudson River ferry and sailing across the river to West Troy.

When Nalle's skiff reached the West Troy shore, he was arrested and taken to a room on the second floor of a building near the dock. The *Daily Times* story continued: "The building was stoned, and the crowd, rushing up into the room under fire from the revolvers of the West Troy officers, seized the prisoner and escaped with him from the building. Nalle was placed in a wagon and driven off."

Abolitionists protected him in a secret location until they raised $650 to buy him from his owner. Nalle then returned to Troy.

Obviously, Nalle's rescue had been carefully planned, with the skiff and the wagon available at the right moment. Harriet apparently was the ringleader.

Recruited as a Spy

In the late fall of 1861, after the onset of war, Gov. John A. Andrew of Massachusetts summoned Harriet to Boston to discuss a critical need. Having previously worked closely with Harriet, he was well aware of her potential as a spy and scout for the Union. A staunch abolitionist, Andrew once said, "I know not what record of sin awaits me in the other world, but this I know, that I was never mean enough to despise any man because he was black." Andrew would be a guiding force behind the creation of some of the first Union army units of black men.

Federal armies had occupied the Sea Islands of South Carolina, Georgia, and Florida in November. The white planters had fled, leaving ten thousand slaves who were now "contraband of war"—free by virtue of military action. "They came flocking into our camps by the hundreds," said one Union soldier, "many of them with no other clothing than gunny-sacks."

These former slaves had no jobs, no money, and no education, but they did have a simple faith that "when they reached Massa Lincoln's soldiers they would be free," noted a Federal report. Not knowing what to do with them, the call went out to abolitionists in the North to come south and help these former slaves to adjust to a new way of life and to keep them from overrunning Union camps.

This call resulted in the formation of the New England Freedmen's Aid Society. They raised money for their "Port Royal Experiment" and sent the first group of missionary teachers on March 3, 1862, to Beaufort, South Carolina. Harriet Tubman arrived two months later. What Governor Andrew said to Harriet before she left is unknown, but given her experience in the Underground Railroad, many believe that the humanitarian aspects of her trip to Beaufort were a cover for her real work as a spy operating within enemy lines.

She later told a neighbor that she agreed to the governor's request to "act as spy, scout, or nurse as circumstances required," but then she said that they changed their request (perhaps to create a cover for her) and asked her to go down and distribute clothes to the contrabands. The rumor among her closest friends was that she was on "some secret service."

Governor Andrew handled arrangements for Harriet's transportation to Beaufort and her assignment to Maj. Gen. David Hunter. He commanded the Department of the South, encompassing South Carolina, Georgia, and Florida, from his headquarters on Hilton Head Island, at the head of Port Royal Sound. Hunter wrote on Harriet's military pass: "Give her free passage at all times, on all Government transports. Harriet…is a valuable woman. She has permission, as a servant of the government, to purchase such provisions from the Commissary as she may need."

At Port Royal, Harriet soon began serving as a spy and an organizer and leader of scouts—a role she would fill through the spring of 1863. With a hundred dollars in "Secret Service money" and the confidence of slaves and former slaves, she selected and paid a core group of nine reliable black scouts. Some were former riverboat pilots and knew every inch of the waterways threading through the coastal lowlands. With training from Harriet, they would prove their ability to gather timely intelligence.

One of their first assignments was to survey enemy territory and map the maze of jagged shoreline and numerous islands of the coast of South Carolina. The marshes and rivers were not unlike those of the Eastern Shore of Maryland.

Harriet's knowledge of them, as well as her experience in covert travel and subterfuge under those conditions, contributed to her effectiveness.

In early May 1862, General Hunter declared all contraband in his region to be free. He then initiated plans to create a regiment of black soldiers. When President Lincoln learned of this, he was outraged. He revoked Hunter's pronouncement on May 19 and reprimanded the general. At this early stage of the war, Lincoln didn't want to do anything to alienate the Border States and cause them to secede.

Harriet was skeptical. "God won't let master Lincoln beat the South til he does the right thing," she said.

With heavy Union battle losses in 1862, Lincoln reconsidered the inclusion of blacks in the Union war effort. By August he was ready to implement a policy permitting his generals to use all the means at their disposal, including available black manpower, to help preserve the Union.

Congress empowered him to do so by passing the Confiscation Act on July 17. Finally, in late August 1862, Brig. Gen. Rufus Saxton put together five regiments of black troops from the Sea Island contraband residents and refugees. Saxton was in charge of Federal enterprises at Port Royal.

Col. Thomas Wentworth Higginson of Massachusetts, a close friend of Harriet Tubman, organized the first authorized regiment recruited from former slaves for Federal service. The regiment consisted of nearly eight hundred men.

Higginson, a Harvard graduate, Unitarian minister, and literary mentor to poet Emily Dickinson, had been a fervent supporter of John Brown. He was one of the Secret Six abolitionists who helped Brown raise money and procure supplies for the intended slave insurrection at Harpers Ferry. When Brown was captured, Higginson launched a fund-raising campaign for a strong trial defense to help him escape from prison, but he was unsuccessful. Prospective donors viewed the matter as a political piranha tank.

Determined to prove the superiority of black soldiers, Higginson praised their first action in January 1863—a nine-day covert operation on St. Mary's River into Confederate territory to seize lumber, bricks, railroad rails, and other supplies. They even acquired a piano, which they gave to a black school in Beaufort. Higginson's success was due in no small part to intelligence provided by Harriet's black spies who knew vulnerable points and locations of Confederate sentinels.

The most controversial figure sent to organize a black regiment was Col. James Montgomery, a tall, rough-and-tumble Kansan who never hesitated to use extreme measures against proslavery populations. Historian Albert Castel described him as "a sincere, if unscrupulous, antislavery zealot." Others described him as wild and vengeful.

Neither Harriet nor Montgomery knew each other, except by reputation, but that alone made them instant allies. John Brown was their common denominator. Montgomery was one of Brown's most trusted lieutenants, and Brown was Harriet's hero.

Montgomery, with Harriet's assistance, raised a regiment of African American infantry in January. It became the 2nd South Carolina Colored Infantry. Meanwhile, Harriet and her nine-man spy team evolved into a kind of special-forces operation for the black regiments. Her team sneaked up and down rivers and into swamps and marshes to determine enemy positions, movements, and fortifications on the shoreline beyond the Union pickets.

When Harriet reported the results of one of these reconnaissance missions to Gen. Saxton, he became so excited that he wired Secretary of War Edwin M. Stanton in Washington and recommended an attack on Jacksonville, Florida. Saxton wrote, "I have reliable information that there are large numbers of able-bodied Negroes in that vicinity who are watching for an opportunity to join us." Stanton authorized the attack, and Saxton assigned the mission to the "fiery westerner," Montgomery, and his 2nd South Carolina Colored Infantry.

Fiery indeed. Montgomery's reputation for slash-and-burn tactics was never more evident. His Jacksonville mission, although successful, was marred by the unnecessary burning of much of the town. Then, in June, Montgomery gained further notoriety by looting and burning the coastal town of Darien, Georgia. Following that raid, Col. Robert Gould Shaw, commander of the 54th Massachusetts, said that Montgomery had declared, "Southerners must be made to feel that this was a real war, and that they were to be swept away by the hand of God, like the Jews of old." Montgomery himself said, "We [black Union regiments] are outlawed, and therefore not bound by the rules of regular warfare."

Harriet's Amazing River Raid

Montgomery drew upon Harriet's team for hard-to-come-by intelligence that enabled him to conduct a series of successful river raids. The most famous of

The Combahee River raid

Montgomery's campaigns was one formulated and guided by Harriet Tubman: the Combahee River raid.

General Hunter asked Harriet if she would go with several gunboats up the Combahee (pronounced kuhm-bee) "to destroy railroads and bridges, to take up the torpedoes [mines] placed by Rebels in the river, and to cut off supplies from the Rebel troops." She said she would go if Colonel Montgomery was appointed to the command. Hunter concurred, and Harriet and Montgomery were, in effect, co-commanders. She led the way. He led about three hundred black soldiers.

Her role was unusual, not just because she was a woman, but also because she was a civilian attached to the Union army and could do pretty much what she wanted. She even had the authority to work secretly on her own and to spend Secret Service funds.

Harriet and her crack team of black scouts sailed upriver on their dangerous reconnaissance to find the torpedoes (the name then used for remotely detonated mines) and to pinpoint the locations of storehouses for rice and cotton. To accomplish both objectives she made her way to slave cabins and found the men who had helped to place the torpedoes. She promised liberation to those willing to tell her where they were. She alerted slaves to listen for the ships' whistles and then to rush to the riverbanks she identified, because if the mission succeeded, Harriet and

Montgomery planned to take the slaves aboard their ships to freedom. With her reconnaissance now complete, she and Montgomery finalized plans for the operation.

The Combahee, a narrow, wiggly river north of Beaufort, emptied into St. Helena Sound, which merged into the Atlantic Ocean. The river bordered and supplied the water for some of the largest, most productive rice plantations in the South—plantations owned by South Carolina's powerful blue bloods. A Spaniard, Lucas Vásquez de Ayllón, discovered the river in 1520 and named it "The River Jordan." In biblical history, the Jordan River was a symbol of the barrier between bondage and freedom. This symbol remained strong on the night of June 2, 1863, when three Federal steam-powered gunboats headed out of St. Helena Sound toward the Combahee.

The troops were primarily from the 2nd South Carolina Colored Infantry. A smaller contingent from the 3rd Rhode Island Heavy Artillery manned the ships' guns. Harriet and Montgomery were on the lead gunboat, the *John Adams*. The *Harriet A. Weed* followed about a quarter of a mile distant, but the third vessel, the *Sentinel*, ran aground in the sound, reducing the force by one-third.

As the two remaining gunboats entered the mouth of the river in the dead of night, Montgomery spotted Confederate sentinels at Fields Point and sent twelve black soldiers to drive them off. As the sentinels fled, they rode frantically to the nearby village of Green Pond to exclaim, "The Yankees are coming! The Yankees are coming!"

Meanwhile, Harriet guided the ships past the mines, which were just below the surface of the water and difficult to see when clouds dimmed the light from the moon. Two miles above Fields Point a company of the 2nd South Carolina landed near a small earthwork at Tar Bluff and deployed into position. The two ships then steamed upriver to the Nichols plantation, where the gunboat *Harriet A. Tweed* anchored.

The *John Adams* carried the two commanders and the remainder of the 2nd South Carolina farther inland. The ship continued to Combahee Ferry, where there was an island, a causeway, and a temporary pontoon bridge. There, they encountered a small band of escaping Confederates riding over the bridge and across the causeway toward Green Pond. The *John Adams* fired at them, and they fled. The ship anchored and deployed troops.

One group from the ship set the bridge on fire. Another detachment crossed the causeway toward Colleton County and sacked and burned several plantations, rice mills, and storehouses—all of which Harriet and her scouts had reconnoitered. A third group advanced up the opposite side to Middleton plantation. They confiscated all supplies they could carry and laid waste to what remained. The regiment's surgeon reported to *Harper's Weekly*: "We broke the sluice gates and flooded the fields so that the present crop, which was growing beautifully, will be a total loss."

The ranking Confederate officer in the area, Major Emmanuel, had been notified of the incursion, but was slow to respond. With malaria, typhoid fever, and smallpox rampant in the low country from spring through early fall, most Confederate troops had been pulled back from the rivers and swamps. Only small detachments remained to guard the river outposts. Nevertheless, Emmanuel ordered his men to repulse the Yankees, so troops from four villages opened fire on the Federals returning to the ships. The Rhode Islanders on the *John Adams* shelled Emmanuel's small force with superior firepower, and the Confederates ran back into the woods.

By this time, Montgomery's troops had set fire to nine plantations and seized thousands of dollars' worth of rice, cotton, corn, potatoes, and supplies. William Heyward later reported that the raiders burned his mansion, mill, stables, riverboats, ten thousand bushels of stored rice, and eight hundred bushels of corn, and that two hundred of his slaves had run off. Plantation owners up and down the Combahee made similar reports. The destruction was unprecedented in the low country.

Confederate commanders kept getting reports of fires at various locations and dispatched troops to each, but in all cases the Union forces were out of reach. All the Rebels could do was retreat to their original positions. Major Emmanuel led a small force to the shoreline with only a single field artillery piece, but he was too late. The ships were steaming back to the sound. He attempted a pursuit, only to become trapped between the river and Union snipers.

While all the damage was being done, the gunboats sounded their whistles, signaling for nearby slaves to rush to the rowboats Montgomery had sent to the riverbank to take them to the gunboats. Montgomery's troops also aroused other slaves and urged them to go to the river and board the rowboats.

When the slaves realized that freedom was within their grasp, they stampeded toward the boats. "I never saw such a sight," Harriet Tubman said later. She described the scene:

*Some was getting their breakfasts, just taking their pots of rice off the fire, and
they'd [carry] the pots, with rice a smokin', young ones hanging on behind....
Some had blankets on their heads with their things done up in them, and
them that hadn't a pot of rice would have a child in their arms, sometimes
one or two holding on to their mother's dress; some carrying two children, one
astride of the mother's neck and another in her arms. Some had bags on their
backs with pigs in them; some had chickens tied by the legs, and so [there
were] children squalling, chickens squawking, and pigs squealing. They all
come runnin' to the gunboats through the rice fields. They [reminded] me of
the children of Israel coming out of Egypt.*

Overseers, armed with guns and whips, tried to stop the fleeing slaves,
but their efforts were useless. Chaos on the shores, however, nearly foiled the
escape. Those who got to the rowboats first climbed in and attempted to cast
off, but other slaves grabbed the boats and wouldn't let go, afraid of being left
behind to face their overseers. The ship's captain yelled to Harriet, "Come and
speak a word of consolation to your people!"

Harriet said later, "Well, they wasn't my people any more than they was
his—only we was all Negroes. I didn't know any more about them than he did.
I didn't know what to say. I looked at them about two minutes, and then I sang
to them: 'Come from the East / Come from the Wes..../ Come along; come along; /
Don't be alarmed. / For Uncle Sam is rich enough / To give you all a farm.'"

The song accomplished what she had hoped. The slaves released their grip
on the boats. Rejoicing, they threw up their hands and shouted "Glory!" Then
the rowboats pushed off. Harriet kept on singing until all were aboard the gunboats. More than seven hundred slaves were rescued that night.

The raid was a huge military success. It struck a damaging blow to a major
food source for the Confederates and opened the river for Union boats to cut
off Confederate supplies. Further, it provided Montgomery with nearly two
hundred new recruits for his regiment (half of whom Harriet brought to the
recruiting office).

Harriet and Montgomery addressed a celebration service near Beaufort,
where they and the slaves were being housed on an abandoned estate christened
Montgomery Hill. It was said that "for sound sense and real native eloquence,
her remarks would do honor to any man."

Reporting on the Combahee River raid, a Boston newspaper, the *Commonwealth*, said the "gallant band of Black soldiers, under the guidance of a Black woman, dashed into the enemy's country, struck a bold and effective blow, destroying millions of dollars' worth of commissary stores, cotton, and lordly dwellings, and striking terror into the heart of rebeldom...without losing a man or receiving a scratch. It was a glorious consummation."

A month later the same publication identified the black woman as Harriet Tubman, thus exposing her work as a spy for the first time. The front-page article by Boston abolitionist Franklin Sanborn praised her work in the Combahee raid and her earlier success in guiding fugitives to freedom. Sanborn said the "whole world" should finally "sing her praises."

The *Wisconsin State Journal* said of Harriet: "Since the rebellion she has devoted herself to the great work of delivering the bondsmen, with an energy and sagacity that cannot be exceeded. Many and many times she has penetrated the enemy's lines and discovered their situation and condition, and escaped without injury, but not without extreme hazard. True, she is but a woman, and a 'nigger' at that, but in patriotism, sagacity, energy, ability, and all that elevates human character, she is head and shoulders above all the copperheads in the land, and above many who vaunt their patriotism and boast their philanthropy."

An official Confederate report blamed Major Emmanuel and his men for the loss. "They were neither watchful nor brave," said the report. "They allowed a parcel of Negro wretches calling themselves soldiers, with a few degraded whites, to march unmolested with the incendiary torch, to rob, destroy, and burn a large section of the country." The report concluded: "The enemy seems to have been well posted as to the character and capacity of our troops and their small chance of encountering opposition, and to have been well guided by persons thoroughly acquainted with the river and country."

That, unknown to the Rebels at the time, was a tribute to the work of the Union's secret weapon, Harriet Tubman, and her black scouts and spies. The combination of their accurate intelligence work and the follow-up action by Union forces produced the most productive and spectacular results of any such combination in the Civil War.

Author Earl Conrad of Auburn, New York (Harriet's future residence), later wrote: "This is the only military command in American history wherein a woman, black or white, led a raid, and under whose inspiration, it was originated and conducted."

After the War

Harriet remained in the South for the next year, helping in various guerrilla activities and tending to newly liberated slaves. She even baked and sold pies and gingerbread to earn money

Harriet Tubman Home for the Aged

to help them. By conversing with all contrabands, she was "able to get more intelligence [from them] than anybody else could," wrote a lieutenant in the 55th Massachusetts Infantry.

During a leave of absence, Harriet visited her parents in Auburn, New York, where she became ill from total exhaustion. After recovering she worked as a nurse for the U.S. Sanitary Commission in Washington and reported on abuses in hospitals.

In 1869 she married a black Civil War veteran, Nelson Davis, who was twenty-two years younger than she. They adopted a baby girl named Gertie. Nelson struggled with tuberculosis until his death in 1890. That same year Congress finally agreed to pay Harriet a pension of twenty dollars a month for her efforts on behalf of the Union during the Civil War. With her small savings as collateral, she purchased land at an auction and later deeded it to an African Methodist Episcopal Zion church for a home for "aged and indigent colored people." When it opened in 1908, Harriet was appalled by the required entrance fee of one hundred dollars. She said: "They make a rule that nobody should come in [unless] they have a hundred dollars. Now I wanted to make a rule that nobody should come in unless they didn't have no money at all." The home was named the Harriet Tubman Home for the Aged.

By 1911 she was so frail and penniless that she was admitted to the home. She died on March 10, 1913, at the age of ninety-two. She was buried with military honors in Auburn.

Frederick Douglass said of her, "Excepting John Brown, I know of no one who has willingly encountered more peril and hardships to serve our enslaved people." Queen Victoria bestowed a silver medal on her. In 1955 the U.S. Maritime Commission launched the SS *Harriet Tubman*, its first Liberty ship ever named for a black woman. In 1978 the U.S. Postal Service issued a stamp in her honor. It was the first in a series on African Americans.

The Smithsonian Institution saluted Harriet in 1982 as "the only American woman ever to plan and lead a military raid." A statue of her was unveiled in the South End neighborhood of Boston on June 20, 1999. A bridge at Combahee Ferry was named for her and dedicated on October 12, 2008.

10

A Teenage Terrorist

Nancy Hart

Newspapers called her a vamp, a spitfire, a bushwhacker, and a voluptuous tomboy. Yankees knew her as a troublesome character who would become one of the most daring and dangerous female spies of the Civil War. Her name was Nancy Hart.

When the war started, Nancy was just fifteen years old. She was an attractive and vivacious West Virginia mountain girl, tall with dark hair and beady black eyes. She couldn't read or write, but she could ride and shoot as well as anyone. Like other mountain girls, she frequently walked barefooted and rode bareback. She hunted squirrels, raccoons, and other fur-bearing animals on and around her family's farm in what is now central West Virginia but was then known as western Virginia. It was a land of narrow valleys, rugged mountains, and tough, independent Scotch-Irish folks.

In this sparsely settled region, most folks were poor, plantations were unheard of, and few mountaineers had ever seen a slave. Yet the region was about equally divided in loyalty to the Union and the Confederacy. The war became a struggle of brother against brother, father against son, sister against brother, and neighbor against neighbor. The Hart family was no exception.

Nancy was one of thirteen children born to Stephen and Mary Hart. Two of their sons joined the Union army. Nancy initially had no interest in politics or in the war. She liked doing "boy" things, like shooting a musket and tracking, fishing, stalking, and taking care of herself. Her parents, however, wanted her to cook, clean, and look after her six younger siblings. But Nancy didn't want to be like other young women who married and lived on farms. To her, marriage meant losing her identity and her individuality. Her parents regarded this attitude as un-Christian, and they realized they had on their hands a rebellious teenager about to become a hardened Rebel.

The Baltimore and Ohio Railroad ran through this area, and Federal troops moved in early in the war to keep it in Union

Nancy Hart

hands. To oppose them and anyone loyal to the Union, Confederate mountain men banded together as "raiding rangers." These Rebel partisans rode at night, usually in groups of ten to fifteen, and attacked Federal soldiers and Union loyalists. "Strike and run" was their tactic. Hit Calhoun County one morning, hit Braxton that night, then Webster the next day, and Nicholas after that.

"We're gonna keep 'em looking over their shoulders every minute," said one raider.

The rangers would charge up to a house occupied by a Unionist family, spray it with bullets, shoot anyone who came to the door or looked through a window, then burn the house, steal the livestock, and move on to pull up railroad ties, burn trestles, and attack Yankee outposts.

Some writers have speculated that many of these acts were more personal than political, and thus they generally were not a credit to the Confederate cause. Some rangers apparently joined a group in order to pay off old scores with Unionist neighbors. But it didn't end there. As the movement grew, and more and more bands developed, civil government broke down, stores were looted, post offices disrupted, and businesses suspended. Each Union loyalist had to depend upon himself or herself for survival.

Considerable military force was necessary to keep the rangers in check and to protect pro-Union persons and property. This was difficult because the rangers scattered after each raid and did not reunite until the next raid. During the war's first two years, many Union troops recruited in the area remained there to combat the guerrillas, but to the rangers' advantage, there were never enough Federal troops, and most of them lacked military savvy and skills.

As one ranger later acknowledged, "They'll be so busy fightin' and lookin' for us, they won't be botherin' Stonewall Jackson and our boys in the Shenandoah Valley."

The most prominent band of Confederate partisans was led by twenty-three-year-old Perry Conley, a six-foot-three muscular menace who could outrun, outfight, and outlift anybody in the area. He titled himself "captain" and called his force the Moccasin Rangers, referring to the moccasin snakes that attacked suddenly and without warning.

In the spring of 1861, rebellious Nancy Hart ran away from home and joined Conley's rangers. Probably the only female guerrilla under Conley, she became his frequent companion and an indispensable asset. She served as both a spy and a guide. She knew the territory. She had ridden over every hill, mountain, and trail, explored every cave, and seen every stream in the region. She supplied Conley with intelligence and occasionally fought in skirmishes with him. Conley liked her partisan spirit and regarded her as "deadly as a copperhead."

As the Moccasin Rangers became even more lethal, so did Nancy Hart. Union sympathizers huddled in their homes in fear for their safety. Word spread about murders committed, property destroyed, women raped, and other atrocities.

Nancy took a brief break from the rangers in October 1861 to visit her sister Mary Hart Price, who was expecting her first child. Mary's husband, William, was a loyal Southerner. He often provided food and other supplies to Confederate troops in the area.

About dusk on October 19, a party of Union soldiers rode into the yard. They told William to come with them to the town of Spencer for a program he should be in. While Price prepared to leave, the soldiers poked around the house. They found Mary in the bedroom with several pillows and a large bolster behind her. They apologized for invading her privacy. Had they looked more closely they would have found Nancy Hart hidden behind the bolster.

Price never got to Spencer. Neighbors found him a couple of days later, his body riddled with bullets. Nancy's sadness turned to intense hatred of the Union. Now that the war had touched her personally, she'd do anything to help the Confederacy, even if it meant fighting against her own brothers.

Later that fall, Conley's Moccasin Rangers raided neighboring Braxton County and were pursued by a detachment of Braxton home guards (Unionist) under Lt. Henry Bender. Bender found some of Conley's band at a home on Stinson Creek and killed one, but the others escaped. The next day Bender searched out their possible hiding places along the West Fork River. As the home guard turned a bend in the road, they came upon Conley and Nancy emerging from the woods on their horses. A member of the home guard fired into the air and yelled, "Halt."

Nancy's mare panicked and reared up. As she sought to control the horse, she looked toward Conley for help. All she saw was Conley cowardly galloping into the brush as bullets whizzed by him.

Almost immediately, the home guard surrounded Nancy and jerked the reins from her hands.

"Why are you botherin' me?" she asked loudly. "I'm jist a farm girl tryin' to visit relatives. I got lost, and that gentleman showed me the way to the road."

Unsure as to what to do with her, they took her back to camp for more questions. At age fifteen she appeared harmless and innocent of any wrongdoing. She was so convincing that the captain in charge said, "O shucks, she's just a farm girl who had some bad luck and got lost. Let her go."

She returned to Conley's camp with loads of information about the home guard and the arrival of regular Federal troops to reinforce them. Eventually, thirty-two home guards were organized and commissioned in Calhoun County to protect Unionist citizens.

Conley's exploits ended abruptly in Webster County in the early summer of 1862 when a detachment of the 30th Ohio Infantry surprised and shot him. Conley was mortally wounded at the first fire, but he continued to return fire until he ran out of ammunition. The soldiers then clubbed him into submission. After his death, the Moccasin Rangers disbanded, and many of them joined Virginia cavalries.

Sixteen-year-old Nancy Hart went through a crash of emotions—rage, bewilderment, and panic—before seeking comfort and love from ranger Joshua

Douglas, a handsome, muscular mountaineer. They married shortly after Conley's demise, but their marital bliss was disrupted by Douglas's decision to sign up with Company A of the 19th Virginia Cavalry. His enlistment was antedated to July 15, 1861, to protect him from prosecution for acts committed while fighting with Conley's band.

Captured—But Not for Long

Nancy moved to a cabin in the mountains of Nicholas County, near Confederate lines. Unwilling to rein in her desire to serve the Confederacy, she posed as an innocent country girl while carrying information to Rebel forces.

Summersville, the county seat of Nicholas, was occupied by sixty Union men of the 9th West Virginia Infantry under the command of Lt. Col. William C. Starr. Starr's headquarters was a two-story frame dwelling abandoned by its owners after the approach of Federal troops. Starr and three other officers occupied the house. Gardens in the neighborhood had been stripped of all vegetation, so the men foraged for fresh vegetables.

On July 10, 1862, a foraging party made up of Starr, two orderlies, Capt. Samuel Davis, and a telegrapher named Marion H. Kerner searched for table luxuries in the region. After riding about three hours, they noticed smoke ascending from a log cabin in the valley below. In front of the cabin they saw two mountain girls crushing corn between two large rocks. When the girls heard horses approaching, they ran into the cabin and barred its heavy wooden door.

As the Federals dismounted, an elderly woman peered through a small, hinged window on one side of the door and yelled to the girls, "The Yankees are upon us!"

Starr gently knocked at the door. Receiving no response he knocked more vigorously. After several vain attempts, he went to the window and assured the old woman that their mission was friendly. He asked her if they would be willing to trade some of their vegetables for a liberal supply of salt. Salt was scarce and expensive. The lady agreed to the trade, and the men filled their sacks with food from the garden.

As they were about to remount their horses and return to Summersville, Colonel Starr paused, as if in thought, and drew from his pocket the description of Nancy Hart, known to be a Rebel guide and spy. The government was offering a substantial award for her capture. Starr consulted with his cohorts. They agreed that one of the girls they had seen matched the description. Starr and Davis returned to the cabin and approached the girls, who had resumed their corn crushing. According to an account by Marion Kerner, Starr laid his hand gently upon Nancy's shoulder and said, "Well, Nancy, at last we've got you!"

The other girl, about Nancy's age, shouted without thinking: "That's not Nancy Hart! Leave her alone!"

And Nancy exclaimed, "What are you going to do with me?"

With these reactions, Starr knew that this girl was, indeed, Nancy Hart. Nancy's friend was arrested as well for harboring an enemy in time of war. She was the granddaughter of the elderly woman, and Nancy was staying with them temporarily.

At Summersville the girls were incarcerated in a dilapidated building formerly used as a jail. Guards patrolled it on all sides. Kerner thought it ungentlemanly to house two teenage girls in "a miserable old building." He appealed to Colonel Starr to transfer them to more comfortable quarters. He suggested the vacant attic in Starr's headquarters. Starr was reluctant but finally consented.

After the transfer, Kerner supplied them with sewing material and illustrated papers. Neither girl could read or write, but they studied the pictures. Kerner also furnished them with dainties purchased from a sutler—a civilian who sold supplies at army posts.

The door of the attic prison remained open during daylight hours so the guard in the hallway could keep an eye on the girls. The guards could talk with them, but they were not allowed to enter the room. Anyone who violated that order or in any way laid hands upon them was to be shot at sunrise. The girls were allowed to close the door at night.

One night, however, Nancy intentionally left the door open. Around three o'clock in the morning she told the guard she couldn't sleep and struck up a conversation with him. In the process, she charmed him and convinced him that she was a sweet country girl who wouldn't harm anyone. She expressed an interest in his musket and asked him if she could hold it. She told him that she had used a rifle to furnish her home with all sorts of game.

The young guard, not much older than she was, could not resist her smile and her soft-spoken voice. Besides, she was a pleasure to look at, and he was lonely and homesick. He handed her the musket. She grasped it, stepped back, pointed it toward a wall, then turned toward him and fired. She shot him through the heart, and he fell dead.

Nancy jumped over the body and ran downstairs and out to the barn. She mounted Colonel Starr's horse bareback and galloped away before the sleeping officials realized what was happening. She left behind her female companion.

Starr ordered a pursuit, but it took his men awhile to get dressed and saddle their horses, giving Nancy a good head start. The Federals checked the cabin where they previously caught her, and they scoured the mountains in all directions, but they did not find her. She had made her way safely to Confederate lines and delivered critical information about Federal forces in and around Summersville.

A week later, on July 25, Nancy returned to Summersville, but she was not alone. She came with two hundred Confederate cavalry under the command of Maj. Augustus Bailey. They had ridden two days and nights along narrow, winding roads through the mountains until they reached a small expanse of open country a mile or so from the village. As they approached, the drowsy Union pickets panicked and ran. The two companies of Federal troops, quartered in several houses, slept soundly.

The Rebels stormed into Summersville at four o'clock in the morning. The lieutenant in charge of Company F heard a single shot from the lone picket at the guardhouse. He jumped out of bed, looked out the window, and saw Confederate cavalry seemingly everywhere. He crawled through a back window and escaped to the woods. Others of his command followed him in their sleeping garments.

The Confederates, meanwhile, surrounded Colonel Starr's headquarters. They captured Starr, Captain Davis, two lieutenants, and others, with little resistance, and rescued Nancy's female companion.

Before leaving the village, the Rebels added to their collection twelve horses, eight mules, and the entire stock of Enfield rifles and ammunition. They burned three houses, including the commissary storehouse.

Among their prisoners was Marion Kerner, who had extended various courtesies to Nancy during her incarceration. To return the favor, she approached Major Bailey and assured him that Kerner was not a Yankee and that he, too, was a Rebel prisoner and should be released. She lied to help her friend.

Bailey, who had no reason to doubt Nancy, released Kerner and allowed him to enter the house and get his effects. In 1882, Kerner wrote the following account for *Leslie's Weekly*:

My first thought upon entering the office was to secure the telegraph instrument. It was still in place. This I did, and placing it under an army blanket which I threw over my arm, I made my way down the turnpike in the direction of Gauley Bridge. I had proceeded about a mile when I came to the place where the wire had been cut by the enemy to prevent communication with the main body of the regiment. Placing the instrument in the circuit and grounding the Summersville side, I found the wire "O.K." to Gauley Bridge.

While in the act of reporting the capture [of Union soldiers] I was surprised by half a dozen mounted men. They approached with carbines leveled at me. They ordered me to desist. I promptly obeyed. They [escorted] me back to Summersville.

When the case was reported to Major Bailey, he flew into a rage and with an oath threatened to "shoot the little Yankee traitor." But Nancy again came to my rescue. What she told the major I never knew, but he put me under guard, and [I was on the way to Libby Prison at Richmond].

The Rebels left Summersville with their prisoners and their various acquisitions. Nancy rode at the head of the column.

She continued to help Confederate units until the end of the war. By day she spied on isolated Federal posts from the forested hills above them. She studied approaches to their sites and estimated their strengths. She also ventured into Yankee strongholds, peddling eggs and vegetables and discovering military secrets from talkative soldiers who couldn't imagine that the teenage girl might be a spy.

Many times at night she led Confederate cavalry or infantry through the rugged terrain to attack Federal outposts. And during daylight hours she guided the cavalry to wagon trains carrying Union supplies. Cautious while spying, but daring while guiding troops, she knew that if she were caught, she would be hanged.

Nancy's husband, Joshua Douglas, survived the war. He and Nancy settled on a mountain farm at the head of Spring Creek in Greenbrier County. Nancy died there in 1902 at the age of fifty-six. She was buried on Mannings Knob, near her home. A pile of stones marked her grave.

Nancy's ability to lure the opposite sex did not stop with her death. Located near her grave was a fire watchtower manned by Ivan Hunter of Richwood, West Virginia. During his lonely vigils at the tower, Hunter apparently thought a lot about Nancy and her exploits. He requested that he be buried beside her. His wish was granted.

In an area where Nancy played when she was a child, on the edge of the West Fork near Nancy's home, is a large stone. The stone is known locally as Nancy's Dancing Rock.

11

"No Sacrifice Too Great"

Antonia Ford and Laura Ratcliffe

What two young female spies did for two young Rebel officers does not show up in any history textbook. But it saved the life of one of them and helped them both become two of the South's greatest heroes.

The story of their interactions and the results that followed seem too remarkable to be real, too romantic to be believable, and at times, too funny to have happened in wartime.

The young men were Brig. Gen. Jeb Stuart and Col. John Singleton Mosby. Stuart, self-confident and flashily dressed, would gain lasting fame by circumnavigating a huge Union army twice to gather intelligence for Gen. Robert E. Lee. Mosby, a small, thin man known as the "Gray Ghost," possessed one of the most brilliant minds in the history of guerrilla warfare. He was so effective that, in the North, he was the most hated Confederate.

The ladies were Antonia Ford and Laura Ratcliffe. They were beautiful Southern belles with brains and spunk. Cousins, they were from prominent families in Fairfax Court House, Virginia, about twelve miles from Washington, D.C. Founded by Laura's great-grandfather, the town was the county seat of Fairfax County. The county was bounded on the north and southeast by the Potomac River and on the south by Bull Run, the site of two major battles in the Civil War.

Antonia Ford

Laura Ratcliffe

Fairfax was a prized target for both the North and the South. It was the first county in the South to be invaded and conquered by the Union army. The Federals occupied it for most of the war, although the population remained sympathetic to the Confederacy.

Laura was twenty-five in 1861, the year the war started. Her father had passed away in 1850, and so she lived with her mother and two siblings ten miles west of Fairfax in the Frying Pan area (present-day Herndon).

Antonia was twenty-three. As a teenager she had attended Coombe Cottage, a private finishing school for girls from wealthy families. She then earned a degree in English literature from the Buckingham Female Collegiate Institute, where she excelled in writing and self-expression.

John Singleton Mosby

Antonia's father, Edward Ford, came from a family long established in the Old Dominion. He was an ardent Secessionist, a prosperous merchant, and the foremost citizen of Fairfax. He owned the finest home in the village.

Before the battle of First Manassas in July 1861, the Fords opened their home to Southern troops stationed near the village. Jeb Stuart and his scout John Mosby were frequent visitors and good friends with the Ford family. But when Brig. Gen. Irvin McDowell's Union Army of the Potomac marched out of Washington toward Manassas, its path took them right through Fairfax Court House, which was midway between the capital and the battlefield. A skirmish at Fairfax resulted in the death of the first Confederate officer in battle—John Quincy Marr—and the takeover of the town by Union troops.

Laura and Jeb: He Liked What He Saw

Twenty-eight-year-old Jeb Stuart first met Laura Ratcliffe on December 21, 1861, when she was ministering to his wounded soldiers at Frying Pan Church after the Union victory at the battle of Dranesville—an engagement of no tactical importance. Of the Confederates' 230 casualties, nearly half resulted from friendly fire. But Stuart's mind wasn't on his defeat. It was on Laura. He liked what he saw. She was a dazzlingly beautiful young woman, refined and gentle, with sparkling dark brown eyes, jet black hair, and a beautiful figure. In fact, it was love (or infatuation) at first sight for the married officer with two children.

In fact, General Stuart planned to have Christmas dinner with her, but on Christmas morning she received this note from him: "A very Merry Christmas to you this bright morning! I deeply regret that duty will prevent me from enjoying the pleasure I so much anticipated of taking my Christmas dinner with you. It so happens that I am obliged

Jeb Stuart

to go in the opposite direction, but in heart and best wishes for your happiness, I will be with you."

Determined to maintain contact with Laura by mail if not in person, he wrote again on January 6, 1862: "A happy New Year. I send you Miss Antonia's friend, Captain Rosser, to escort you to the camp for dinner, and hence to Fairfax to spend a night with Mrs. Ford [Antonia's mother]. Be assured I sacrifice a great personal pleasure in forgoing this visit."

On January 30 he sent his regrets again, this time to both Laura and Antonia: "My Dear Ladies—It is such a muddy day that I refrain from visiting you because I would dislike to appear in such an unpresentable costume as the roads would give me. Nevertheless, you may expect me soon, rain or shine."

After that, more letters followed to Laura and Antonia, along with more excuses.

Jeb Rewards Antonia for Covert Actions

For self-protection, the Fords also entertained Federal officers in July 1861 and allowed them to use the house as a gathering place. Federal officers were as impressed with the Ford home as had been the Confederates, and several blue-coats became paying guests.

While the Federal men stayed, Antonia viewed their presence as an opportunity to serve her beloved South through covert activity. Since Stuart and Mosby were friends of the family, she would report any information to them. Before each party or gathering she would primp before a large mirror in her room, trying on various dresses, arranging her lustrous light brown hair, and cultivating a sweet and subdued voice—all to make herself more seductive. Reportedly, she also visited a phrenologist to enhance her ability to win friends and influence powerful figures.

She charmed officers without appearing inquisitive. She never talked about military affairs, but impressed her admiring guests with her intelligence and her pretended loyalty to the Union. She kept their attention not only with her good looks and genteel personality, but also as an amusing and entertaining conversationalist and companion. The Union's spy chief, Lafayette Baker, later described her as a "decidedly good-looking woman with pleasing, insinuating manners." One observer said she received all sorts of information "in an apparently no-interest-to-me-I-assure-you manner, which quite deceived the men."

Consequently, the army officers, anxious to be around her, talked freely. They bragged about their troop strengths and strategies to whip the Rebels. They revealed military secrets. She listened carefully and reported as much as she could to Stuart, whose troops were in the area, and to Mosby, who would become the war's most famous partisan ranger. She sometimes passed information through other field operatives, and apparently was part of Rose Greenhow's spy organization in Washington (see chapter 1).

In one of the soirees at her home, Antonia learned that the Yankees suspected leaks to the Confederates and planned to conduct a sunrise house-to-house search. When they arrived at her residence, they saw Antonia reading in the parlor, her crinoline skirts spread wide around her chair. In her quiet manner, she told them to search where they wished. When they finished, the officer in charge stood before her and asked her to get up. Her piercing brown eyes glared at him: "I thought not even a Yankee would expect a Southern woman to rise for him." The embarrassed officer went out, not knowing that valuable documents were hidden under her skirts.

Two days before the First Battle of Manassas on July 21, 1861, Antonia borrowed a horse and rode to a Confederate camp to warn Gen. P. G. T. Beauregard that McDowell's army would attack the Confederate left, crossing Bull Run over the Stone Bridge. Her message came three days after Beauregard had heard from Rose Greenhow, and for whatever reason, Beauregard's staff assumed that Antonia was a Union spy trying to trick them. They arrested her. After twenty-four hours under guard, Antonia returned home, taking back roads to avoid the bluecoats. Meanwhile, the Federal position was confirmed by Stuart's Washington spy, John Burke.

Although this episode was humiliating for Antonia, Virginia author John Esten Cooke wrote her for details and included them in his novel *Surry of Eagle's Nest*. Cooke, who was thirty-two and a native of Winchester, had strong romantic feelings for Antonia, and she seemed to feel the same way about him. Antonia's superstitious nature probably encouraged the romance. She had dreamed that the initials of her true love were "J.C." and that they surely meant John Cooke.

By the fall of 1861 Antonia's patriotism, secret reports, and loyalty to the cause drew the admiration of Stuart, who himself had attracted the attention of the Confederate government by leading a crucial and courageous charge on the Federal forces at First Manassas. In recognition of Antonia's services to the South, Stuart awarded Antonia a mock commission as his honorary aide-de-camp on October 7, 1861. Because of "special confidence in the patriotism, fidelity, and ability of Miss Antonia Ford," Stuart directed that she be "obeyed, respected, and admired by all the lovers of a noble nature." She hid the citation under her mattress.

Moonstruck Poetry and the Secret Rock

As much as Stuart respected Antonia, he was enamored with her cousin Laura. In late winter and early spring of 1862, Stuart waltzed with Laura, took her on horseback rides, went sleighing with her, and composed moonstruck poetry to her.

On March 3, he penned his first romantic and patriotic poem for Laura and included it in a leather-bound, gold-embossed album he presented to her with this preprinted inscription on it: "Presented to Miss Laura Ratcliffe by her soldier-friend as a token of his high appreciation of her patriotism, admiration of her virtues, and pledge of his lasting esteem."

The album was ten and a half inches high, eight inches wide, and one and a half inches thick. Its pages were blank except for Stuart's poem and two others on the life of soldiers written by Scottish poets Thomas Campbell and Lord Byron. Stuart also gave her his watch chain with a gold dollar attached. In addition to demonstrating his affection, he probably was trying to impress her so that she would want to gather information for him.

Laura drew lines for calling cards on the album's blank pages and collected signatures

The cover page of a leather-bound album that Jeb Stuart presented to Laura as a gift.

on them, then a common way of gathering autographs of important people. When found after her death, the album contained forty signatures—twenty-six by Confederate soldiers and fourteen by civilians. Among others, the signatures included Stuart, Mosby, Fitzhugh Lee, and some of the men who fought with them.

Stuart's poem to Laura included these lines:

> *To Laura—We met by chance; yet in that 'ventful chance*
> *The mystic web of destiny was woven:*
> *I saw thy beauteous image bending o'er*
> *The prostrate form of one that day had proven*
> *A hero fully nerved to deal*
> *To tyrant hordes—the south avenging steel....*
> *I saw thee soothe the soldier's aching brow*
> *And ardently wished his lot were mine*
> *To be caressed with care like thine....*
> *And when this page shall meet your glance*
> *Forget not him you met by chance.*

Laura received a long letter from Stuart dated March 17. Here are portions of it:

> *My Dear Laura—*
> *I have thought of you long and anxiously since my last tidings from you.... You no doubt will find opportunities to send me an occasional note. I need not say how much it will be prized. Have it well secreted and let it tell me your thoughts, freely and without reserve. Can I ever forget that never to be forgotten good-bye? Will you forget it? Will you forget me? I am vain enough Laura to be flattered with the hope that you are among the few of mankind that neither time, place, or circumstance can alter—that your regard, which I dearly prize, will not wane with yon moon that saw our last parting, but endure to the end. That whatever betides...you will in the corner of your heart find a place in which to stow away from worldly view the 'young Brigadier..... If you know how I would prize a letter, you would write me every opportunity. Have you forgotten?*

Stuart wrote again on April 8 while on his way to Yorktown to fight in the Peninsula campaign. In this letter he boasted of "glorious" Confederate victories and added: "I have thought of you much."

Several months passed before he corresponded again, primarily because of his increasingly important cavalry command in Robert E. Lee's Army of Northern Virginia. On a four-day, 150-mile mission in June on the Virginia Peninsula, Stuart and his carefully selected twelve hundred cavalrymen circumnavigated Maj. Gen. George B. McClellan's Union Army of the Potomac to find its weakest positions. Stuart met no serious opposition from the Union cavalry, coincidentally commanded by his father-in-law. In the process Stuart destroyed wagonloads of Union supplies and captured 170 soldiers and 260 horses and mules. In Richmond, Stuart was greeted with flower petals thrown in his path and a promotion to major general.

During a lull in the fighting, Stuart withdrew his forces into bivouacs north of Chantilly in western Fairfax County and visited Antonia Ford's family in Fairfax Court House.

On December 28, he passed through Frying Pan and stopped at the home of Laura Ratcliffe and her mother. During this visit he gave Laura his second

Federal cavalry scouting in the neighborhood of Fairfax Court House. Fairfax County was the first county in the South to be invaded and conquered by the Union army. The Federals occupied it for most of the war.

original poem, titled "To Laura." Its closing two lines were: "When friends are false save one whose heart beats constantly for thee / Tis then I ask that thou wouldst turn confidingly to me."

On December 29, Stuart returned to the Ratcliffe home with Capt. John Mosby, hoping to persuade Laura to be helpful as a spy to both of them.

Mosby had told Stuart at a meeting that week, "I did not want to rust away my life in camp." He requested permission to remain in northern Virginia with a nine-man unit of partisan rangers and continue operations there while Stuart's cavalry was in winter quarters west of Fredericksburg. Stuart agreed. Mosby's mission, as he stated in his memoirs, was to launch raids to impede and disrupt Union operations and "to weaken the armies invading Virginia by harassing their rear." He believed correctly that "every soldier withdrawn from the front to guard the rear is so much taken from its fighting strength."

Laura and Mosby had much in common and undoubtedly liked each other almost instantly. Both were well educated. Mosby was twenty-nine, intelligent, and thoughtful; some called him a walking dictionary of the classics. Laura was quiet and refined. Mosby was usually reserved. He spoke in a low voice, slowly and distinctly, but he could become quite talkative and animated. He had studied at the University of Virginia and was admitted to the bar in 1858. He also was happily married to a Kentucky girl, Pauline Clarke.

The meeting at the Ratcliffes' home was significant. With Laura and Mosby now knowing and liking each other, they both envisioned opportunities for her to help him. Laura told Mosby she wanted to show him what she thought might be a good hiding place for messages and a rendezvous point for his men. They walked about a mile through the woods to the top of Squirrel Hill. Before them was a great rock about ten feet in diameter. It was conveniently located near Frying Pan Church on the western edge of Fairfax County. With various trails leading from it, the rangers could quickly scatter, if necessary.

Mosby was impressed with the rock, with Laura, and with the plan she presented. In time, the rock was named Mosby's Rock, and Laura was called Mosby's Pet. Mosby and his operatives used the rock as a drop for letters and documents. When Laura acquired secrets about the movements of Union forces, she communicated them to Mosby either in person or under the rock. When she carried messages, she concealed them in a false-bottomed egg basket.

Laura also served as a banker to Mosby's Rangers and hid money and supplies near the rock. After one raid, several thousand dollars were turned over to Laura for safekeeping, and she secured it beneath the rock. When she could safely do so, Laura placed the money in proper hands. Union officers searched the area, but they never found the cash.

On many occasions Mosby used the Ratcliffe farm as his area headquarters and as a storage site for confiscated Union material and money until it could be safely transferred to the proper Confederate authorities. He also used Frying Pan Church, near Laura's home, as a hospital and a secret meeting place.

The G. M. *Hopkins Atlas of Washington* for 1879 explains how Mosby's Rock got its name. It states that Mosby's men frequently met there after successful raids and divided the spoils. They then "dispersed to their houses, as was their custom after making one of their famous dashes." The atlas also emphasized Laura's role in using the rock to assist Mosby and referred to her "as a maiden lady of great intelligence and high accomplishments and [a person who] is well spoken of by all the surrounding neighbors."

Mosby Relies on Laura; She Saves His Life

On February 8, 1863, Mosby faced a near-death situation, saved only by the daring exploits of Laura Ratcliffe.

In Mosby's memoirs he related how he had planned to attack a Union cavalry picket at Frying Pan Church, not knowing it was a trap that would surely have led to his death or capture. Hiding in a thick grove of pines was a large body of Union cavalry ready to pounce on the partisan rangers and bag all of them on the spot.

On the same day two Union soldiers stopped at the Ratcliffe home for fresh milk and eggs. One of them bragged about the clever trap they had set for Mosby. He said with a smirk: "I know you would give Mosby any information in your possession, but since you have no horses and the mud is too deep and the weather too cold for women folks to walk, you can't tell him. So the next time you hear of your 'pet,' he will either be dead or our prisoner."

Laura waited anxiously for the soldiers to leave. She and her sister then bundled up, put on their boots, and went out on foot across the muddy fields to reach the home of her cousin George Coleman and ask him to find and warn Mosby. In a remarkable coincidence, their path crossed Mosby's as if it had been timed perfectly. And she warned him herself. In Mosby's memoirs, he wrote:

> *We were proceeding toward Frying Pan, when I heard that a cavalry picket was stationed there and waiting for me to come after them. I did not want them to be disappointed....When I got within a mile of it and had stopped for a few minutes to make my disposition for attack, I observed two ladies walking rapidly toward me. One was Miss Laura Ratcliffe, a young lady to whom General Stuart had introduced me a few weeks before. Fortune brought them across my path. But for meeting them, my life as a Partisan would have ended that day.*

From that time onward, Laura worked in closer cooperation with Mosby, and he more frequently relied on her for shelter and intelligence. Her timely information on Union troop movements led to his successful raids on Union outposts, communications, and supply lines. He could trust her, and she never let him down.

Over a period of two years, Mosby's Rangers conducted more than a hundred raids or skirmishes, derailed trains, and seized thousands of soldiers, horses, and arms. They usually escaped barely scathed by the encounters.

"Hurrah for Mosby!" exclaimed the usually reserved Robert E. Lee. "I wish I had a hundred like him."

Lt. Gen. Ulysses S. Grant, frustrated by Mosby's successes, issued an edict in 1864: Mosby and his men were to be designated as outlaws and hanged without trial if captured.

Antonia Aids Mosby's Amazing Feat

Union Gen. Irvin McDowell's aide-de-camp, Maj. Joseph Clapp Willard, arrived in Fairfax Court House during an unusual snowstorm on April 9, 1862. McDowell had sent him from Washington to obtain a house for the general's headquarters. It was not a difficult assignment. The home of Antonia Ford was the town's finest, and Willard chose it. He was a quiet, handsome, forty-one-year-old businessman/

soldier who was co-owner of the prestigious Willard Hotel in Washington. As he inspected the Fords' home, he and Antonia eyed each other. A mutual attraction was obvious. Years later, he wrote in his diary: "A snowstorm today—as on the day 22 years ago that I first saw my dear-dear Antonia."

Just before the Second Battle of Manassas in late August 1862, Antonia saved Southern troops from certain disaster. From Union officers staying at her home, she learned of a Union plan to use Confederate flags to draw Rebels

Major Joseph Clapp Willard

away from their assigned positions. Unable to find anyone to deliver the message to Jeb Stuart's camp, she and her aunt hitched up a team of horses and proceeded tediously for twenty miles over rough roads on a stormy night. They dodged prowling Federal troops to complete the mission.

Following the battle—another victory for the Confederates—McDowell's staff again stayed at the Fords' home, and McDowell ordered Major Willard to protect the house. "The whole family gave me their thanks," he wrote in his diary. He added: "Miss Ford says if I am taken prisoner I must come to her house."

In December 1862 the Federals changed forces at Fairfax Court House and brought in Brig. Gen. Edwin Stoughton and the 2nd Vermont Brigade to protect and defend the area. Stoughton, a twenty-four-year-old West Point graduate, was the youngest general in the Federal army. He set up his headquarters at the residence of Dr. William Gunnell, a few hundred yards from the village courthouse.

The next three months were relatively quiet, the monotony broken only by Stuart's cavalry attacks and by gossip about the lovely Virginia girl General Stoughton was keeping company with. That young lady was Antonia. They had met at a soiree at her home. Stoughton was smitten, but her only interest in him was as a source for enemy intelligence. Thus, she teased him enough to lead him on.

Antonia and Stoughton were often seen riding in the country on horseback and talking in low tones. Even the general's own troops became concerned and wondered about his common sense. They feared that she was after military secrets to be passed along to Mosby, whose guerrilla warriors were nearby. One soldier wrote to a friend in Vermont about Stoughton being intimate with a pretty girl in the village by the name of Ford, and he wondered "why our people do not send her beyond the lines....If he gets picked up some night he may thank her for it."

From this relationship Antonia obtained important details about the number and disposition of Stoughton's command, the location of his troops and pickets, and even the countersign used at the time. She knew that Mosby would eagerly devour this intelligence. He did, and he acted upon it.

In February 1863 Mosby rode into Union-occupied Fairfax Court House alone. Dressed in civilian clothes, he went directly to Antonia Ford's home and spent three days and nights as her parents' guest—at the same time that Federal officers were housed there. When they saw Antonia sitting on the gallery with the lean, unimpressive-looking civilian, they assumed he was a "simple, green, raw" countryman. According to a report in the *Washington Star* Antonia even gave Mosby a tour of the town, pointing out locations where Federal officers resided and cavalry horses were stabled. She also described the number and position of enemy forces and the location of depots where supplies were stored.

The purpose of his visit was not social. He was gathering intelligence from Antonia for a daring raid that would make him a legend in the South. He was determined to capture Sir Percy Wyndham, a Union cavalry colonel quartered at Fairfax Court House. Wyndham had accused Mosby of being a horse thief, and Mosby could not tolerate the insult. The two men despised each other.

Mosby had recruited a Federal deserter, Sgt. James Ames, to serve as his guide. Ames knew the locations of Union encampments in the area outside Fairfax and could direct Mosby around them. Then, once in the town, the information supplied by Antonia would complete the required intelligence.

The raid was planned for the night of March 8–9, 1863, the same night that General Stoughton hosted a champagne party at Antonia's home to celebrate his new position. His mother and sister came from Georgetown

In 1863, Harper's Weekly learned that two years earlier, Jeb Stuart had presented Antonia Ford with a mock commission as his honorary aide-de-camp. They ran this "Cartoon of the Day" on April 4 with the following caption: "The rebel cavalry leader, Stuart, has appointed to a position on his staff, with the rank of Major, a young lady residing at Fairfax Court House, who has been of great service to him in giving information."

and stayed with the Fords. All the villagers were invited, but none of the Secessionists showed up. They missed an elaborate party, which included a regimental band for dancing. The last of the guests departed around one o'clock in the morning.

The night was cold and wet. Mosby and the twenty-nine men he had handpicked for the raid wore Federal-issue ponchos as a disguise and for protection from the weather. They snaked their way, unchallenged, past three thousand Yankee troops and through drowsy pickets. Well inside Federal lines, they entered Fairfax Court House around 2:00 a.m.

"We are going to mount the skies tonight or sink lower than plummet ever sounded," the Confederate commander told his men. "My fate was trembling in the balance," he later recalled. "If we should get caught, it would end my career as a partisan; everybody would say that I had tried to do what I ought to have known to be impossible."

It was pitch dark when they approached the courthouse yard.

A picket called out: "Who goes there?" A ranger threw a coat over the soldier's head and pulled it tightly around his neck.

Next, they captured the telegraph operator and cut the telegraph wires. From these men Mosby learned that Colonel Wyndham was in Washington, but General Stoughton was in the Federal camp.

Mosby divided his forces into squads of four and five men, some to collect horses, others to capture guards and army officers in their homes. Mosby took five men with him to snatch Stoughton from the two-story brick home where he slept.

Dismounting in front of the house, Mosby banged on the front door with his sword hilt. A drowsy aide asked what they wanted.

"Fifth New York Cavalry bearing dispatches for the general," Mosby replied.

A guard opened the door and was greeted by Mosby and a Colt revolver. One of the Rangers clapped a hand over the guard's mouth.

Mosby pointed the revolver at his head and demanded: "Take me to the general's bedroom."

Stoughton was deep asleep and snoring loudly. Empty champagne bottles lay near the bed. Mosby pulled back the blanket, raised the general's nightshirt, and slapped him hard on the rump. Stoughton snorted and opened his eyes.

"Are you General Stoughton?" Mosby asked.

Stoughton, seeing men with pistols, replied, "Yes, what do you want?"

"Did you ever hear of Mosby?" the Ranger asked.

"Yes!" exclaimed Stoughton, who thought he was talking to his own men. "Have you caught the son of a bitch?"

"No, but he has caught you!" replied Mosby. "I am Mosby, and you are my prisoner. Get dressed. You are coming with me."

Mosby then picked up a piece of coal from the fireplace and wrote his name on the wall. He took the prisoner outside and joined the other Rangers. Besides

Stoughton, they had captured two captains, thirty enlisted men, and fifty-eight horses without firing a shot or losing a man.

As the raiding party began to leave, a man shouted from an upstairs window, "Halt! The horses need rest. I will not allow them to be taken out."

No one replied. He yelled even louder. "I am commander of this post, and this must be stopped." He was Col. Robert Johnstone, commander of the cavalry brigade in Wyndham's absence.

Mosby ordered two men to take him prisoner, but the colonel's wife blocked them at the front door, fighting and scratching them. Johnstone, clad only in his nightshirt, fled by the back door. He found a hiding place beneath the outhouse in the backyard, but he lost his nightshirt in the process. He stayed under the outhouse, naked, for several hours. Johnstone drew the nickname "Outhouse Johnstone" from his men. Embarrassed, he left the service in December.

Mosby, not wanting to scuffle with Johnstone's wife, withdrew his men and led the contingent out of town, riding in a column of fours, pretending to be Union cavalry. The Rangers returned to their camp, from which Stoughton was delivered to Libby Prison in Richmond.

Stoughton, a West Point graduate from a prominent Vermont family, was devastated. The *New York Times* called the capture "utterly disgraceful." The *Baltimore American* referred to Stoughton as "the luckless sleeper at Fairfax who was caught napping." The *Washington Star* reflected the national mood with its statement: "There is a screw loose somewhere." Lincoln told reporters he did not mind losing the general, since he could create another one with the stroke of a pen, but he hated to lose the horses, because "they cost a hundred and twenty-five dollars apiece."

Jeb Stuart commended Mosby for his "daring enterprise and dashing heroism" in accomplishing "a feat almost unparalleled in the war, performed in the midst of enemy troops."

Two months later, Stoughton was exchanged for a Confederate general. But he saw no further service, as the Senate had not confirmed his initial appointment. His career was ruined, and his health along with it—partly from the humiliation and partly from his imprisonment. He died five years later.

After the Stoughton episode, it was rumored but never confirmed that the planks were removed each night from some Washington bridges to prevent Mosby from sneaking into Washington to kidnap Lincoln.

A Counterspy Tricks Antonia

In Washington, Stoughton's capture by Mosby drove Secretary of War Edwin M. Stanton ballistic. He sent for Lafayette Baker, chief of the National Detective Police, and ordered him to determine the cause of Stoughton's capture and to arrest everyone involved. Baker surmised that the plot was perpetrated by a spy in cahoots with Mosby. He reported: "Mosby's knowledge of the number and position of our forces, of the exact localities of officers' quarters, and of depots of Government property all point unmistakably to the existence of traitors and spies within our lines, and their recent communication with Confederate officers."

Baker had seen the earlier article in the *Washington Star* about the intimate relationship between Antonia Ford and Stoughton, and he had heard numerous speculations. But he didn't know about the Yankee deserter who had assisted Mosby. Baker instead focused on local Secessionists. With Antonia Ford's reputation, she had to be investigated. Perhaps, Baker pondered, she was a cunning female spy capable of extracting information from unsuspecting heart-struck officers. So Baker assigned the mission to one of his most trusted female operatives, Frankie Abel. If the spy was a woman, he speculated, then let a woman find her and expose her clandestine activities.

Around March 11, Frankie Abel showed up at the Fords' home posing as a distressed Confederate refugee fleeing from Union-occupied New Orleans. She wore an old calico dress that had been out of style for years. She said she had been stranded in Union-held territory since the beginning of the war. When she finally received a pass to go to Virginia, she said she went through Washington, where a friend gave her a secret message to deliver to Maj. Gen. Fitzhugh Lee at Culpeper Court House.

Frankie appeared to be shy, timid, and embarrassed. Antonia felt sorry for her and treated her like a beloved sister. All of the Fords received her with open arms. At dinner they served some old-fashioned corn muffins, and the visitor exclaimed how wonderful it was to have real Southern food and how terrible it was to live among the damn Yankees.

After dinner Antonia offered some of her own clothes to the visitor, who gladly accepted them. And at bedtime, Antonia took her guest to the bedroom and talked for hours about the cause. The guest spoke proudly of her work for the Confederacy. Then Antonia slipped up. She boasted about her covert accomplishments for Mosby and Stuart. Beaming with pride, Antonia reached her arm beneath the mattress, pulled out a document, and showed it to her guest. It was the commission issued by Stuart for her "patriotism and fidelity."

Frankie remained with the Fords for several days, gathering more evidence. Antonia spoke of her pretended romance with Stoughton, of flirting with other army officers to get information, and of briefing Mosby while he was in civilian clothes in Fairfax.

As Frankie prepared to leave, ostensibly to deliver her message to Fitzhugh Lee, she and Antonia embraced and kissed each other on the cheek. Frankie departed with a tearful good-bye, wearing Antonia's expensive clothes.

The next visitors to the Fords' home arrived on Sunday, March 15. They were secret agents from Colonel Baker's headquarters. They asked to see Antonia. She was in bed with a severe migraine headache, but she put on a housecoat and came down the stairs. The agents introduced themselves and requested that she take the oath of allegiance to the Union. She refused. They arrested her and searched the house. They found six thousand dollars in Confederate money, private letters from Union officers, and numerous papers from Confederate officials, including Antonia's commission as aide-de-camp to General Stuart.

Washington newspapers later reproduced Stuart's document. Meanwhile, the Vermonter who had received a letter from a soldier at Fairfax about Stoughton's relationship with Antonia sent it, along with his own criticism, to the *New York Times*. The loss at Second Manassas, he charged, resulted from the Union's failure to identify and capture spies. He wrote: "[The] Belle Boyds and Antonia Fords have more to do with these Stuart raids than the Government is aware of. They are 'rebel Majors' in disguise. They pass unchallenged by our sentries. They mingle in our camps of officers. They are the Delilahs who betray our Samsons."

The *Times* added: "Miss Ford of Fairfax was unquestionably [Mosby's] local spy and actual guide in his late swoop upon that village."

Concerned that some of Mosby's men might attempt to rescue Antonia on the way to prison, the Federal agents escorted the young Virginia belle under heavy guard to the railway station. She was hidden in a boxcar and taken to Washington during the night.

Her arrest sheet stated: "Antonia Ford is a native of Virginia—aged 25 years—resident of Fairfax C.H. Va.—rather delicate in appearance—is a defiant rebel—pleads especially for her family, and says she alone is responsible for her sentiments and actions—has a Rebel Commission from the Rebel General Stuart which she declares he gave her as a compliment and as a personal acquaintance. She acknowledges the will but asserts her physical inability to participate in any manner in this national strife, and positively denies having done a single act for or against either part, but claims having assisted the sick and wounded of both sides."

Baker didn't buy her denial. Antonia, after all, had shown the commission to Frankie and bragged about telling Mosby of the Union positions in and around the village. Those incriminating statements were sufficient to incarcerate her at the Old Capitol Prison in Washington.

Upon arriving in the capital city, the agents took Antonia directly to the provost-marshal's office. She had not eaten for nearly twenty-four hours and was tired and haggard from a sleepless night. She sat in tears, observed to her surprise by Maj. Joe Willard, who was now on the provost marshal's staff. Willard had not forgotten this lovely lady in whose home he had stayed a year earlier.

For the next two months—from March 15 to May 14—Antonia was confined in the Carroll Prison, an annex to the Old Capitol Prison. In this dingy, stinking environment, Antonia's health suffered. Bedbugs and lice inhabited her straw mattress. Meals of greasy beans, fat, and bad meat took their toll. She lost weight and became a mere shadow of her former self.

The *Washington Star* wrote on March 17:

It turns out that the woman Antonia J. Ford, of Fairfax Court House, was the principal spy and guide for Colonel Mosby in his successful recent raid upon that village. Col. L. C. Baker, the War Department's provost marshal, ordered her arrest, having obtained positive information that Mosby (in disguise) slept at the house of Ford in Fairfax Court House, and that Ford's daughter went round with him and pointed out the houses which General Stoughton, Colonel Wyndham, and Colonel Johnstone occupied as their quarters, and that she certainly aided Mosby in planning and executing his raid. She was accordingly brought here on Sunday last and consigned to the Old Capitol Prison.

Acting out of love for Antonia, Major Willard, along with another of Antonia's dear friends, John Esten Cooke, headed a campaign to secure her release. Jeb Stuart did his part too. He asked Mosby to deny Antonia's involvement in his capture of Stoughton, which Mosby did. Some historians have used his statement to discredit Antonia's spy work, but in reality, spymasters never reveal the identity of their spies. By denying Antonia's complicity in any covert operations, they were simply protecting her, assuring her future usefulness as a spy and hopefully aiding in her release.

Meanwhile, Willard sought to cheer up Antonia with frequent gifts and newspapers. Almost daily he pleaded with her to take the oath of allegiance to the Union. But she would not.

Antonia's mother, Julia, knew the prison superintendent, and he granted her permission to send Antonia several items: bows, a china mug, tea, spool cotton, plumes, buckskin gloves, stationery, the music of "Bonnie Blue Flag" and "Dixie," and the book *Les Misérables*.

Two months after her incarceration, the prison superintendent abruptly announced: "Miss Ford, you are to be sent for exchange to Fortress Monroe, and then to City Point, Virginia. Pack everything as quickly as possible."

On that same day, she and twelve other female prisoners were transported by train to Baltimore, and from there, down Chesapeake Bay to Virginia.

Willard's Confession to Antonia

Before leaving the prison, Antonia had a disturbing conversation with Major Willard. "There is something I must tell you," he said. She looked into his eyes but was unable to smile, not knowing what to expect.

"I am married."

Surprised, stunned, and overcome with emotion, she said nothing for a few moments. She then stood up and approached him. She wanted to slap him, but she restrained herself. They had been very close for nearly a year. He had declared his undying love for her. He had claimed to be a Christian. She was not, but she had strong moral values. She had flirted with officers to acquire information, but she had never had an affair. Antonia was angry.

Willard tried to explain. He said his marriage to Caroline had been a failure, that they had no children, and that they had been separated for some time. He said he had traveled to California to get away from his wife with the hope of striking gold. His brother Henry had written him in 1857, scolding him for not telling his friends or his wife where he was. His two years in California were financially disappointing, he said, and he returned to Washington to work with his brother in expanding the hotel they had acquired. He said he had wanted to get out of the marriage for some time, but that his wife had resisted.

Antonia told Willard she would "prayerfully consider" his explanation, but she did not know if she could agree to ever see him again. Antonia returned to her cell and cried inconsolably.

Within minutes the guard returned to take Antonia and the other exchangees to catch the train to Baltimore and the ship to Fort Monroe. The next morning they boarded a steamer for City Point, Virginia, near Petersburg. From there they traveled by train to their destinations, with Antonia getting off at Culpeper Court House, about fifty miles southwest of Fairfax. She was hungry, weary, and frail.

Culpeper, then under Southern control, witnessed more than a hundred battles during the war. Most houses in town were used for military lodging or hospitals. Antonia checked into the Old Virginia Hotel and waited for mail and advice from her family farther north.

About a month later—on June 18—General Stuart's chaplain notified her not to go to Middleburg or to Fairfax, which were still occupied by the Yankees. Instead, at his suggestion, she traveled to Warrenton and stayed at the home of Mr. and Mrs. William H. Gaines. He was the town's former mayor.

While she was there, Joe Willard showed up one day. During their conversation, he said he was not yet divorced because Congress only authorized divorces in Washington in and after 1860, and the only grounds for divorce were adultery, bigamy, lunacy, and impotence. Willard said he would use lunacy as the charge against Caroline. They strolled around town for a while, and then he left.

Antonia remained in Warrenton until mid-September, when she returned to her home in Fairfax Court House. She had been away for six months. Major Willard escorted her. Antonia had not told her parents that he was married, but that changed when she blurted it out after Willard's departure. She acknowledged her love for Willard and their plans to marry. Her father was disappointed; he could not imagine his daughter marrying a Yankee officer. But Antonia was sure they could overcome the major obstacles.

However, the next Sunday both Antonia and her father were arrested for not having taken the oath of allegiance to the Union. So it was back to the Old Capitol Prison for Antonia—this time with her father.

Upon arriving at the prison they were taken to the visitors' room, where Major Willard embraced Antonia. He asked her if she was ready to take the oath. Although she had already decided to do so, she saw an opportunity to gain a concession from him.

"I will do so if you promise on your honor to resign your commission in the Union army." He agreed to start the process immediately. But he didn't.

Antonia and her father both took the oath, and on September 18, 1863, they were freed. To prevent further harassment, they displayed a Union flag from a front window of their home.

For the next six months Antonia and Joe Willard carried on a steamy correspondence. She continued to ask why he hadn't resigned and why he hadn't secured a divorce, but he dodged both issues.

In 2009, attorney Charles W. Vernon III of Virginia researched this strange situation and discovered why Joe refused to discuss the divorce. He had lied to Antonia about his intent to charge Caroline with lunacy. She was the one seeking a divorce, and she was building a case of adultery against him. While married to her, and while courting Antonia, Joe Willard was having numerous affairs at his hotel, at his home, and at houses of prostitution. This was a sordid, well-hidden secret Antonia never knew. Published for the first time, here is the background Vernon uncovered.

Willard and Caroline were married in 1849, but by 1853 were ready to split. Still, they waited nine years before signing an article of separation. It stated that they intended to live apart for the rest of their lives. This separation agreement provided for an immediate cash payment to Caroline of ten thousand dollars, a very large amount for that time. Caroline also was given lifetime possession of their residence in Washington, which was across the street from the Willard Hotel. Finally, the agreement provided that their slave Cecilia was to be delivered to Caroline.

Two years later, in February 1864, Caroline filed a petition for divorce on the grounds of adultery. According to documents in the National Archives, Caroline alleged that Joseph Willard, from time to time, had sexual relations with women of damaged reputations who had been guests at the hotel. The petition further stated that, in the spring of 1860, Joseph introduced into their private residence Caroline Rosekrans, with whom Joseph had committed adultery on several occasions. In Joe Willard's answer to the divorce petition, he denied committing adultery with any guest of the hotel. He did admit to adultery, but he did not state the name of the woman or provide other details. Attorney Charles Vernon reported the outcome of the case for the film *Spies in Crinoline*, which was released in 2009:

Like most divorce laws, the District of Columbia law required proof before a divorce on the grounds of adultery could be granted. For the Willards' divorce, the required proof was provided through the testimony of the Willards' former slave, Cecilia. Her statement, made under oath, described in some detail Joseph's relationship with Caroline Rosekrans in the summer of 1860. Cecilia stated that Joseph had visited Caroline's room, which he had provided in the Willards' residence, on numerous occasions and had frequently spent the night with her. On March 2, 1864, the Chief Judge of the Supreme Court of the District of Columbia issued an order granting the divorce. The divorce order provided that the terms of the 1862 separation agreement were confirmed.

These proceedings were taking place at the time Joe and Antonia Ford were exchanging love letters. Perhaps with her background as a spy, Antonia should have investigated Willard before agreeing to marry him. But their two hearts were divided in every way but one—their love for each other. Had she discovered Joe's amorous conquests of other women, the tone of her love letters and the direction of the rest of her life probably would have been different.

In December 1863, nearly two months before Willard's wife filed the divorce petition, Willard asked Antonia for "a private marriage." Her response, written on New Year's Eve, was both resolute and loving:

You know I love you but I can never consent to a private marriage. My parents and relatives would be mortified and distressed to death; acquaintances would disown me; it would be illegal; and above all it would be wrong. I cannot claim to be a Christian (unfortunately) but I have a conscience, and am governed by it. I dislike to say 'no' to one so dear, but there is no alternative in this case. I will grant any request which is right and proper, and would make you the happiest man in the world if I could without compromising myself....I [will not] place a barrier between myself and all friends. It would be wrong for you as well as for me. Neither of us could be happy, for the curse of God would cast upon us.

You ask for my "heart and hand." The heart is yours already. When your
hand is free and you can claim mine before the world, then that also is yours.
Notwithstanding my unalterable determination in this matter, I love you
dearly, and will love you as long as I live. I wish you a very happy New Year,
so happy that all your preceding life may seem darker than ever by contrast.

Willard resigned his military commission on February 12, 1864, at about the same time his wife filed for divorce.

A few days after the divorce decree was granted on March 2, Antonia's father received this note from Willard: "I shall come for Antonia on the morning of the 10th of March."

The couple took a carriage to Alexandria and then the train into Washington. They were married at the Metropolitan Hotel in Washington, D.C., on March 10, 1864. He was forty-four; she was twenty-six. Interestingly, her dream of marrying a man with the initials J. C. had come true. Her husband's full name was Joseph Clapp Willard.

When asked by a friend why she had married a Yankee, Antonia jokingly replied, "I knew I could not revenge myself on the nation, but I was fully capable of tormenting one Yankee to death, so I took the Major."

They had three children—all sons—but only the first, Joseph Edward, survived infancy. The third died during childbirth. Antonia died five days later, on February 14, 1871, at age thirty-two, after only seven years of marriage. She never knew the true reason for Willard's divorce.

Antonia's funeral was at the historic New York Avenue Presbyterian Church in Washington, and presided over by its pastor, Dr. Phineas Gurley, who had married Antonia and Joseph. Gurley, also known as Lincoln's pastor, had delivered Lincoln's funeral sermon at the White House in 1865.

Perhaps the most memorable and relevant statement in Antonia's obituary was the following line: "Whatever she thought to be right she considered no sacrifice too great to accomplish it."

Jeb Stuart's Obsession with Laura Ratcliffe

During the spring of 1864, Laura Ratcliffe seldom heard from Jeb Stuart, who, by all accounts, was still romantically obsessed with her. One historian claimed Stuart proposed to her, and that she "threw him out of the house."

Rumors apparently reached his wife, Flora, about his attention to young women, and he felt compelled to try to explain his actions.

In summary, he said that generals were expected to have a flamboyant public life and to get away with activities that would not be tolerated in subordinates. Stuart's staff officer, Maj. W. W. Blackford, put a slightly different perspective on it: "Though he dearly loved, as any good soldier should, to kiss a pretty girl, and the pretty girls dearly loved to kiss him, he was as pure as they."

Author Emory Thomas supported this view in his book *Bold Dragoon*, writing that Stuart "idealized women" but he "did not deflower" them.

But Stuart's amorous advances to Laura seem to be on a different level than that referred to by Blackford and Thomas and could hardly be called appropriate military behavior. Unquestionably, he loved Laura, and he demonstrated that feeling time and time again.

But when it came to flirting with Northern girls, that was regarded as serious military business. Stuart constantly prodded his officers to do so and promised that "funds will be placed at your disposal with which to purchase military intelligence."

On May 11, 1864, Jeb Stuart was killed at the battle of Yellow Tavern north of Richmond. General Lee gave him an epitaph worthy of a great spy: "He never brought me a piece of false information." That was due in no small part to the intelligence provided to him by Antonia Ford and Laura Ratcliffe.

After the War

Laura Ratcliffe, like many Southerners, was destitute after the war, but she inherited a comfortable home in 1873. In 1890, at the age of fifty-four, she married for the first time. He was a wealthy Union veteran—her neighbor and friend Milton Hanna. Many men had sought her hand in marriage, but she had refused all of them. Now, she said yes to a former Yankee soldier, replicating the marriage of Antonia Ford to a Union officer.

Seven years after their wedding, Milton was killed in a farming accident.

Strangely, the marriages of both Laura and Antonia were of equal length. In Laura's case, she found herself in charge of not only her holdings but his properties as well. That made her a very wealthy woman.

In 1910, when she was seventy-four, ninety-six of Mosby's men held their annual reunion in Herndon. According to the *Washington Post*, Congressman

C. C. Carlin addressed the group and praised "the service rendered to Mosby by Miss Laura Ratcliffe, a venerable woman, who gave the guerrilla leader valuable information as to the movements of Federal troops."

On August 8, 1923, she died at the age of eighty-seven and was buried on her property in a small family plot. Her home, Merrybrook, is one of the few antebellum homes that has survived real estate developments in the heavily trafficked Herndon area. The house is listed on the National Register of Historic Places.

A Virginia historical highway marker honors Laura. It is located on Virginia Route 228 in Herndon, near her grave site. Within two miles another marker describes Mosby's Rock.

12

MOSBY'S MERRY CHRISTMAS

Roberta Pollock

The Union had a lot to smile about in December 1864. On December 16, the Confederate Army of Tennessee was decimated at the battle of Nashville. On December 22, Maj. Gen. William T. Sherman sent his famous message to President Lincoln: "I beg to present you, as a Christmas gift, the city of Savannah." In Virginia, the Federals possessed Warrenton, a town near the Blue Ridge Mountains, and were developing plans to capture Col. John Singleton Mosby. Mosby's Rangers were based in northern Virginia and noted for their lightning-quick raids and ability to elude pursuers.

A local teenage girl, Roberta Pollock, picked up some scuttlebutt about mysterious goings-on among the Federals and wondered what was brewing. She was the sixteen-year-old daughter of the Reverend Abram David Pollock, a Presbyterian minister. Although a native of Pennsylvania, Reverend Pollock had become a Southerner, and his daughter was a committed Rebel.

Roberta learned that a black man and Federal officers had been seen on their way to the provost marshal's office. Determined to find out what the hubbub was all about, she approached the guard in front of the office on the main floor and said she wished to see some black people who lived in the basement. When he hesitated, she offered him a few coins from her small purse, and he waved her into the building.

The basement was damp and dark, but Roberta found her way to a room just below the provost marshal's office. She heard clearly the conversation above.

Warrenton, Virginia, in 1862

The black man told the officers he could easily guide them to Mosby's head-quarters and to the houses where many of his men stayed. He said he also knew where Mosby had stored a huge quantity of corn. The officers then debated the best time to surprise Mosby and capture most of his men. It would either be that night, December 22, or the next. Then they laughed, congratulated each other on their plans that carried so much promise, and talked of a great Christmas celebration.

Roberta left the building and walked through the town to the Union picket station. As she approached the picket, she took the last of her coins from her purse and bribed the soldier on duty to allow her to pass through. He probably thought that this young, pretty girl couldn't cause the Federals any problems.

The weather was bitter cold, with several inches of snow. Unperturbed, Roberta walked two miles to the home of a neighbor. "Could I please borrow a horse?" she inquired. "I must warn Colonel Mosby. The Yankees are planning to attack him tonight or tomorrow night." The neighbor readily provided a horse.

This was the shortest day of the winter. It would soon be dark and colder. Strong, biting winds roared across the fields of snow. Continuing on her mission,

Roberta reached the home of a family from her father's church and went inside to warm up. A teenage girl loaned Roberta warmer clothes and wraps, and the girl's younger brother offered to accompany her as an escort and guide. He climbed up behind her on the horse, and they headed for the backwoods, where Roberta expected to find some of Mosby's Rangers, to whom she might deliver her message.

Two or three hours later they came upon a large campfire and found more friends there. That was the good news. The bad news was that she had ridden nearly ten miles but was only four miles from Warrenton. She had been riding in a circle. Her friends pointed her in the right direction, and the moon broke through the clouds to light the way.

The boy riding with her looked toward their right and exclaimed: "There are soldiers approaching. See the V-shaped formation!"

Their carbines were pointed straight ahead. Roberta thought the best thing to do was to keep moving, as if the presence of the soldiers meant nothing to them. The plan worked, and they passed without incident. That was surprising, but Roberta took a deep breath and said a quick prayer of thanks.

Soon after, a single horseman approached them. He pointed his carbine directly at Roberta and shouted, "Halt!"

The gutsy teenager yelled back, "Surrender or I'll blow your brains out!"

Jarred and hoodwinked, the rider turned and sped off at a fast gallop.

Roberta spurred her own horse and reached the top of a hill. To her frustration and astonishment, she could see below the lights of Warrenton. The borrowed horse was trying to return home. Roberta had two choices—stay on the same road and encounter Federal outposts or fight the horse and change direction, uncertain of where it might lead. The following lines came to her mind:

God shall charge his angel legions
Watch and ward o'er thee to keep,
Though thou walk through hostile regions,
Though in desert wilds thou sleep.

She had a mission to accomplish, and she did not falter. Putting Warrenton behind her, she and the boy turned toward the darkness.

Within a mile, they were stopped by a Federal picket. He grabbed the reins of their horse and demanded: "Where are you going?"

"I am trying to go to Salem to see a sick friend," Roberta answered. "It was later than I thought. I lost my way in the night."

The picket frowned. "Well, it is my painful duty to take you to the reserves. You will be detained all night and then taken to headquarters in the morning."

"You shall not do so," said Roberta sternly. "Shoot me on the spot if that is what you have to do. But I will not spend the night unprotected among your soldiers. And you wouldn't either if you were a sixteen-year-old girl."

The picket wasn't much older than Roberta, and he seemed to understand what she was saying. It wouldn't be right to put her under arrest at night and surround her with soldiers.

"All right, then, I will not do what I am supposed to do." After a short pause, he added, "See that light in the distance. Go to that house. No one will be so cruel as to turn you away on such a night as this."

Using the light as her reference point, she found the house, identified herself with a false name, and was allowed to spend the night. The family didn't know what to think of them and wondered why two youngsters would be out so late at night. But they provided comfortable beds and hot bricks to warm their feet.

In the morning Roberta saw several Yankee soldiers riding up to the house and assumed they were coming to arrest her. She was relieved when they just wanted to buy milk and eggs. Chatting amicably, the captain mentioned an incident that had occurred during the night. He said that the Rebels wanted to attack his men and tried to fool him by sending one soldier ahead, pretending he was alone. The Rebels, he said, must have expected us to fire on him, thereby revealing our location and thinking we would not expect more of them to come up. But, he added, his force was too sharp for them and didn't fire at all. That made the Rebels afraid to try anything.

Obviously, the Yankees had mistaken Roberta and her guide for Confederates, but they saw only one of them.

Roberta, trying to find out if Mosby had been captured, asked the captain if they had taken any prisoners during the night. When the captain replied that there were no raids and no captures, Roberta knew she still had time to contact Mosby. But she had to reach him that day.

Fortunately, in discussions at the breakfast table, Roberta found out that her hosts were as strongly pro-Confederate as she was. She told them her real name and the mission she had to complete.

"We can help you with that," said the lady of the house, according to Roberta's notes. "We have friends who reside in the hills, and they will know where to find some of Mosby's men. I'll accompany you and introduce you."

Roberta hoped the lady would be a better guide than the boy by her side. And, thankfully, she was. On the way they encountered several members of Mosby's guerrilla band. Roberta explained the danger they were in. They thanked her, and her two guides reversed their direction and returned to their homes.

The Yankees made their raid that night, but the plan that had carried so much promise turned into a miserable failure.

On Christmas Eve, some of Roberta's friends came over to spend the night with her. Near midnight, as the girls were undressing around the fire in an upper room, they heard a gentle tapping on the window below. Roberta's mother came upstairs smiling and told Roberta that a man at the door wanted to see her without delay. Calmed by her mother's smile but concerned about what awaited her, she threw on the nearest dress and walked down the stairs.

Waiting at the door was Mosby with a few of his men. His remarks, as remembered by Roberta, were: "Ma'am, we are indebted to you for saving us and for spoiling the Yankees' Christmas surprise. I just want to express a very sincere 'thank you' and to wish you and your family a Merry Christmas."

And then they were gone, somehow eluding the Federal pickets and returning to their hideouts and safe houses for their own joyous Christmas Day.

MOSBY'S POSTWAR TURNABOUT

Col. John Singleton Mosby, the incredible partisan ranger, survived the Civil War thanks in part to the intelligence provided by young female spies such as Roberta Pollock. But Mosby's life after the war surprised and astounded diehard supporters of the Lost Cause. Their wartime love for him turned into a rage that threatened Mosby's life.

During the war, Gen. Ulysses S. Grant's hatred of Mosby's successes was so strong that he ordered Mosby to be hanged without trial if captured. Yet after the war, Mosby became a Republican and campaigned for Grant in the presidential elections of 1868 and 1872. It was the best way to help the South, he said in his memoirs. Grant wrote in his autobiography: "I have come to know Colonel Mosby personally and somewhat intimately. He is a different man entirely from what I supposed. He is able and thoroughly honest and truthful."

Mosby's friendship with Grant made him highly controversial in Virginia. He suffered the loss of much of his law practice; he was shot at as he stepped from a train in Warrenton in 1877; and his boyhood home was burned down. Through Grant's intercession with President Rutherford B. Hayes, Mosby was appointed U.S. Consul to Hong Kong, a position he held for seven years, from 1878 to 1885. He then served as a lawyer in San Francisco with the Southern Pacific Railroad. During these years, Mosby met a ten-year-old boy named George S. Patton Jr. and shared secrets of guerrilla warfare with him. The boy became a famous U.S. general in World War II. Later, Mosby worked for the U.S. Department of the Interior, first enforcing federal fencing laws in Omaha, then evicting cattle barons who used federal land to graze their cattle. He served as an assistant attorney general in the U.S. Department of Justice from 1904 to 1910.

Many years after the war, Mosby explained why, although he disapproved of slavery, he fought on the Confederate side: "A soldier fights for his country—right or wrong. He is not responsible for the political merits of the course he fights in. The South was my country."

Today, in Virginia, schools, subdivisions, highways, restaurants, and a public housing complex are named after him. Thirty-five monuments and markers in northern Virginia are dedicated to actions and events related to Mosby's Rangers. The John Singleton Mosby Museum was founded at Warrenton, Virginia, in his honor. Some sources credit him with coining the term, "the solid South." He used it in an 1876 letter to the *New York Herald*, supporting the candidacy of Republican Rutherford B. Hayes for president. And in 2008, a computer game titled Mosby's Confederacy was produced by Tilted Mill.

13

A SECESH CLEOPATRA

Belle Boyd

Belle Boyd had her way with young men in uniform. A glance, a smile, and men would do almost anything for her and give her almost anything she wanted. That made her an exceptional femme fatale.

As a tall, slim, well-proportioned seventeen-year-old, she turned heads and drew men to her. Because of a long nose set in a dour face, she probably would not have won any most-photogenic awards, but there was a special allure about her that prompted a friend of author Charles Dickens to call her "disturbingly attractive." To him, her somewhat irregular face suggested "joyous reckless-ness." Others commented that her gray blue eyes could be tenderly warm, brightly aflame, or as cold as ice. Without a doubt, she was fearless, self-reliant, and instinctively able to make the most of any situation. Add to that a musical and vibrant voice, a lighthearted and merry laugh, well-read intelligence, and a witty conversationalist, and the total package made her an instant favorite in Washington society and in Virginia.

Underneath these outward appearances was a spunky girl with a zest for adventure. Going against the social customs of the period, Belle would walk streets unchaperoned, dance and flirt with Federal and Confederate officers, visit military camps on both sides, and even call on commanders in their tents. For Belle, it was all part of a logical way to learn military secrets: attract and maintain their interest, obtain information, and convey it to the Confederates.

The most exciting years of Belle's life were from ages seventeen to twenty-one. It was during this time that she achieved lasting fame as a great heroine of the South.

She was born in 1844 in historic Martinsburg, Virginia (now West Virginia), the first of eight children for shopkeeper Benjamin Boyd and Mary Rebecca Glenn. Situated along the old Cumberland Trail—a major route west during the 1700s and 1800s—Martinsburg was the northern gateway to the Shenandoah Valley. The city and villages to the south—Winchester (twenty-two miles) and Front Royal (thirty-seven miles)—were strategically located and thus changed hands frequently during the Civil War. Baltimore was seventy-five miles due east of Martinsburg, and Harpers Ferry, with one of the largest and best arsenals in America, was only fifteen miles southeast.

Belle Boyd

Belle described their home in Martinsburg as "a pretty two-story house, the walls of which are completely hidden by roses and honeysuckle in most luxuriant bloom. At a short distance in front of it flows a broad, clear, rapid stream; around it the silver maples wave their graceful branches in the perfume-laden air of the South."

She passed her childhood as many happy children usually do, petted and caressed by a father and mother, and adored and beloved by her brothers and sisters. But that did not restrain her mischievousness. At age eleven, she reportedly rode her horse into the dining room to protest her exclusion from an adult gathering. "Well," she declared, "my horse is old enough, isn't he?"

At age twelve she was sent to Baltimore's Mount Washington Female College, where she studied classical literature, European languages, music, and the social graces. Belle left her mark by carving her name on the ground-floor window of a campus building. She finished the elite boarding school at age sixteen in 1860, the year Abraham Lincoln was elected president. Belle wrote in her memoir: "At sixteen my education was supposed to be completed, and I made my entree into the world of Washington, D.C., with all the high hopes and thoughtless joy natural to my time of life. I did not then dream how soon my youth was to be 'blasted with a curse'—the curse of civil war."

In the spring of 1861 Belle and her mother returned to Martinsburg to learn that Belle's father had enrolled in the 2nd Virginia Infantry. Mother and daughter raised funds to arm and equip them. On the colors, they inscribed, "Our God, Our Country, and Our Women." The regiment belonged to that section of the Southern army afterward known as the Stonewall Brigade.

On the morning of July 3, 1861, residents of Martinsburg were startled by the roar of artillery and the rattle of musketry. Following a skirmish that lasted five hours, a Federal army of twenty-five thousand under Maj. Gen. Robert Patterson occupied the town.

Belle wrote in her memoir: "It was to us a sad, but an imposing sight. On they came (their colors streaming to the breeze, their bayonets glittering in the sunlight), with all the pomp and circumstance of glorious war....The doors of our houses were dashed in; our rooms were forcibly entered by soldiers who might literally be termed 'mad drunk.' They left our homes mere wrecks, utterly despoiled and mutilated. Shots were fired through windows; chairs and tables were hurled into the street."

Belle recalled "without one shadow of remorse" an act by which she saved her mother from insult and their house from destruction.

A group of soldiers found its way into their home and began to pillage. The angry Federals resolved to hoist a large Federal flag over the house to indicate submission to their authority. That strained Mrs. Boyd's patience. Moving toward the pillagers with a firm step, she said, very quietly, but resolutely: "Men, every member of my household will die before that flag shall be raised over us."

One soldier then thrust himself forward and cursed Mrs. Boyd and Belle in the filthiest of terms. Belle, knowing that violence often follows invective, wasn't about to wait for the soldier's action. "I could stand it no longer," she wrote in her memoir. "My indignation was roused beyond control; my blood was literally boiling in my veins."

So the Southern belle drew out her derringer and shot the Yankee solider. It was not unusual for Southern ladies to carry guns when their male relatives were away. The ladies were prepared to protect themselves from insult and outrage.

The soldier was carried away, mortally wounded.

The Boyds thought they were rid of the pillagers, but once outside, some of the soldiers chose to seek vengeance and prepared to burn down the house. Belle wrote: "The prospect of being burned alive naturally terrified us, and, as a last resource, I contrived to get a message conveyed to the Federal commander."

One of her family's servants delivered the message to the nearby Federal office, and Union officers responded promptly. They arrested the lurking incendiaries before they could accomplish their purpose.

At Federal headquarters, other officers fumed when they learned about the shooting, and some demanded Belle be hanged immediately. The commanding officer was more diplomatic, however. Along with several members of his staff, he called at the Boyd residence to investigate. He examined witnesses and inquired into all the circumstances with strict impartiality. He concluded that Belle had "'done perfectly right."

To avoid further trouble, he posted sentries around the house. Federal officers called every day to assess the situation and to ask the Boyds if they had any complaints. When they came, Belle always spoke to them and developed close friendships with many of them.

She carried on flirtations with numerous Union officers, some of whom she had met at social gatherings in Washington before the war. These men responded by sending her love letters, flowers, and other gifts. But what she really wanted was information she could pass on to Confederate officials. Whatever she learned she committed to paper (something a spy usually never does), and whenever an opportunity developed, she sent her secret dispatches by trusted friends to Brig. Gen. Jeb Stuart or some officer in command of Confederate troops. She sewed messages into soles of shoes and packed them inside loaves of bread, heads of dolls, and hollowed-out fruit. She later confided to one of her friends, Charles Archer:

There was a young Union officer at our house. He fell in love with me, but I had refused to kiss him goodnight. I wanted his papers, and one night, when he pressed me for a kiss, I saw these papers sticking from his pocket. Here was an opportunity, and have them I must. I kissed him and at the same time deftly removed the packet of papers, and he never missed them until long after he had gone. So you see, it was the "kiss of Judas" after all. Fortune favored me. Those papers were more valuable than I had imagined.

With the papers in her hands, she saddled her favorite horse, Fleeter, and galloped away to deliver the news she had stolen from her lover. A well-trained horse, Fleeter could kneel on command, thereby helping to conceal Belle from Union patrols.

Belle did not always deliver messages directly; teenage girls often assisted her. One in particular is identified only as Sophia B. She once walked seven miles to carry reports to Stonewall Jackson's headquarters, and then walked back. Two slaves devoted to Belle also served as couriers: her personal maid, Eliza, and an elderly man who folded messages to fit inside an old watch.

Through accident or by treachery, one of Belle's missives was intercepted by the Yankees. It was not written in cipher, and carelessly, Belle had written it herself. She was summoned to appear at headquarters, where she was threatened and reprimanded. As a final scare tactic, they read the following article of war to her and warned that they had the authority to carry it out: "Whoever shall give food, ammunition, information to, or aid and abet the enemies of the United States Government in any manner whatever, shall suffer death, or whatever penalty the honorable members of the court-martial shall see fit to inflict."

Belle wrote in her memoir: "I was not frightened. I listened quietly to the recital of the doom which was to be my reward for adhering to the traditions of my youth and the cause of my country. I made a low bow, and, with a sarcastic 'Thank you, gentlemen' I departed; not in peace, however, for my little 'rebel' heart was on fire, and I indulged in thoughts and plans of vengeance."

Remarkably, the army officers let her go. But from this hour, Belle was a suspect to be watched. The Federals realized she was potentially dangerous and kept her under strict surveillance, but still she found ways to get her vengeance and, in the process, to supply weapons to Confederate forces.

Soldiers tended to remove their heavy sabers, as well as belts and pistols, at social gatherings and hang them with their coats and hats. Then, when they were in another room, Belle would hide as much arsenal as she could under her hoop skirt and store them in secret chambers.

She later wrote: "I confiscated and concealed their pistols and swords on every possible occasion, and many officers looked everywhere for their missing weapons, little dreaming who it was that had taken them, or that they had been smuggled away to the Confederate camp, and were actually in the hands of their enemies."

For a small town, Martinsburg perhaps had more spies per capita than any place in Virginia. Two female spies for the Union—a Miss Hickey and a Miss Frances—were detected and arrested in December 1861. Among the more prominent Union spies was David Hunter Strother, a local artist who had known Belle Boyd since she was a little girl. Strother, who worked for *Harper's Weekly*, was allowed to wander around Confederate camps. On one visit he learned that Gen. Joseph E. Johnston planned a carefully screened withdrawal from the Valley to support Confederate forces at Manassas. Strother went immediately to Gen. Robert Patterson's headquarters to report this vital information. But Patterson didn't believe him and ignored the report. Had he acted upon it, he could have attacked Johnston's rear and stopped or delayed his march. Without Johnston's forces as last-minute reinforcements at Manassas, the battle would likely have been a Union victory.

In October 1861, Belle and her mother visited the Confederate camp at Manassas, about sixty miles southeast of Martinsburg. For several weeks they lived in a house occupied by wives and daughters of Southern soldiers. During this time, Belle made contacts that led to her appointment as a courier between Gens. Thomas J. "Stonewall" Jackson and P. G. T. Beauregard and their subordinates. Belle was a fine equestrian and longed to play a man's role in the war. As a courier (often referred to as a land blockade-runner), she had to ride undetected through enemy lines, carrying letters, dispatches, and contraband sewn in her riding habits and coiled in her hair. She also smuggled much-needed quinine for soldiers ill with malaria.

When winter settled in, the need for couriers dropped, and a period of quiet normalcy allowed the people of Martinsburg to relax. The Federals had withdrawn a few miles, and the Confederates regained possession of the village. Col. Turner Ashby and his 7th Virginia Cavalry established headquarters there. He and his men mingled with Belle and other young women at balls, sleigh rides, and various seasonable activities. It was said that Belle was the "belle of the ball." And Colonel Ashby, dashing, well dressed, and handsome, was looked upon admiringly by all the ladies.

As Jackson's main source for enemy intelligence, Ashby would become one of the most heroic and chivalrous

Thomas J. "Stonewall" Jackson

figures the South had ever produced. His cavalry and the people of the Valley, especially Belle Boyd, supplied the vital military information Jackson needed to achieve his spectacular successes. By the end of May, Belle had risked her life at least twice to deliver the information Jackson demanded.

Before Ashby's cavalry left Martinsburg in early 1862, Belle's father, who was home on sick leave, grew concerned about her safety as the Yankees again began moving southward along the Shenandoah Valley. He sent Belle to stay at her uncle's hotel in Front Royal, a picturesque village at the western base of the Blue Ridge Mountains.

Had Belle's father known that Front Royal would soon be occupied by Northern forces, he probably would not have been so insistent. And had he known that her uncle and aunt, James and Mary Stewart, would flee Front Royal on March 12 to escape the Yankees, he definitely would never have broached the subject.

The Stewarts had two daughters about Belle's age, and one of them, Fannie, fled with her parents to seek refuge in Richmond. That left Belle, her cousin Alice, and their grandmother, Ruth Burns Glenn, to run the hotel and direct the staff.

No Fun to Travel

Within two weeks, on March 23, 1862, Jackson was defeated at Kernstown and driven back, far beyond Front Royal. When a Yankee force under Brig. Gen.

James Shields occupied the town, Belle decided to return to Martinsburg to be with her mother. General Shields graciously provided the required passes for Belle and her faithful servant, Eliza.

They had to pass through Winchester to get to Martinsburg, and that should not have been a problem. But as she and Eliza entered a train car for the last leg of the trip, a Federal officer named Captain Bannon stopped her and asked: "Are you Miss Belle Boyd?"

Perturbed, she answered, "Yes."

Apparently, someone had denounced Belle as a spy, and the local Federal provost marshal wasn't going to allow her to get by him.

Captain Bannon told her: "'I am the assistant provost, and I regret to say that orders have been issued for your detention, and it is my duty to inform you that you cannot proceed until your case has been investigated."

"Sir," Belle replied indignantly, "here is a pass which I beg you to examine. It is from General Shields. You will find that it authorizes my maid and me to pass on any road to Martinsburg."

Bannon faced the predicament of which general to obey: his boss, who had ordered him to arrest her, or Shields, who had issued the pass. Bannon had some prisoners to take to Baltimore, so he chose to take Belle with them and hand her over to Maj. Gen. John A. Dix, who commanded the departments of Maryland and Pennsylvania. Defiantly, Belle waved a small Confederate flag en route.

Fortunately for Belle, General Dix opposed the arbitrary arrest of civilians without strong evidence of guilt. While he investigated her case, he confined her at the Eutaw House, one of Baltimore's best hostelries, and treated her courteously. Finding nothing against her, he released her after five days and sent her home to Martinsburg.

Even so, her hometown was under Federal occupation and control, and the officials there were far less lenient. They placed her under surveillance and forbade her from going beyond the village limits.

Mrs. Boyd, who could be as rambunctious and persistent as her daughter, appealed to the local provost marshal, Maj. Charles Walker. He seemed as anxious to get Belle out of his territory as she was to get away. So he gave her mother a pass for both of them to go to Front Royal by way of Winchester. From Front Royal they hoped to obtain a pass to continue on to Richmond to visit Belle's aunt and uncle.

With the usual military inconsistency or inefficiency of the era, the Boyds found that a pass issued by one Federal authority could be voided by another. That happened in Winchester when the local provost marshal, Lt. Col. James S. Fillebrown, said they couldn't go to Front Royal because General Shields had forbidden travel between the two towns. But after seeing the women's distress, he changed his mind and told them to go ahead. It was the worst blunder of his career.

When they reached the aunt's hotel in Front Royal a few hours after sunset, they were surprised to find it brightly illuminated and occupied by Yankee soldiers. Belle learned that General Shields and his staff had taken over the hotel and were using it as his headquarters. Cousin Alice and Grandmother Glenn had been relocated to a small cottage in the hotel courtyard, and Belle and her mother joined them there. The location, adjacent to Federal headquarters, was the perfect spot for a Confederate spy in Front Royal.

After dinner, Belle sent a card to General Shields, and he visited her promptly. Shields was a handsome man who fancied himself irresistible to women while always being respectful of them. In this situation, however, he denied Belle's request for a pass to Richmond, implying a major battle was in the works. He stated emphatically that Jackson's army would be annihilated in a few days.

Shields was accompanied by his aide-de-camp, Capt. Daniel J. Kelly, a young Irishman. Belle must have captured his attention because shortly thereafter he besieged her with flowers and romantic messages. She also acquired from him unwittingly what she later described as "a great deal of very important information," and she passed it on to her countrymen.

The Hole That Saved Jackson

The Federals had hatched a scheme to hastily assemble their scattered forces in or near the Valley and outflank and capture Jackson's army. Jackson had about twenty thousand troops. He would be outnumbered two to one.

Apparently from Captain Kelly, Belle learned that Shields would hold a final "council with the officers" in the hotel in what had been the drawing room of Belle's aunt. Belle knew that just above the parlor was a bedroom with a small closet, and that a hole in the floor of the closet extended through the ceiling of the drawing room. The hole looked like a knothole, but Belle wrote in her memoir that it was "a hole that had been bored, whether with a view to espionage or not I have never been able to ascertain."

Belle crept quietly upstairs, lay on the floor with her ear to the hole, and found that she could hear everything. As the council ended around one o'clock in the morning, the general announced: "We'll march at sunrise. Before noon we'll attack Jackson in the flank."

Belle wrote down in cipher everything she had heard. She then went straight to the stables, saddled Fleeter, and with a pass through Federal lines obtained months earlier from a paroled prisoner of war, she galloped toward Confederate lines in the mountains.

Speed was critical; if Jackson acted promptly on what she overheard, he could move his army and avoid capture. Twice she was stopped by Federal sentries, and twice they accepted the pass and allowed her to continue.

Once clear of the sentries, she galloped fifteen miles, finally arriving at the home of a Mr. M., where she expected to find Colonel Ashby, Jackson's cavalry leader and scout she had befriended earlier in Martinsburg.

The house was quiet and dark. She pounded on the door. Mr. M. opened it and recognized Belle. "My dear, where did you come from? And how on earth did you get here?"

"Oh, I forced the sentries, but I have no time to explain. I must see Colonel Ashby immediately. Where can I find him?"

With that, a door on her right swung open, and Ashby walked into the room, having been awakened by the noise. "Good God! Miss Belle, is that you? Am I dreaming?"

Belle assured him that he was awake. She proceeded to narrate what she had overheard in the closet and handed him her ciphered notes. Ashby immediately saddled up and began the ride to Jackson's headquarters. Belle left too, returning to the cottage after a two-hour ride.

Before sunrise, Union bugles blew in Front Royal, and Shields and his army marched out, convinced they were about to surprise and defeat Jackson and his "demoralized army." Shields proceeded to where his scouts said they'd find Jackson. One problem: Jackson wasn't there, and he was nowhere to be found.

After Shields and his command left Front Royal, another Federal force marched in. Belle observed their positions and waited anxiously for news about Jackson. The next several days would be the most adventurous of Belle's life.

The Important "Little Note"

On May 20, Belle learned that a Confederate spy in Winchester needed to see her immediately. She described him only as "a gentleman of high social standing." He was probably Lt. Col. William R. Denny. To secure a pass, Belle submitted her request to Major Tyndale, the provost marshal in Front Royal. He said no at first, then yes, and told her to pick it up the next morning. When she returned to pick it up, he was "gone on a scouting mission" and had not left a pass.

Her skills as an expert flirter now paid off. She called on "Lieutenant H," a Federal officer who could travel to Winchester at any time. Equally important, the pickets guarding Front Royal reported to him. They would not dare bother him or any lady he escorted.

Belle appealed to him with all the sweetness and urgency she could muster, saying, "You profess to be a great friend of mine. Prove it by assisting me [to] pass through the pickets."

He hesitated but then agreed. Mounting the box of her carriage, he drove Belle, her maid, and a girl cousin to Winchester.

On May 22, she made contact with the Confederate agent. He handed her two packets of papers. "This one," he said, tapping it with his index finger, "is of great importance." He also gave her "a very important little note." Belle was to deliver these items "to Jackson or some other responsible Confederate officer."

At this time Jackson's ragged army was advancing secretly northward toward Front Royal. No one in the Union army was aware of his approach. They thought he was at Harrisonburg, farther north. Belle knew he was headed toward Front Royal, but she didn't know how close he was.

First, she had to get the papers out of Winchester. She gave the most important packet to her maid and kept the other packet and the note. The unsuspecting Union lieutenant took the packet Belle had given to her slave girl and placed it in his pocket. He noticed that Belle had written "Kindness of Lieutenant H" on both packets.

Next, Belle needed a pass to go to Front Royal. So she sent her old acquaintance Colonel Fillebrown a bouquet and a request for the pass. He was Winchester's provost marshal who had helped her earlier. She received the pass immediately along with a note thanking her "for so sweet a compliment." But he was being sly.

When the spy in Winchester had handed the papers to Belle, a black man had observed the transaction and reported it to Federal authorities. Consequently, as Belle's carriage reached the picket line, two mounted men rode up. "We have orders to arrest you."

"For what?" asked Belle.

"Upon suspicion of having letters."

And so they returned to Winchester and the headquarters of the 10th Maine Infantry.

"Do you have any letters?" asked Col. George L. Beale.

With an air of girlish innocence, Belle drew out of her basket the least important packet and handed it to him. That might have settled the matter had it not been for the words, "Kindness of Lieutenant H."

"This scribbling means nothing," Belle assured the colonel. "It was a thoughtless act of mine."

The lieutenant finally sensed that he had been duped into chauffeuring Belle to Winchester and could be in big trouble. He produced the package he had taken from the slave girl, which also was marked "Kindness of Lieutenant H."

Colonel Beale opened it and found a copy of the anti-Federal *Maryland News-sheet*, a publication so vitriolic that no one in the North dared to be seen carrying a copy. Beale glared at Lieutenant H, regarded him as complicit, and served him a steaming plateful of invective. Pausing to catch his breath, he turned toward Belle and noticed a piece of paper in her hand.

"What is that you have in your hand?" he asked sternly.

The Confederate agent in Winchester had told Belle it was the most important of the three documents. Now, she had to make it appear insignificant.

"What—this little scrap of paper? You can have it if you wish: it is nothing." She approached the colonel as if to give it to him, but intended to swallow it if he reached out to take it. The colonel, however, was so angry with the lieutenant that he waved her off and showed no further interest in the paper.

Belle and her party were allowed to drive back to Front Royal. She was to be kept under surveillance, an order that became irrelevant within hours. The lieutenant was court-martialed, ending his military career.

As for that important little note, Belle would personally deliver it the next day, May 23. Shortly after noon on that day, a servant rushed into Belle's room with exciting news. Jackson was less than a mile away. Belle gave a firsthand account of what happened next:

I immediately went to the door. The servant's report was true. The streets were thronged with Yankee soldiers, hurrying about in every direction in the greatest confusion.

I asked a Federal officer, who just then happened to be passing by, what was the matter. He answered that the Confederates were approaching the town in force, under Generals Jackson and Richard S. Ewell, that they had surprised and captured the outside pickets and had actually advanced within a mile of the town without the attack being suspected.

"Now," he added, "we must get the ordnance and the quartermaster's stores out of their reach."

"But what will you do," I asked, "with the stores in the large depot?"

"Burn them, of course!"

"But suppose the Rebels come upon you too quickly?"

"Then we will fight as long as we can, and if defeated retreat to Winchester, burning the bridges as soon as we cross them, and link up with General Banks's force."

I returned to the house and hurried to the balcony. With the aid of my opera-glasses, I saw the advance-guard of the Confederates at the distance of about three-quarters of a mile, marching rapidly upon the town. My father was one of them.

My heart beat alternately with hope and fear. I was not ignorant of the trap the Yankees had set for my friends. I had obtained important information. If I could only get it to General Jackson, our victory would be secure. Without it I anticipated defeat and disaster.

The intelligence I possessed [about Union forces] indicated that Maj. Gen. Nathaniel Banks was at Strasbourg with four thousand men, that the small force at Winchester could be readily re-enforced by Brig. Gen. Julius White, who was at Harper's Ferry, and that Generals James Shields and John Geary were a short distance below Front Royal, while John Frémont was beyond the Valley; further, and this was the vital point, that all these separate [Union] divisions were to unite to defeat Jackson.

I had to get this information to Jackson. I put on a white sunbonnet, and ran down the street amidst Federal officers and men. I soon cleared the town and reached open fields. Though tired I kept running, hoping to escape observation until I reached the Confederate line, which was still rapidly advancing.

I had on a dark-blue dress, with a little fancy white apron over it. This contrast of colors, being visible at a great distance, made me far more conspicuous than was just then agreeable. The skirmishing between the outposts was sharp. The main forces of the opposing armies were disposed as follows:

The Federals had placed their artillery on a lofty eminence that commanded the road by which the Confederates were advancing. Their infantry occupied in force the large hospital buildings, from which they kept up an incessant fire.

The Confederates were in line, directly in front of the hospital, with their artillery-men throwing shells with deadly precision into the structures.

At this moment, the Federal pickets, who were rapidly falling back, saw me and fired upon me.

My escape was most providential; for, although I was not hit, the rifle-balls flew thick and fast about me, and more than one struck the ground so near my feet as to throw dust in my eyes. Nor was this all: the Federals in the hospital, seeing in what direction the shots of their pickets were aimed, followed the example and also opened fire upon me.

My life was spared by what seemed to me to be little short of a miracle; for, besides the numerous bullets that whistled by my ears, several actually pierced different parts of my clothing, but not one reached by body. Besides all this, I was exposed to a crossfire from the Federal and Confederate artillery, whose shot and shell flew whistling and hissing over my head.

At length, a Federal shell struck the ground within twenty yards of my feet; and the explosion sent the fragments flying in every direction around me. I had just time to throw myself flat upon the ground before the deadly engine burst; and again Providence spared my life.

Springing up when that danger was passed, I pursued my mission, still under a heavy fire. I shall never run again as fast as I ran on that memorable day. Hope, fear, the love of life, and the determination to serve my country conspired to fill my heart with more than feminine courage, and to lend unnatural strength and swiftness to my limbs. I often marvel, and even shudder, when I reflect how I cleared the fields, and bounded over the fences with the agility of a deer.

As I neared our lines I waved my bonnet to our soldiers, to intimate that they should press forward. The First Maryland "Rebel" Infantry and [Harry T.] Hay's Louisiana Brigade gave me a loud cheer, and, without waiting for further orders, dashed upon the town.

They did not then know who I was, and they were naturally surprised to see a woman on the battlefield, and on a spot where the fire was so hot. Their cheers rang in my ears for many days afterwards, and I still hear them frequently in my dreams.

At this juncture the main body of Confederates was hidden from my view by a slight elevation. And I feared that the force I saw was too weak to be any match for the Federals, and that the gallant men who had just been applauding me were rushing upon a certain and fruitless death. Overcome by fatigue and the feelings that tormented me, I sank upon my knees and offered a short but earnest prayer to God.

Suddenly I was inspired with fresh spirits and a new life. Despair and fear vanished. My only thought was how to fulfill my mission.

I proceeded but a short distance, when, to my indescribable joy, I caught sight of the main body fast approaching....

Among the Confederates, Belle recognized an old friend, Col. Henry Kyd Douglas. He gave his perspective of the moment in his book, *I Rode with Stonewall*:

I observed almost immediately the figure of a woman in white glide swiftly out of town on our right and, after making a little circuit, run rapidly up a ravine in our direction and then disappear from sight. She seemed, when I saw her, to heed neither weeds nor fences, but waved her bonnet as she came on trying, it was evident, to keep the hill between herself and the village. I called General Jackson's attention to her movement, but just as a dip in the land hid her, he sent me to meet her and ascertain what she wanted. That was just to my taste, and it took me only a few minutes for my horse to carry me to the romantic maiden whose tall, supple, and graceful figure struck me as soon as I came in sight of her. As I drew near, I [realized] she was Belle Boyd whom I had known from her earliest childhood. She was just the girl to do this thing.

Belle's narrative continues:

Colonel Douglas rode up, recognizing me, and cried out while he seized my hand:

"Belle, what is it? What are you doing here?"

When I had sufficiently recovered myself, I produced the "little note," and told him all I knew: "The Yankee force is very small, one regiment of Maryland infantry, several pieces of artillery, and several companies of cavalry. I know because I went through the camps and got it out of the officers. Tell Jackson to charge right down, and he will catch them all. And urge him to seize the bridges before the retreating Federals have time to destroy them."

Douglas instantly galloped off to report to General Jackson.

Though the depot building had been fired, and was burning, our cavalry reached the bridges barely in time to save them from destruction. So hasty was the retreat of the Federals that they left all their killed and wounded in our hands.

The day was ours. And I had the heartfelt satisfaction to know that it was in consequence of the information I had conveyed at such risk to myself. With that information General Jackson made the flank movement that led to such fortunate results.

The Confederates, following up their victory, crossed the river by the still-standing bridges, and pushed on toward Winchester.

Two days later Jackson wiped out nearly half of General Banks's army near Middleton, and the remainder rushed through Winchester and Martinsburg and finally crossed the Potomac River at Williamsport, Maryland. Jackson then returned to Front Royal.

During the hasty flight General Banks halted for a few minutes in the main street of Martinsburg. A number of girls chatted on the sidewalk. One of them was Belle's little sister, Mary. Recognizing General Banks's aide-de-camp, Mary walked up to him and said, "Captain, how long are you going to stay here?"

"Until Gabriel blows his horn," he replied.

Belle's sister quietly rejoined, looking him in his face, "Ah, Captain, if you were to hear Jackson's horn just outside the town, you would not wait for Gabriel's."

Nor did they wait, for the echo of the Confederate general's bugles was enough to put them on the run out of town.

When Belle returned from the battlefield, the Confederates were filing through the town. She was greeted with enthusiastic hurrahs. Belle's hometown friend, Major Douglas, noted Belle's appearance after the battle: "Her cheeks were rosy with excitement and recent exercise, and her eyes all aflame as she pinned a crimson rose to my uniform bidding me to remember that it was blood-red and that it was her colors."

Just before Jackson's troops continued through Winchester, Belle's duped "buddy," Colonel Fillebrown, the provost marshal, was preparing to remove his personal effects from Winchester.

A gentleman of high social position and Southern proclivities stepped into his office and said, "Colonel, how on earth did you get into such a trap? Did you know nothing of the advance of the Confederates?"

Colonel Fillebrown turned, and pointing to the bouquet Belle had sent him only a day or two before. He said: "That bouquet did all the mischief. The donor of that gift is responsible for this misfortune."

Belle wrote in her memoir that she had "the satisfaction of being of some service to my country and that neither a desire for fame nor notoriety had motivated my action. I was not prepared, however, for the note I received on the very day my services occurred. I value it far beyond anything I possess."

The note was from Stonewall Jackson. Addressed to Belle, it stated:

Miss Belle Boyd,
   I thank you, for myself and for the army, for the immense service that you have rendered your country today.
   Hastily, I am your friend,
   T. J. Jackson, C.S.A.

While May 23, 1862, constituted Belle Boyd's finest hour, it was also Jackson's first significant battlefield victory, and he was clearly elated beyond measure. In this campaign, he took three thousand prisoners, thousands of small arms, and more than three hundred thousand dollars' worth of abandoned Federal supplies.

Unfortunately for the Confederates, Jackson could only spare one regiment to protect the village, and it wasn't enough. A week after his victory, the Federals retook Front Royal. Shortly, the Confederate army retreated southward, and much of the Shenandoah Valley fell into Federal hands.

The Northern Press Reacts

Belle's exploits launched a flotilla of absurd stories in the Northern press. Several newspapers called Belle the "Secesh Cleopatra." On May 31, 1862, the Associated Press referred to her as "an accomplished prostitute who had figured largely in the Rebel cause." The story was nonsense and libelous and probably a knee-jerk reaction to Jackson's stunning victory at Front Royal. The *Philadelphia Inquirer* complained that Belle had exercised her wiles upon young and inexperienced lieutenants and captains and that, from them, and by pumping new arrivals, she was able to identify Federal regiments and learn their strength. The *Washington Evening Star* noted that she "managed in diverse ways to recommend herself to our officers."

Furious with these attacks on her character, Belle did what she should not have done—what no smart spy had ever done. She granted an interview with a reporter to talk about her work in espionage. In a widely syndicated interview of June 4, 1862, Nathaniel Paige of the *New York Tribune* wrote: "In personal appearance, without being beautiful, she is very attractive. [She] is quite tall, has a superb figure, an intellectual face, and dresses with much taste. That she has rendered much service to the Rebel army, I have not the least doubt, and why she should be allowed to go at will through our camps, flirt with the officers, and display their notes and cards to visitors, I am at a loss to know."

Why, the reporter wondered, did a woman with a proven record of espionage have easy access to Union troops? He surmised that "her feminine getup" caused some soldiers to discount her threat. He described her attire and offered an opinion: "She wears a gold palmetto tree branch beneath her beautiful chin, a Rebel soldier's belt around her waist, and a velvet band across her forehead, with seven stars of the Confederacy shedding their pale light therefrom. It seemed to me, while listening to her narrative, that the only additional armament she required to render herself perfectly beautiful was a Yankee halter encircling her neck."

Diarist Kate Sperry of Winchester wrote of the same attire, adding that her dress was finished with "a colonel's shoulder straps" and a gold palmetto breast pin. Sperry concluded that Belle was "the fastest girl in Virginia or anywhere else for that matter"—a girl with unacceptably lurking sexuality.

Equating Belle's spying with sexuality, a Union brigade surgeon, Washington Duffee, recommended using her salaciousness as a counterintelligence tactic—as a legitimate, calculated means of obtaining intelligence. Duffee wrote on July 30, 1862: "The celebrated Belle Boyd, the Rebel Spy, has fallen in love or is anxious to make a victim of the medical director of the first army corps [Dr. Rex], with whom she is in correspondence. Were that used by higher authority at the War Department, Jackson and all the Rebel officers with whom she is in direct communication might be trapped. I mention these facts that the Government may make what use they think proper of them, and I know that the Medical Director will, with Maj. Gen. Franz Sigel's cooperation, use this woman for our common cause."

While Federal army officials pondered this possibility, local women in Martinsburg rebuffed Belle for "unladylike behavior" and "manly ways." And the Northern press, while belaboring her sexuality, also wrote of her "protruding jaw" and large "manly" nose—a sarcastic comment from opponents who resented her fame.

Arrested "On Suspicion" Twice

In Belle's memoir, she recounts sitting in her parlor one morning and noticing two Confederate soldiers standing near the provost marshal's tent. Belle walked to the tent and asked the provost who they were. He said they were paroled Confederate soldiers procuring passes to go south. Belle then asked if they might be permitted to dine with her family and friends.

"Certainly," replied the provost.

The two soldiers readily assented. One of them was quite handsome and accomplished, and Belle gave him her attention.

After dinner the two of them stood side by side and sang "Bonnie Blue Flag" and other Southern songs. Confident of his loyalty to the South, Belle asked him if he would take a letter to General Jackson. He agreed to do so.

When Belle went upstairs to write the dispatch, one of her servants stopped her suddenly and exclaimed: "Miss Belle, dat man ain't no Rebel; I seen him 'mong de Yankees in de street. If he has got secesh clothes on, he ain't no secesh. Can't fool Betsy dat way—dat man's a spy."

Belle thought differently and wrote a long, friendly letter to Jackson, including in it information about movements of the Union army. But before she gave it to the soldier, she asked him outright if he were a Yankee spy.

"Oh no," he insisted, "I assure you of that."

After the man left with the message, Belle learned that her servant was right. He was a Union detective sent to spy on her. His name was C. W. D. Smitley, and he went straight to Maj. Gen. Franz Sigel and gave him Belle's letter. The general, in turn, forwarded it to Secretary of War Edwin M. Stanton in Washington. It was Stanton who had resorted to this trickery to trap Belle. He regarded her as too dangerous to be allowed to roam at large.

In a few days—July 30, 1862, to be exact—two men showed up at the house and asked to see Belle Boyd. One of them was a Federal detective from the Secret Service. Belle described him as "coarse in appearance, with a mean, vile expression of countenance, and a grizzly beard." On Stanton's orders, they had come to arrest Belle. The nineteen-year-old girl was escorted by about five hundred cavalry to Martinsburg, where she was put on a train to Washington and taken to the Old Capitol Prison. One newspaper exulted, "The Secesh Cleopatra Is Caged at Last!"

That night she was visited by Col. Lafayette Baker, the chief of national detectives. He left her door open as he addressed her: "Ain't you pretty tired of your prison a'ready? I've come to get you to make a free confession now of what you've done against our cause; and, as we've got plenty of proof against you, you might as well acknowledge it."

"Sir," Belle replied, "I do not understand you; and furthermore, I have nothing to say. When you have informed me on what grounds I have been arrested, and given me a copy of the charges preferred against me, I will make a statement; but I shall not now commit myself."

Baker then noted the enormity of her offense and asked her to take the oath of allegiance to the Federal government. "Remember," he said, "Mr. Stanton will hear all of this. He sent me here."

The government never stated what her exact offense was, however, as Stanton and Baker arrested anyone they considered suspicious.

Belle responded with two memorable statements: "Tell Mr. Stanton I hope that if I am forced to commence the oath of allegiance that my tongue may cleave to the roof of my mouth; and that if ever I sign one line that will show to the world that I owe the United States Government the slightest allegiance, I hope my arm may fall paralyzed by my side."

"Well," said Baker, "if this is your resolution, you'll have to lay here and die; and that will serve you right."

"Sir," she retorted in a loud voice, "if it is a crime to love the South, its cause, and its president, then I am a criminal. I am in your power; do with me as you please. But I fear you not. I would rather lie down in this prison and die, than leave it owing allegiance to such a government as yours. Now leave the room; for so thoroughly am I disgusted with your conduct towards me, that I cannot endure your presence longer."

When she finished her defiance, she heard cheers and cries of "Bravo!" piercing the walls in all directions. Instead of lamenting her fate, she closed what she called her "first day in a dungeon" by reciting to herself the poem that includes the lines, "Stone walls do not a prison make / Nor iron bars a cage."

A month later Belle was sent to Fortress Monroe on the tip of the Virginia Peninsula, and from there to Richmond, as part of a prisoner exchange. Officials in the Confederate capital held a parade in her honor and made her an "honorary captain of the Confederacy." She reviewed the troops as they marched along.

In the spring of 1863 Belle returned to Martinsburg. It was again under Federal control. Placed on parole, and forbidden to leave her home, she was arrested in late August "on suspicion," allowable under suspension of habeas corpus. Again, she was taken to Washington. This time she was confined in the Carroll Prison, an annex of Old Capitol Prison.

Never one to stay inactive, Belle communicated with another prisoner by enclosing notes in rubber balls. And she helped other prisoners escape by instructing an inmate in another section to yell "Murder! Murder!" As guards rushed to the scene, the escaping prisoners climbed through a hole in the roof and slid down an incline outside. In the evenings, crowds often gathered outside the prison to hear Belle sing "Carry Me Back to My Own Sunny South," "Dixie," and other songs. These acts raised public opinion of her and public support for her release.

Several weeks after her incarceration, she contracted typhoid fever, and the reports of her condition were reported in the press. As her health improved, Stanton planned to transfer her to a term of hard labor. Hearing this, Belle became deathly ill—perhaps real, perhaps feigned. Whatever the case, public opinion was so great in her favor that her jail sentence was commuted, and she was banished from Federal soil. She was told that she would face a death sentence if she was caught in Federal territory again.

Overseas Adventures

Twenty-year-old Belle Boyd returned to Richmond and offered her services to Jefferson Davis. He welcomed her interest and asked if she would consent to bear dispatches to Confederate agents in Europe. He warned her that crossing the Atlantic in a blockade-runner would be dangerous, but Belle had never known the meaning of fear. She accepted the challenge.

Traveling as Mrs. Lewis, on May 8, 1864, Belle boarded the blockade-runner *Greyhound*, which sailed under the British flag. The vessel slipped out of her berth late at night and appeared to be well on its way. But before daybreak the USS *Connecticut* spotted the *Greyhound*, gave chase, and captured her.

Union Lt. Samuel Hardinge took command of the *Greyhound*. Belle, realizing she could be hanged, resorted to her feminine wiles and focused all her energies on Hardinge, whom she called "a gentleman I had met in my hour of distress." She described him in her memoir as well mannered and refined, with "dark hair hanging down on his shoulders." She wrote: "My Southern proclivities, strong as they were, yielded for a moment to the impulse of my heart and I said to myself: 'Oh, what a good fellow he must be.'"

Before long, Hardinge came under her spell. He bowed to Belle and requested permission to enter her cabin. "Certainly," she replied. "I know that I am a prisoner."

"I am now in command of this vessel," said Hardinge, "and I beg you will consider yourself a passenger, not a prisoner."

He visited her cabin daily but behaved with Victorian decorum, even though her energy and demeanor lit up the room and fired up his passion. To Belle, he was a ray of sunshine, illuminating her gloomy scenario. Before the *Greyhound* reached New York, Hardinge proposed twice to her.

Not wanting to appear overly anxious, she was noncommittal the first time. When he proposed again, "I said I would marry him," she wrote in her memoir, "if he would agree to give me his signal book, covering every flag of the United States naval code, leave the Navy, enter the service of the Confederacy, and help the Confederate captain of the *Greyhound* to escape. He must have been deliriously in love because he accepted the conditions, all of which made his own situation perilous."

Hardinge's orders were to deliver the *Greyhound* to a prize court in Boston and the prisoners to Federal authorities. The Boston press reported the arrival of the vessel and its famous passenger, Belle Boyd. The *Boston Post* called her "a female of intelligence and quick understanding" and said that people were curious to see her.

She was held under surveillance several days, until her husband-to-be intervened on her behalf. He persuaded authorities that since she was under sentence of banishment, they could not imprison her in Boston. They would have to send her to Canada instead. This they did, while forbidding her to return to the United States. If she returned, she would be shot.

Hardinge then faced the charges against him. He was court-martialed for allowing the Confederate captain to escape and dismissed from the navy for "neglect of duty." His father disinherited him. With his military obligations gone, Hardinge boarded a ship for England, where he and Belle had agreed to meet and marry.

Federals Play Hardball

On August 25, 1864, Belle and Hardinge exchanged vows at St. James Church in Piccadilly before a crowd of Confederate friends and English sympathizers. The wedded couple was toasted by the leading socialites of London.

In November, Hardinge sailed back to America for reasons that are unclear. Instead of boarding a blockade-runner, he took a ship to Boston. Surely, both he and Belle realized that he would be arrested if he was found on Northern soil. Aside from the *Greyhound* episode and his marriage to Belle, newspapers had reported his promise to Belle to serve the South.

He visited his parents in New York and her family in Martinsburg and even slept in Belle's bedroom. Later, he wrote in the journal he kept for Belle:

When, at last, I retired to sleep, it was in your own room; and as I entered it I thought of you. This was your room. Here you had been held a prisoner and had suffered the torture of an agonizing doubt as to your fate. Here lay your books just as you had left them. Writings, quotations, every thing to remind me that you were here. I do not know how long I stood gazing about me in silence [before] a Negro servant broke my silence by saying, "No one's ever slept in dis room since Missy Bel' been gone—Missus says you're de only person as should." So, when I retired to bed that night, I lay for a long time looking into the fire that glimmered and glared about the room, picturing you here, there, and everywhere about the chamber, and thinking of you sadly, far away from me in England—the exile, lonely and sad.

On his way back to Baltimore, Hardinge was arrested on December 2, 1864. He was taken to Harpers Ferry, accused of being a spy, and ordered to turn over Confederate dispatches. He didn't have any. He was conveyed to Washington's Old Capitol Prison and then to Carroll Prison, and finally to Fort Delaware, near Wilmington, which held more than thirty thousand Confederate soldiers and Southern sympathizers under notorious conditions. More than three thousand died there. Hardinge undoubtedly would have too had he not been released on February 3, 1865. He was so weak he could scarcely move. But on February 8 he managed to set sail for England, arriving in Liverpool on February 19. Hardinge's return was a joyous occasion for both Belle and Hardinge, but his illness and harsh treatment in prison had taken their toll, and he died within the year.

During his three months in America, Federal agents had intercepted all financial drafts sent to Belle by her agent. With her funds cut off, she had no income

Belle wrote this letter to President Lincoln threatening to "tell all" in her forthcoming book if he did not release her husband, Samuel Hardinge, by March 1865. The former Federal navy officer was released on February 3, 1865.

and was in a state of poverty. She pawned jewelry and wedding gifts and moved into a dingy boardinghouse.

On the advice of friends, she began writing the story of her life. It was published in New York and London and sold well. Its royalties, along with gifts from friends, enabled Belle to live comfortably.

After the War

After her husband died, Belle switched careers, became an actress, and was featured in a play in Manchester, England. With the war over, she returned to America and performed in theaters in St. Louis, New York, Cincinnati, Houston, and Galveston.

She married a former British army officer, John Hammond, in 1869, and moved to California. They had two daughters and two sons. She divorced Hammond in 1884 for reasons unknown and then married a man much younger than herself, an actor named Nathaniel High, from Toledo, Ohio. He was twenty-four. She was forty.

For the next sixteen years she gained notoriety as a platform lecturer, giving a dramatic narrative of her exploits as a Confederate spy. Her first performance was at the People's Theatre in Toledo. She wore a Confederate-gray uniform and a broad, low-crowned hat with a large,

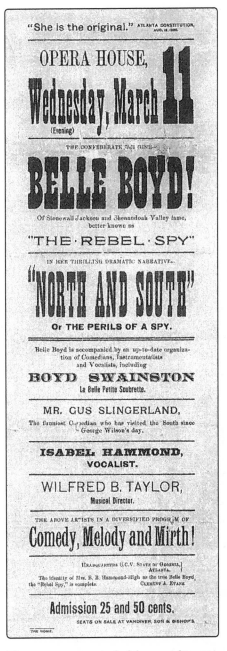

This poster was typical of those used in cities throughout the country to announce the appearance of Belle Boyd, "The Rebel Spy," and her dramatic readings on "The Perils of a Spy." She debuted in Toledo, Ohio, on February 22, 1886.

flowing black plume, reminiscent of Jeb Stuart. She spoke for two hours, reliving the misery, suffering, and splendor of the war in a way that drew tears, laughter, and applause. She concluded by stressing the unity of the nation with the words, "One God, One Flag, One People—Forever!" For both the blue and the gray, she became "Our Belle"—not a Southerner, but an American.

On June 9, 1900, she arrived at Kilbourn (now Wisconsin Dells), Wisconsin, to speak on June 13 for the local post of the Grand Army of the Republic. On the evening of June 11 she suffered a severe heart attack and died. She was fifty-six years old but didn't look a day over forty, according to a Wisconsin newspaper.

Her death received considerable attention in the nation's press, much of it erroneous. The usually reliable *National Cyclopedia of American Biography* stated that she married the outlaw Cole Younger and two Choctaw Indians. Not true. Other publications have confused Belle Boyd and Belle Starr. Some historians have questioned the reliability of her memoir, *Belle Boyd in Camp and Prison*, but at least two highly competent authorities have stamped it as genuine. Carl Sandburg accepted her account without question in his biographical masterpiece *Abraham Lincoln—The War Years*. And Douglas Southall Freeman, in his book *Lee's Lieutenants*, canonized her historically as "one of the most active and most reliable of the many secret agents of the Confederacy."

14

THE CLEVER
MASQUERADER

Emma Edmonds*

Tomboyish and hard to control, Emma Edmonds annoyed her parents with a tough, stubborn, active, and mischievous demeanor. She was Canadian and grew up as a farmer's daughter near Fredericton, New Brunswick, about 125 miles northeast of Bar Harbor, Maine. She was one of five children—four girls and a boy.

Recalling her childhood, Emma wrote in her diary: "I heard my mother once tell a Scotch Presbyterian clergyman that she was afraid I would meet with some violent death for I was always in some unheard-of mischief [like climbing the tallest trees, riding the meanest horses, and swimming raging rivers]."

With only one boy in the family—a boy with epilepsy—the girls had to get out of the house and do heavy farm work, from plowing fields to chopping wood. In the process, Emma developed a strong body and skills in horseback riding, shooting, and hunting.

As she grew into her teens, she blossomed into an attractive young lady but never lost her rugged qualities. A neighbor liked what he saw, and with

*Note: This chapter is based primarily on Sarah Emma Edmonds's memoir titled *Memoirs of a Soldier, Nurse, and Spy: A Woman's Adventures in the Union Army*, published in 1865 by W. S. Williams and Company in Hartford, Connecticut. Much of this chapter is told in Emma's own words.

a nudging from Emma's father, he decided he wanted to marry the seventeen-year-old girl. He proposed, but to his surprise, Emma refused. He was, after all, twice her age. Emma had other plans, and she probably wouldn't have married anyone at this time of her life.

Emma Edmonds

Her father was shocked and angry. He had arranged the marriage and could not allow his daughter to avoid it. He had always been dictatorial, tyrannical, and verbally abusive to his wife and children. When he gave Emma a threatening scolding, she feared for her life.

"Alright," she said, "I will marry him."

But when her father went outside to do his chores, Emma appealed to her mother.

For probably the first time in her life, Mrs. Edmonds defied her husband, and she did so behind his back. She contacted an old friend, Annie Moffitt, in Salisbury, a town ninety miles to the east, and arranged for Emma to become an apprentice in her millinery shop. Secretly, Emma and her mother planned Emma's escape from home.

Emma confided only to her best friend, Linus Seelye. Concerned about a young woman traveling alone, he suggested a disguise and gave her a set of his clothes to wear. On a dark night in 1858 she snuck out the back door and walked on back roads to Salisbury. She evaded disclosure for a year while learning the millinery business, and then she opened her own shop.

One day Emma received terrifying news in a letter from her mother. Her father had discovered her whereabouts. He was likely to come after her with a gun and force her into the unwanted marriage. Emma could not allow that to happen. She moved eighty miles south to St. John and changed her identity. She cut her hair short, had a large mole surgically removed from her left cheek, dressed herself in men's clothing every day, and changed her name to Franklin Thompson. With small breasts, a stature of five feet six inches, and a deep voice, she believed she could easily pass for a man.

She tried selling Bibles for a year, made some money, but then lost it. In November 1859, with only five dollars in her pocket and snow on the ground, she started walking to the United States. Except for a few sleigh and carriage rides, she walked much of the distance of 450 miles to Hartford, Connecticut, arriving with frostbitten feet, ragged clothes, and nearly soleless boots. She pawned her watch to buy men's clothing and took a job as a bookseller and publisher's agent for Hurlbut and Company, for whom she had sold Bibles in Canada. Nine months later she followed the advice of the time to "Go west, young man." She stopped at Flint, Michigan. She was there when the Civil War began.

When President Lincoln called for seventy-five thousand troops to put down the rebellion, Emma, disguised as Frank Thompson, did what most folks in that day would regard as plumb crazy. She enlisted as a man. She knew there'd be no physical exam; the army was taking anyone who "could carry a musket without falling down." She was accepted as a three-year recruit and shortly was assigned duty as a male nurse in the 2nd Michigan Infantry. She was twenty-one.

"I had inherited from my mother a rare gift of nursing," she later wrote, "and when not too weary or exhausted, there was a magnetic power in my hands to soothe the delirium."

The first few months in the army were nerve-racking—avoiding discovery, stealing a bit of privacy when she needed it, marching for hours, and crawling through dirt and underbrush. Male nurses were classed as noncombatants, but all recruits had the same training.

At the regimental hospital in Alexandria, Virginia, in October 1861, male nurse Jerome Robbins struck up a friendship with Thompson (Emma), and they spent hours talking about human nature and religion. Shortly, Emma fell in love with him and then revealed her identity. Robbins was stunned. He told her he had his own special affection for a woman named Anna back home. Emma reacted poorly. In December 1861 Robbins noted sadly, "I am fearful our natures are not as congenial as I first supposed."

Meanwhile, the 2nd Michigan was busy defending Washington, D.C., before seeing action at Blackburn's Ford, Virginia, on July 18, 1861. Three days later they covered the escape route as the Union army retreated after the battle of First Manassas. Private Thompson had hospital duty in a small stone church about five miles from the action. This was Emma's first contact with the horrors of war. As she treated the wounded and the dying, many of them gave her personal items to send to their wives, mothers, and sweethearts. One mother later wrote a note to Emma: "Oh, how I want to kiss those hands that closed my darling's eyes, and those lips which spoke words of comfort to him in a dying hour."

Emma Edmonds disguised as Frank Thompson.

Following the Union disaster at Manassas, President Lincoln appointed Maj. Gen. George B. McClellan to command and rebuild the Army of the Potomac. During McClellan's extended period of retraining the army, Emma (as Thompson) transferred from hospital duty to the more dangerous position of regimental postmaster and mail carrier. With extensive travel on horseback, she would often be within the range of enemy fire, but to her, that was better than working with Robbins, her unrequited love.

When McClellan landed his huge army of one hundred thousand at Fort Monroe on the tip of the Virginia Peninsula, Pvt. Frank Thompson went with the troops, her masculine masquerade still intact. Again serving as a nurse, she worked in the tent hospital. She loved this work and earned the respect of doctors and other nurses, all of whom were male. Then, two unexpected events changed her life forever.

Disguised as a Male Slave

Emma had learned that an old friend, Lt. James Vesey, was in nearby Company B. She received permission to visit him. In earlier years she and this tall man with black, wavy hair and a bushy moustache had shared many good times and may have been romantically involved. Maintaining her disguise to see if he'd recognize her, she approached Company B. In the distance she noticed a cluster of soldiers standing around a mound of earth. Emma paused near a soldier watching the service and asked, "What happened?"

"It's sad," he replied. "Lieutenant Vesey took out a patrol last night and ran into Rebel cavalry. He took a musket ball in his neck and was killed." Numb, Emma sobbed. She felt sick. That night she knelt beside his grave and vowed to get revenge for his death. She was no longer satisfied with being a nurse. Now she wanted to do more—something significant.

Within days one of General McClellan's top spies was captured in Richmond and sentenced to be hanged. When McClellan announced he was looking for another agent, Pvt. Franklin Thompson applied. Here was an opportunity to make a difference in the war, to avenge Vesey's death, and to test the limit of her courage. After interviews with three generals, Thompson became part of McClellan's intelligence network.

Emma's first mission was to infiltrate Confederate fortifications around Yorktown and report the troop strength, gun placement, and layout of defenses. She was given three days to prepare.

She knew that hundreds of slaves accompanied Rebel armies and that these slaves did much of the heavy work, from digging trenches to cleaning stables. If she could disguise herself as one of them, she probably wouldn't be noticed, she opined. Thus, she would be a male slave.

She secured silver nitrate and mixed it with a stain to darken her skin color. She acquired patched overalls, an old red bandanna, a gray flannel shirt, and heavy shoes. A barber shaved her head.

Needing the wooly hair of a typical slave, she ran toward the docks where ships cruised the Chesapeake Bay to link Fort Monroe with Washington. Finding the mail boat ready to leave, she handed money to its captain and asked him to buy a minstrel wig. Minstrel shows, popular in the capital, were performed by white men with blackened faces and black woolly wigs. The following afternoon, the captain returned with one. Emma tried out her disguise on a close friend, the chaplain's wife, who did not recognize her.

The next day, Emma delivered a memo from headquarters to her supervisor. It detached her from the hospital for "special assignment." She then transformed herself from Franklin Thompson into a slave named Ned. Carrying only a few hard crackers and a revolver, Emma began the mission. She later wrote about it in a book published in 1865:

Emma disguised as a male slave.

> *I started on foot, without even a blanket or anything which might create suspicion. At half-past nine o'clock I passed through the outer picket line of the Union army. At twelve o'clock I was within the rebel lines, but had not been halted by a sentinel. I had passed within ten rods of a rebel picket, and he had not seen me. I took this as a favorable omen, and thanked heaven for it.*
>
> *As soon as I had gone a safe distance from the picket lines I lay down and rested until morning. The night was chilly, and the ground cold and damp.*
>
> *The first object [I saw] in the morning was a party of Negroes carrying hot coffee and provisions to the rebel pickets. This was another fortunate circumstance, for I immediately made their acquaintance, and was rewarded... by receiving a cup of coffee and a piece of corn bread. I remained there until the darkies returned, and then marched into Yorktown with them without eliciting the least suspicion.*
>
> *The Negroes went to work immediately on the fortifications...All day long I worked in this manner until my hands were blistered from my wrists to the finger ends....*
>
> *Notwithstanding the hardships of the day I had had my eyes and ears open, and had gained more than would counterbalance the day's work.*
>
> *Night came, and I was released from toil. I was free to go where I pleased within the fortifications, and I made good use of my liberty. I made out a brief report of the mounted guns which I saw that night in my ramble round the fort: fifteen three-inch rifled cannon, eighteen four-and-half-inch rifled*

cannon, twenty-nine thirty-two pounders, twenty-one forty-two pounders, twenty-three eight-inch Columbiads, eleven nine-inch Dahlgrens, thirteen ten-inch Columbiads, fourteen ten-inch mortars, and seven eight-inch siege howitzers. (I also recorded the location of "Quaker guns." These were wooden logs painted to look like guns to fool the enemy.) This information, together with a rough sketch of the outer works, I put under the inner sole of my contraband shoes and returned to the Negro quarters....

The second day was much pleasanter. I had only to supply one brigade with water. That did not require much exertion, for the day was cool and the well was not far distant; consequently I could lounge among the soldiers, and listen to important subjects discussed.

In that way I learned the number of reinforcements which had arrived from different places and the total size of the force around Yorktown.

When Gen. Joseph E. Johnston arrived, a council of war was held, and things began to look gloomy. A report circulated that the town was to be evacuated.

Having a little spare time I visited my sable friends and carried some water for them. After taking a draught of the cool beverage, one young darkie looked up at me in a puzzled sort of manner, and turning around to one of his companions, said: "Jim, I'll be darned if that feller ain't turnin' white." I felt greatly alarmed at the remark, but said, very carelessly, "Well, I'se always 'spected to come white some time; my mudder's a white woman." This had the desired effect, for they all laughed and made no further remarks.

As soon as I could conveniently get out of sight I looked at my complexion with a small pocket looking-glass—and sure enough, I was really turning white. I was only a dark mulatto color now, whereas two days previous I was black as coal. However, I had a small vial of nitrate of silver in weak solution, which I applied to prevent the remaining color from coming off.

Upon returning to my post with a fresh supply of water, I saw a group of soldiers gathered around some individual who was haranguing them in real Southern style. I went up quietly, put down my cans of water, and of course had to fill the men's canteens, which required considerable time, especially as I was not in any particular hurry just then. I thought the voice sounded familiar, and upon taking a sly look at the speaker I recognized him at once as a peddler who used to come to the Federal camp regularly

once every week with newspapers and stationery, and especially at headquarters. He would hang round there, under some pretext or other, for half
a day at a time.

There he was, giving the rebels a full description of our camp and force.
He also brought out a map of the entire works of McClellan's position. He
wound up his discourse by saying: "They lost a splendid officer through my
means. It was a pity though to kill such a man even if he was a damn
Yankee." Then he went on to tell how he had been at headquarters and
heard Lieutenant Vesey say he was going to visit the picket line. Knowing
that, the peddler had hastened away to inform rebel sharpshooters and
encourage them to capture him and probably obtain valuable information.
Instead of this, however, they watched for his approach and shot him as soon
as he made his appearance.

I thanked God for that information. I would willingly have worked with
those Negroes on that parapet for two months, and have worn the skin off
my hands half a dozen times, to have gained that single item. The peddler
was a fated man from that moment; his life was not worth three cents in
Confederate scrip. Fortunately he did not know who I was, and it was well
that he did not.

On the evening of the next day I was sent, in company with the colored
men, to carry supper to the outer picket posts on the right wing. This is just
what I wished for, and had been making preparations during the day.…
[After supper] I remained a while with the pickets, and the darkies returned
to camp without me.

Not long after sunset an officer came riding along the lines, and seeing me
inquired what I was doing there. One of the pickets replied that I had helped
to carry out their supper, and was waiting until the Yankees stopped firing
before I started to go back. Turning to me he said, "You come along with
me." I did as I was ordered, and he turned and went back about fifty rods,
stopped in front of a petty officer, and said to him, "Put this fellow on the post
where that man was shot until I return." I was conducted a few rods farther,
and then a rifle was put into my hands, which I was told to use freely in
case I should see anything or anybody approaching from the enemy. Then he
grabbed me by the coat-collar and shook me, saying, "Now, you black rascal,
if you sleep on your post I'll shoot you like a dog."

"Oh no, Massa, I'se too sceerd to sleep," was my only reply.

The night was very dark, and it was beginning to rain. I was all alone now. [Rebel pickets are strung along, one in each place, from three to four rods apart.] But how long before the officer might return with someone to fill my place I did not know, and I thought the best thing I could do was to make good use of the present moment.

After ascertaining as well as possible the position of the picket on each side of me, each of whom I found to be enjoying the shelter of the nearest tree, I deliberately and noiselessly stepped into the darkness, and was soon gliding swiftly through the forest toward the "land of the free," with my splendid rifle grasped tightly lest I should lose the prize.

I did not dare to approach very near the Federal lines, for I was in more danger of being shot by them than by the enemy; so I spent the remainder of the night within hailing distance of our lines. With the first dawn of morning I hoisted the well-known signal [a small white cloth] and was welcomed once more to a sight of the dear old stars and stripes.

I made out my report immediately and carried it to General McClellan's headquarters, together with my trophy....The rifle was sent to Washington, and is now in the Capitol as a memento of the war.

Three days later McClellan ordered an all-out attack, and the Rebels began to fall back. That changed when Confederate Gen. Joseph E. Johnston sent thousands of reinforcements to defend Yorktown. McClellan then dug in for a long siege, fierce battles, and numerous casualties. At the Union hospital, Thompson was among the surgeons and staff that worked long hours amputating limbs, cleaning wounds, and comforting the dying.

Five weeks after Emma's spy mission, McClellan's Army of the Potomac finally took Yorktown. Then, moving slowly and cautiously, he pushed the Rebels up the Peninsula to within six miles of Richmond. When heavy rains stalled his advance, only half of his army had crossed the Chickahominy River before it became impassable. McClellan ordered a bridge to be built, but it would take weeks to complete. The general didn't know where the Rebels were setting up defenses or where or when they might attack. He needed intelligence—an agent to slip across the river, penetrate enemy lines, make observations, and report back. He chose Pvt. Frank Thompson.

Disguised as an Irish Female Peddler

This time Emma disguised herself as Bridget, an Irish peddler selling cakes and pies to soldiers. She wore a heavy skirt that reached to the floor, an old sweater, a fringed shawl, and a big bonnet. She carried a basket of peddler's goods for the soldiers—spools of thread, needles, matches, scissors, soap, corncakes, and packets of tea.

The mission began on May 20, 1862. Her description of it follows:

The bridges were not finished across the Chickahominy when I was ready to cross the river, so I packed up my new disguise in my cake-and-pie basket, and my horse and I plunged into the cold water of the Chickahominy. After crossing the river, I dismounted, and led him to the edge of the water—gave him a farewell pat, and let him swim back to the other side, where a soldier awaited his return.

It was now evening; I did not know the precise distance to the enemy's picket lines, but thought it best to avoid the roads, and consequently I spent the night in the swamp, as the only safe retreat. It required some time to don my new disguise and feel at home in the clothes. I did not [plan] to pass the enemy's lines in the night, but to present myself at the picket line in the morn-ing and request passage as a fugitive fleeing from the approach of the Yankees, which was a usual thing.

In crossing the river I had my basket of clothes and other items strapped on my back and was surprised that its contents were completely drenched. I had been suffering from slight ague chills during the day, and feared the consequences of spending the night in wet clothing, especially in that malaria-infested region. However, there was no alternative, and I was obliged to make the best of it. I had brought a patchwork quilt with me from the hospital, but that, too, was wet. Yet it kept off some of the chill night air....

That night I was attacked by severe chills—chills beyond description. During the latter part of the night the other extreme presented itself, and it seemed as if I should roast alive, and I had not a single drop of water to cool my parched tongue. My mind began to wander, and I became delirious....

Morning at last came, and I was aroused by the roar of cannon and screaming of shell through the forest. But there I was, helpless as an infant, equally unable to advance or retreat....

The cannonading was only the result of a reconnaissance, and in a few hours ceased altogether. But not so my fever and chills; they were my constant companions for two days and two nights in succession. At the end of that time I was an object of pity. With no medicine, no food, and consequently little strength, I was nearly in a state of starvation. My pies and cakes were spoiled in the basket, in consequence of the drenching they had received in crossing the river, and now I had no means of procuring more. But something must be done; I could not bear the thought of starving to death in that inglorious manner; better die upon the scaffold at Richmond, or be shot by rebel pickets; anything but this.

It was around nine o'clock in the morning of the third day after crossing the river when I started, as I thought, towards the enemy's lines. I traveled until five o'clock in the afternoon, and was then deeper in the swamp than when I started. I knew not which way to go. It was a dark day in every sense of the word—and I had neither sun nor compass to guide me.

At five o'clock the glorious booming of cannon reverberated through the dense wilderness, and to me, at that hour, it was the sweetest and most soul-inspiring music that ever greeted my ear. I now turned my face in the direction of the scene of action, and was not long in extricating myself from the swamp which had so long enveloped me.

Soon after emerging from the swamp I saw, in the distance, a small white house, and thither I bent my weary footsteps. I found it deserted, with the exception of a sick rebel soldier, who lay upon the floor in a helpless condition. I went to him, and assuming the Irish brogue, I inquired how he came to be left alone, and if I could render him any assistance. He could only speak in a low whisper, and with much difficulty said he had been ill with typhoid fever a few weeks before, and had not fully recovered when he was ordered to rejoin his company for action. He participated in a sharp skirmish, in which the rebels were obliged to retreat; but he fell out by the way, and fearing to fall into the hands of Yankees, he crawled along as best he could, sometimes on his hands and knees, until he reached this house.

He had not eaten anything since leaving camp, and he was truly starving. I did not dare say to him "ditto," but thought so, and realized it most painfully.

He also told me that the family who had occupied the house had abandoned it since he came there, and that they had left some flour and cornmeal,

*but had not time to cook anything for him. This was good news. Exhausted
as I was, I soon kindled a fire, baked a large hoe cake, and heated water in
a saucepan, for there was no kettle to be found. After searching the premises
I found some tea and earthenware. My cake being cooked, and tea made, I
fed the poor famished rebel as tenderly as if he had been my brother, and he
seemed grateful for my kindness.*

*It is strange how sickness and disease disarm our antipathy and remove
our prejudices. There lay before me an enemy to the government for which
I was daily and willingly exposing my life and suffering unspeakable priva-
tion. He may have been the very man who took deadly aim at my friend
and sent the cruel bullet through his temple. Yet, as I looked upon him in his
helpless condition, I did not feel the least resentment or entertain an unkind
thought toward him personally. I looked upon him only as an unfortunate,
suffering man, whose sad condition called forth the best feelings of my nature.
I longed to restore him to health and strength, not considering that the very
health and strength I wished to secure for him would be employed against
the cause I espoused.*

*After examining his pulse, I could tell that he was fast sinking....He asked
me to pray with him. I knelt down beside him and prayed for grace to sustain
him in that trying hour and for the triumph of truth and right.*

*He looked up suddenly and saw me weeping—for I could not restrain my
tears. Looking startled he exclaimed, "Am I dying?"*

*Oh, how often have I been obliged to answer that awful question in the
affirmative! "Yes, you are dying, my friend. Is your peace made with God?"
He replied, "My trust is in Christ. He was mine in life, and in death He will
not forsake me"—almost the very words I heard a dying Federal soldier say, a
few days before, at the hospital in Williamsburg. A few weeks previous those
two men had been arrayed against each other in deadly strife; yet they were
brethren; their faith and hope were the same; they both trusted in the same
Saviour for salvation.*

*Then he said, "I have a last request to make. If you ever pass through the
Confederate camp between here and Richmond inquire for Major McKee of
General [Richard] Ewell's staff and give him a gold watch you will find in my
pocket; he will know what to do with it; and tell him I died happy, peacefully."
He then told me his name was Allen Hall and identified his regiment.*

He died about twelve o'clock—his hand clasping mine in the painful grip of death, my arm supporting him, and his head leaning on my bosom like a wearied child....I drew his blanket close around him and left him in the silent embrace of death.

Then I enveloped myself in my patchwork quilt and slept soundly until six o'clock in the morning. Feeling much refreshed I arose. I cut a lock of hair from his temple, took the watch and a small package of letters from his pocket, replaced the blanket reverently, and bade him farewell.

[Before leaving] I found a number of items to improve my disguise. There was mustard, pepper, an old pair of green spectacles, and a bottle of red ink. Using the mustard I made a strong plaster about the size of a dollar, and tied it on one side of my face until it blistered thoroughly. I then cut off the blister and put on a large patch of black court plaster. I gave my pale complexion a deep tinge with some ochre I found in a closet, and with the ink I painted a red line around each eye. I put on my green glasses and my Irish hood. It came over my face about six inches.

Next, I toured the house from garret to cellar, looking for household fixings an Irishwoman would carry with her—for I expected to be searched before I was admitted through the lines. I packed both my baskets, for I had two now, and was ready for another start. But [first] I thought it best to bury my pistol and other things that might arouse suspicion. Then I left the house, taking the nearest road to the rebel picket line. I felt perfectly safe in doing so, for the rebel soldier's watch was a sufficient passport in daylight, and a message for Major McKee would ensure me civility at least.

I followed the Richmond road about five miles before meeting anyone. At length I saw a sentinel in the distance. I displayed a flag of truce—a piece of a cotton window curtain which I brought from the house. Upon coming up to the guard, instead of being dismayed at his formidable appearance, I felt rejoiced, for there stood before me an immense specimen of a jolly Englishman, with a smile on his good-natured face, provoked, I presume, by the supremely ludicrous figure I presented.

He mildly questioned me with regard to my hopes and fears, whence I came and whither I was going, and if I had seen any Yankees. I told him my sorrowful story and applied the peppery handkerchief to my eyes, causing tears to run down my face without the least effort on my part. The good-natured guard's sympathy was excited, more especially as I was a foreigner like himself, and he told me I could pass along and go just wherever I pleased....

After thanking the picket guard for his kindness, I continued toward the rebel camp. I had not gone far when the guard called me back and advised me not to stay in camp overnight, for, said he, "One of our spies has just come in and reported that the Yankees have finished the bridges across the Chickahominy, and intend to attack us either today or tonight." He went on to tell me how many masked batteries they had prepared, and said he, "There is one," pointing to a brush heap by the roadside, "that will give them fits if they come this way."

Feeling in a hurry, I started once more for the rebel camp....I went directly to headquarters and inquired for Major McKee. I was told that he would not be there before evening. "He's gone to set a trap for the damned Yankees."

I knew I had to find out as much as possible before night, and make my way back before the impending battle came on. Upon looking around the camp I saw a shanty where some Negro women were cooking meat. I went and told them I was hungry and would like to have something to eat. "Oh yes, honey, we'se got lots o'meat and bread, but hain't got no salt; but reckon ye can eat it without."

I thought it would be well to look a little smarter before I presented myself at headquarters again, so that I could gain their confidence. My patched and painted face made it impossible for anyone to define the expression of my countenance. My blistered cheek was becoming very painful due to the court plaster. I took off my glasses and bathed my face in clear, cold water. That did not remove much of the color, but it made me a shade more like myself. Then I succeeded in getting one of the colored women to go to the doctor's quarters and get me some unguent (a healing salve) to dress the blister. My eyes were sufficiently disfigured by this time to dispense with the glasses, so I laid them aside.

I had no difficulty in finding out the size of the enemy's force and their plans for the coming battle, for everyone seemed to talk of nothing less.

Five o'clock came, and with it Major McKee. I lost no time in presenting myself, and with a profound Irish courtesy I delivered the watch and package. I did not require any black pepper now to cause tears, for the sad mementoes I had just delivered to the major so forcibly reminded me of the past night that

I could not refrain from weeping. The major, rough and stern as he was, sat there with his face between his hands and sobbed like a child. Soon he rose to his feet, surveyed me from head to foot, and said, "You are a faithful woman, and you shall be rewarded."

He then asked: "Can you go direct to that house and show my men where Allen's body is?" I answered in the affirmative—whereupon he handed me a ten-dollar Federal bill, saying, as he did so: "If you succeed in finding the house, I will give you as much more." I thanked him, but positively declined taking the money. He did not seem to understand the philosophy of a person in my circumstances refusing money, and when I looked at him again, his face wore a doubtful, puzzled expression, which alarmed me. I was actually frightened. Bursting into a passionate fit of weeping, I exclaimed vehemently:

"Oh, general, forgive me! But me conshins wud niver give me peace in this world nor in the nixt, if I wud take money for carrying the dyin missage for that sweet boy that's dead and gone—God rest his soul. Och, indeed, indeed, I nivir cud do sich a mean thing, even if I'm a poor woman."

The major seemed satisfied and told me to wait until he returned with a detachment of men.

When they arrived, I told him I did not feel able to walk that distance. I requested a horse, stating the fact that I had been sick for several days, and had slept but little the night before. He ordered a horse saddled immediately....

We made our way toward the house cautiously, lest we should be surprised by the Federals. I rode at the head of this band of rebels as their guide, wondering if I was leading them into the jaws of death every step we advanced, and if so it would probably be death for me as well as for them. Thus, we traveled those five miles silently, thoughtfully, and stealthily. The sun had gone down behind the western hills, and the deepening shadows were fast gathering around us as we came in sight of the little white cottage in the forest.

The detachment of twenty-four men halted to rest and to make arrangements before approaching the house. The men were divided into squads, each of which was to take its turn carrying the body of their late captain upon a stretcher. Having settled things satisfactorily among themselves, we again resumed our movement and were soon at the gate. The sergeant then ordered the corporal to proceed to the house with a squad of men and bring out the corpse, while he stationed the remaining men to guard all approaches to the house.

He asked me to ride down the road a little way, and if I should see or hear anything of the Yankees to ride back as fast as possible and let them know. I assented, and joyfully complied with the first part of his request. This was a pleasant duty for which I mentally thanked the sergeant a thousand times. I turned and rode slowly down the road, but not "seeing or hearing anything of the Yankees," I thought it best to keep on in that direction until I did.

I was like the Zouave after the Battle of Bull Run who said he was ordered to retreat but not being ordered to halt at any particular place, he preferred to keep on until he reached New York! So, after getting out of sight of the rebel guards I made that horse go over the ground faster, I think, than he had ever run before—which seemed to give him a bad impression of Yankees in general, and of me in particular. I kept him galloping at a fast pace until I reached the Chickahominy, where I reported to the Federal general.

I had no desire to have those rebels captured, and consequently said nothing about it in my report; so the sergeant and his men were able to return to the rebel camp unmolested bearing with them the remains of their beloved captain.

Forever after, in regard to the horse I rode, it was as much as a person's life was worth to saddle him; at every attempt he would kick and bite most savagely.

The day after Emma made her report, General McClellan issued orders for the Army of the Potomac to advance beyond the Chickahominy.

Disguised as a Male Detective

In February 1863, Emma (still in disguise as Frank Thompson) was granted permission to go with Maj. Gen. Ambrose E. Burnside's 9th Corps to Louisville, Kentucky. It was a slaveholding Border State that stayed with the Union. Its citizens, however, were about equally divided in their loyalties. They generally supported slavery but did not want to secede.

Shortly, Emma (as Thompson) was given a special assignment as a detective serving inside Union lines. "There were many spies in our midst who were daily giving information to the enemy," Emma wrote, "and they had baffled all attempts at discovery." Her mission was to identify them.

Emma acquired a man's suit and pasted on a neat moustache. Looking dapper in her new disguise, she proceeded to Louisville, mingled freely with the citizens, and made many secesh acquaintances. Among them was a merchant Emma later described as "the most bitter in his denunciations of the Yankees that it has ever been my lot to meet." Thinking he would be a good person to know, she walked into his store one morning and inquired about a job. He said that one of his clerks was about to leave and, yes, he would need help in a few days. The merchant hired Thompson, who began work immediately in order to learn from the other clerk before he left.

Several days passed, and then the merchant asked Thompson to go out to the nearest camp and sell pocketknives, combs, and suspenders to the soldiers. Emma did this very well, selling everything, which pleased the merchant.

"Things went on this way for two weeks," Emma later wrote, "and through the good merchant's assistance I succeeded in finding a clue to the identities of three rebel spies then within our lines."

She said she was "often questioned by my employer about my political sentiments," but she professed no knowledge of politics and no interest in the terms *Federal* and *Confederate*. Emma reported the outcome of this venture in her *Memoirs*.

I expressed a desire to enter the Confederate service, and asked the merchant how I should manage to get through Yankee lines if I should decide to take such a step. After a long conversation, and much planning, we decided that I should go through [Federal] lines the next night with a person who was considered by [Federal] troops [to be] a thorough Union man, as he had taken the oath of allegiance to the Federal government—but who was in reality a rebel spy.

That afternoon I was sent out again to dispose of some goods to the [Federal] soldiers. While [at the camp] I informed the provost marshal of my intended escape [to Confederate lines] the following night together with the rebel spy.

I advised the provost marshal to send someone to the store the next day to purchase some trifle, so that I might enclose in the parcel any new information I might have. I went back to the store and my employer told me to get ready for my journey. This I did, and soon returned.

[Shortly, the spy showed up at the store, although he wasn't identified as such. And the merchant assured him of my allegiance to the Confederacy.]

The provost marshal himself came in a few minutes later. I had my docu-
ment ready. It stated what time we would start and what direction we were
to take.

The night came, and we left about nine o'clock. As we walked along toward
the rebel lines the spy seemed to think that I was a true patriot in the rebel
cause. He entertained me with a long conversation concerning his exploits in
the Confederate Secret Service; and of the exploits of the other two spies who
he said were still in the Union camp. He said one of them was a sutler, and
the other sold photographs of our generals.

We were pursuing our way in the darkness, talking in a low, confidential
tone, when suddenly Union cavalry dashed upon us. They took us both pris-
oners (so as not to reveal my identity). We were searched. Documents found
on my companion condemned him as a spy.

[We were taken back to Louisville, and he was put under guard. The
general's staff found the sutler and arrested him. The dealer in photographs
had escaped.]

I dared never to go back to Louisville again. My life would pay the penalty
if I did.

Thompson Ceases to Exist

That spring, Emma requested a leave of absence, but it was denied. On
April 19, 1863, Frank Thompson suddenly disappeared from the Union army.
He was AWOL and never to be heard from again. Stories vary as to why
Emma deserted. She may have contracted malaria and feared discovery of
her sex if confined in a hospital. Among those surprised by her unexplained
absence was her unrequited love, male nurse Jerome Robbins.

Within a few weeks, Robbins received an unusually warm letter from Emma,
postmarked Washington, D.C. Emma apparently no longer resented his rejec-
tion of her love. She wrote: "Oh, Jerome, I do miss you so much. There is no
person living whose presence would be so agreeable to me this afternoon as
yours." No record exists of his response, but the two former comrades corresponded for several months.

Emma next surfaced in Oberlin, Ohio, where she continued to serve the
army as an army nurse—a female hospital nurse—under the auspices of the U.S.
Christian Commission. This time she used her real name.

Near the end of the war, while working as a nurse at Harpers Ferry, she met an old friend from Canada, Linus Seelye. He was the person who had assisted her escape from home at age seventeen. When Emma moved back to Ohio after the war, Linus followed her and proposed to her. She happily accepted. They were married in Cleveland on April 27, 1867. They had three children, all of whom died in childhood, and then they adopted two boys.

In 1882, Emma attended a reunion of her regiment and stunned them when she revealed her masquerade as Frank Thompson. They quickly accepted her and supported her application for a veteran's pension. It was approved, and she was granted a pension of twelve dollars a month. Subsequently, she received an honorable discharge. The charge of desertion was removed from her records.

In 1898, at age fifty-seven, she became the only woman soldier accepted as a regular member of the Grand Army of the Republic. She died a few weeks later, on September 5, reportedly after suffering repeated malaria attacks and paralysis. She was buried with full military honors in Washington Cemetery in Houston, Texas.

Three years later, in an address to the veterans of the Second Michigan, Col. Frederick Schneider paid tribute to Emma Edmonds Seelye. He praised her "daring bravery, heroic fortitude…and extraordinary patriotic devotion to the cause of her adopted country in the greatest crisis of its history." He said that no one had surpassed "her zeal for the cause of humanity," that "her whole life [was] devoted to the alleviation of human suffering, and that the whole world [was] made better for her having lived in it."

15

Trapped in a Sting Operation

Clara Judd

Clara Judd's hard-luck story masked her effectiveness as a spy and smuggler for the Confederacy. She was a Northerner who married an Episcopalian clergyman in Minnesota, had eight children, and moved to Winchester in middle Tennessee in 1859. She was probably in her late thirties in 1861 when her husband and one child were killed in an accident while he was on business in Nashville. With very little money, she obtained jobs for her oldest sons in a government factory to support the family and keep them from being conscripted into the army. For this act, she said she was "censured very much" by her neighbors in Tennessee.

Claiming severe heart disease, she wrote that she needed "to preserve their lives to take care of the younger children."

During 1861 and 1862 Federal armies took possession of Winchester five different times. Clara later wrote that she "always treated them as brothers [and] had a house full every time they were there." She added that she never had a Confederate soldier in her home.

When Union forces under Union Maj. Gen. George H. Thomas occupied Winchester, Clara learned they had been ordered to destroy all of her crops "except enough to last six weeks." She said that a Union officer advised her to leave Winchester as soon as possible. "I could not stay to dispose of any of my property," she said. Her meager holdings included three cows, seven acres of crops, and her deceased husband's library.

With what she said was borrowed money, Clara allegedly took the three youngest children to Minnesota, but then supposedly fled from Indian uprisings and returned south to Louisville and put them under the care of one of her sisters.

Thereafter, Clara made several trips north after obtaining passes through Union lines "to visit her children." She also traveled frequently to Atlanta "to see her son who was working in a factory there." Apparently, these trips were funded by Confederate sources for the purpose of obtaining intelligence and contraband of war.

The Federal Army of the Cumberland, then in control of Nashville, was under orders to take all of Middle and East Tennessee and was preparing for action against Braxton Bragg's Confederate Army of Tennessee. Brig. Gen. John Hunt Morgan, the famous Confederate raider, hoped to distract and disrupt Union plans by leading some twenty-five hundred troops through the heart of Kentucky by way of the Louisville and Nashville railway and then into Indiana and Ohio.

General Morgan, aware of Clara's clandestine work, got word to her in December 1862 that he needed to know the location and strength of Federal forces controlling the railroad. He asked if she would try to obtain this information. She said she would.

On her way north, she was detained at Murfreesboro, Tennessee, for three days, waiting for a pass to Nashville. When she finally obtained one, she could not find transportation and began walking toward the state's capital city. Shortly, Clara was approached by a man in a buggy who claimed to be a paroled prisoner with a pass from General Bragg to enter Nashville. He was actually a Northern counterespionage agent. He gave his name as Delos Thurman Blythe.

He invited the neatly dressed lady to ride with him, and she accepted. They had traveled nearly to Nashville when they came to a Union picket line at which Federal and Confederate officers were conferring under a flag of truce. Blythe's pass was accepted, but Clara was required to obtain a permit from headquarters in Nashville. During the delay, Blythe overheard one of the Confederates tell Clara: "If they won't let you in, you can go across the country—about four miles—to my father's and there they will run you through the lines." This made Blythe suspicious.

At headquarters, Clara told Federal authorities that she was on her way to her home in Minnesota after having visited one of her seven children in Atlanta. She seemed sincere, and the judge gave her a pass to Louisville.

Clara secured lodging for the night at the home of an acquaintance and wrote a note to Blythe, requesting that he call upon her "for important private business."

Blythe, meanwhile, had reported his suspicions about her to Federal authorities and told them that she was probably a spy. Returning to his hotel he was handed her note. He walked to the house where she was staying.

Following the usual pleasantries, she blurted out: "Are you loyal?"

"Yes, absolutely," he said without hesitation.

She incorrectly interpreted that to mean he was loyal to the Confederate cause. The mistake would be devastating for her. She confirmed his suspicions by disclosing her identity and her mission to obtain military information for John Hunt Morgan so he could determine the best points of attack. She said she'd deliver the information to Morgan through friends in Gallatin, Tennessee, on her way back to Murfreesboro. She also said she planned to buy quinine, morphine, nitrate of silver, and clothes in Louisville for the Confederate army, and that Morgan's men were to assist in getting her baggage of contraband through Federal lines by loading it on a wagon and covering it with fodder and straw.

To accomplish all of this and meet her contact in Gallatin at the prearranged time, Clara needed to leave Nashville a day earlier than indicated on her present pass. She asked Blythe if he could exchange the pass. He said he would try.

Blythe went straight to the office of the Federal provost marshal and reported what Clara had told him. "Assist her in carrying out her plans," he said, "but don't encourage her and don't restrain her."

Blythe returned to Clara with the new pass. "You are engaged in a dangerous enterprise," he told her. "But it is important work, and I would like to set aside my usual business and accompany you to Louisville. I will even sit with you in the ladies' car."

She replied: "That is gallant of you. It would add to my pleasure to have you with me."

At each train stop on the way to Louisville, Clara leaned out of the window and asked bystanders about the troops stationed there and their means of defense. When she first did this, Blythe begged her to stop.

"For God's sake," he exclaimed, "please sit down and be quiet. Such conduct could get us arrested as spies."

"But I must do this," she replied. "It is the most important part of my duty to General Morgan."

At Louisville, Blythe was her constant companion. He pampered her, took her to dinner, complimented her, held her hand, and helped her with all of her purchases of medicines and clothes. The ruse worked. She fell in love with him.

One day in Louisville, Blythe pretended to be ill, and Clara took care of him in the most warmhearted and loving manner. She trusted him completely.

When he recovered sufficiently to move about, he excused himself to run an errand. Completely devoted to him, Clara did not ask about his business or why he wanted to go alone. Blythe, however, was setting a trap. He telegraphed his superiors in Nashville, advising them to arrest him and his companion at Mitchelsville, one of the stops before Gallatin.

As Clara started to pack her goods in a trunk with a false bottom, he advised: "Don't go to all that trouble. It isn't necessary. I can get your trunks passed without inspection. I will take care of everything." He did.

On the return trip, Blythe told her to be careful and cautious. "If anything should happen to you," he warned, "it would get me into trouble and that would make you feel bad. I am concerned that you may already be under suspicion."

"I realize that possibility," she replied. "There is a man on this coach who has been watching us for some time."

At Mitchelsville, both Clara and Blythe were arrested by the army police, and he was roughed up in the process, per the plan. She seemed more upset about him than she was about herself. Their baggage was seized and examined, and the contraband was discovered. Authorities also found a Bible inscribed "To Delos Blythe." It was obviously a present for him.

In Nashville—on the Monday before Christmas—the Federals placed Clara under guard in a hotel and falsely told her that Blythe would be court-martialed the next day. In tears she testified on his behalf. "He is innocent," she said in a broken voice. "The responsibility is mine alone."

Blythe, of course, was released without her knowledge. She never learned that his love for her was part of an act and that she was the victim of a sting operation he had directed.

Clara was imprisoned at Alton, Illinois, on a charge of espionage. The provost-judge, John Fitch, had declared that "she is a dangerous person," that cases of this kind involving females were too frequent, and that she should be committed to the military prison at Alton for trial. The trial was never held. Eight months later she was paroled because of "poor health" and instructed to go to Minnesota and stay there.

Her capture probably delayed Morgan's infamous raid into Kentucky more than five months. And it deprived the Confederate army of a huge quantity of drugs and supplies. She never saw Delos Blythe again. But other Confederate female spies did. He snared several while serving as chief of detectives in Louisville.

16

SARAH'S DEADLY REVENGE

Sarah Lane Thompson*

She couldn't spell or write a complete sentence, but Union spy Sarah Lane Thompson brought down a legendary Confederate cavalry commander: Brig. Gen. John Hunt Morgan.

Sarah was born in eastern Tennessee in Greene County, not far from the borders of North Carolina and Virginia. Greene County was also the birthplace of Davy Crockett, a celebrated nineteenth-century American folk hero known as the "king of the wild frontier."

Sarah never became a folk hero, but she did accomplish what the Union army had tried to do for three years. For Sarah, it was revenge. Morgan's men had killed her husband.

Sarah Lane married Sylvanius Thompson in 1854, when she was sixteen. They had two daughters before the start of the Civil War. The family supported the Union, although the state had seceded in 1861. Thompson enlisted but had to travel to Barberville, Kentucky, to sign on with the 1st Tennessee Cavalry (US). His first assignment was to serve as an army recruiter in Tennessee.

Sarah worked closely with her husband in his recruitment efforts. They established designated places for Union loyalists to gather secretly at night.

---

*Note: Quotes in this chapter attributed to Sarah Lane Thompson have been edited for readability.

Sarah and Sylvanius would then lead them some seventy miles across the state line to Kentucky, where they would be sworn in. The Thompsons were responsible for enlisting more than five hundred men.

In 1863, while carrying a dispatch for Maj. Gen. Ambrose E. Burnside in Knoxville, Tennessee, Sylvanius was captured and taken to Belle Island Prison in Richmond, Virginia. It was a camp with no barracks. Prisoners slept in tents or on the ground in all kinds of weather. Somehow, Sylvanius escaped and rejoined his regiment in Tennessee. A few months later, on January 10, 1864, he was ambushed and killed near Greeneville by one of Morgan's raiders.

Sarah's mourning for Sylvanius morphed into motivation. As she wrote years later: "I devoted all my strength and energy to aid the Union cause." She swore she would get even.

The Saga of Morgan's Raiders

In the summer of 1863, Morgan set off on the campaign that would become known as Morgan's Raid. His cavalry rode more than a thousand miles and covered a region from Tennessee to northern Ohio. He struck fear in the civilian population of several Northern states and distracted tens of thousands of Federal troops from their normal duties. The raid almost ended on July 19, 1863, at Buffington Island, Ohio, when approximately seven hundred of his men were captured while trying to cross the Ohio River into West Virginia. On July 26, Morgan and his remaining soldiers—exhausted, hungry, and saddlesore—were forced to surrender.

Four months later, Morgan and six of his officers escaped from their cells in an Ohio penitentiary by digging a tunnel into the inner yard and ascending a

Brigadier General John Hunt Morgan

wall with a rope made from bunk coverlets and a bent poker iron. They eventually made it safely to the South. On August 22, 1864, Morgan was placed in command of the Trans-Allegheny Department, embracing at the time the Confederate forces in eastern Tennessee and southwestern Virginia.

The men assigned to him were in no way comparable to those he had lost. When he once again began raiding into Kentucky, his men wreaked havoc wherever they went. Morgan seemed unwilling or unable to control them.

He then began to organize a raid aimed at Knoxville, Tennessee. On September 23, 1864, Morgan and sixteen hundred raiders rode into Greeneville, roughly seventy miles from Knoxville. He and some of his officers stayed overnight in the spacious home of Mrs. Lucy Williams, the widow of Dr. Alexander Williams, who had built the mansion. Sarah Thompson described it as "a handsome southern home with a beautiful yard and garden and a very large vineyard in the rear of the house."

The Williams family consisted of a daughter and three sons, all but one of whom were loyal Confederates. One son, in fact, was on Morgan's staff. The youngest son, Joe, supported the Union and was married to a Unionist named Lucy. Some writers credit this Lucy with the sequence of events to occur that night. But they are wrong. She was visiting relatives elsewhere in east Tennessee.

Twenty-six-year-old Sarah Thompson took note of the Rebel guards posted in town and around the Williams mansion. It didn't take many inquiries to find out that General Morgan was about to arrive. Sarah's challenge was to notify Federal cavalry stationed at Bull's Gap, fifteen miles from Greeneville. That required getting past Confederate soldiers who were guarding all the roads out of town.

She grabbed her sunbonnet and a pail and rushed to the home of a Confederate colonel she knew in Greeneville. Sarah later wrote in her diary:

I asked him to tell the sentry to issue me a pass out of town so I could milk my cow, as there were several cows on the hill. Obligingly, he told the guard to pass me out and to pass me in when I returned, and I would give him some milk. So I got through the enemy's lines and went after the cow. When I got to her, I threw [something] at her, and she ran down the hill, and I followed her. When out of sight, I crossed through a corn field and went to the house of a friend who had aided me before.

Sarah borrowed a horse from her friend and then followed the railroad tracks to the Union camp at Bull's Gap, arriving around midnight. The commander, Brig. Gen. Alvan Gillem, was sleeping and unhappy at being awakened by the loud voice of a young woman. He did not believe her report. He said it was "a woman's tale."

Fortunately, two of his officers were aware of Sarah's past service for the army, and they vouched for her. One of them, Lt. Edward J. Brooks of the 10th Michigan Infantry, supported Sarah's request for a pension twelve years later. He wrote: "She was the person who conveyed the information of the presence of General Morgan in Greeneville—the information resulting in the move upon Greeneville....She was very often engaged as a spy. Earlier she had been on a spying expedition for us [in Wytheville, Virginia] and brought information to us at Strawberry Plains, Tennessee."

A hundred Union cavalrymen saddled up for the ride to Greeneville. They were accompanied by Sarah, who was given a fresh horse.

General Morgan was asleep as the Federal troops approached the town. A sentry sounded the alarm, and a guard shook Morgan to wake him. The general dashed down the stairs in his nightclothes. Mrs. Williams was in the front hall.

"Where are the Yankees?" he asked.

She responded: "Everywhere. They are everywhere."

He ran out the back door, looking for a place to hide. First, he crouched behind a hotel. Feeling insecure, he sneaked into the adjacent church and darted into its cellar. That didn't satisfy him either. He went out the back of the church, returned to the Williams's yard, and slid under a white fence next to some grapevines.

Sarah had anticipated his efforts to hide or escape. As she noted in her diary: "I paid a colored woman 25 cents to watch him, and when I got back and found he had gone, I asked her where he was. She said, 'Come,' and after going through the house she pointed to a man under a grapevine in the middle of the garden. 'That is Morgan,' she said."

Sarah flagged down the first Union trooper she saw, Pvt. Andrew Campbell of the 13th Tennessee Volunteer Cavalry. Quietly, Sarah took him to the fence.

"Pull back a board or two," she whispered.

He followed her instructions and discovered the general cowering in the grapevines. Morgan jumped up and started to run.

"Halt and surrender!" shouted the cavalryman.

"I will never surrender!" Morgan exclaimed.

As Morgan reached for his gun, Campbell fired his rifle, hitting him in the chest.

"Oh, God!" were Morgan's last words.

Nearly all of Morgan's sixteen hundred men escaped. Only seventy-five were taken prisoner. One hundred were killed.

After the Federals returned to their camp, some of Morgan's men sneaked into Greeneville and surprised and captured Sarah. She described the situation in her diary: "The rope was there to hang me on the same limb where [two other Yankees] hung for three days. And as the trains would pass, the Rebels would strike their dead bodies with canes. But God has so often cared for me, and he did now. Suddenly, bullets fell like hail, and Lt. Edward Brooks of the 10th Michigan and a number of others came and rescued me. And I stepped back into my house to my two children to enjoy the freedom of a free American woman again."

After this episode, Sarah fled to Knoxville, then under Union control, and served as an army nurse. Later she relocated to Cleveland, Ohio.

After the war she married twice and was widowed twice. In 1899, Congress awarded her a pension of twelve dollars a month for her war service. She died in 1909 after being trapped between two trolley cars and suffering a skull fracture. Her burial at Arlington National Cemetery was with full military honors.

17

HIRED TO FIND HERSELF

Loreta Velazquez

L oreta Velazquez never liked being a woman. "I was especially haunted with
the idea of being a man," she wrote in her memoir. "I wished that I was
a man—such a man as Christopher Columbus or Captain Cook—and could
discover new worlds or explore unknown regions of the earth."

As a teenager she was so consumed with her desire to be a man that, late at
night when everyone in the house had gone to bed, she dressed in men's clothes
and promenaded before a mirror.

Not being a man, she chose to model herself after Joan of Arc, who led the
French army to an astounding series of victories in the Hundred Years' War.
"My imagination fires with a desire to emulate [her] glorious deeds," Loreta
wrote, calling Joan "the greatest and noblest" of women who had distinguished
themselves in battle.

Loreta descended from fiery and headstrong Castilian nobles connected
with impressive episodes of Spanish history. Her father was an accomplished
Latin, French, and German scholar. Her mother was the daughter of a French
naval officer and a wealthy American lady. Her grandfather supposedly was the
world-renowned Spanish portrait painter Diego Velazquez.

Loreta was born in 1842 in Havana, Cuba, where her father was a Spanish
government official. When she was one year old, her father fell heir to a
large estate in Texas (then a part of Mexico) and moved there. He fought

for Mexico in the 1846–48 war against the United States. After Mexico's defeat, he abandoned his estate and returned to Cuba rather than become a U.S. citizen.

In 1849, when Loreta was seven, her parents sent her to New Orleans to live with her aunt and attend a school conducted by the Sisters of Charity. During this period Loreta said that she "expended [her] pocket money not in candies and cakes, as most girls are in the habit of doing, but in the purchase of books [about] the lives of kings, princes, and soldiers."

When she was fourteen, her parents prearranged her engagement to a young Spaniard. This Spanish custom was unappealing to Loreta, who had learned from her American classmates in New Orleans that a young lady should pick her own husband. But she had mixed emotions about the arrangement: "The fact is, that the majority of young people really do not know their own minds, and they often fancy themselves in love when they are not. Marriage undeceives them, and then they wish that they had exercised more discretion, and had not been in such a hurry. On the other hand, in a marriage of convenience, if the parties are at all suited to each other, and are disposed to make the best of the situation, they soon become affectionate, and love after marriage is, perhaps, in reality, the most likely to be enduring."

Regardless, she rejected her parents' wishes and broke off the engagement. Then, still fourteen, she stole the boyfriend of a classmate and eloped with him after her father refused to consent to their marriage. Further alienating her parents, Loreta left the Catholic Church and converted to Methodism, her husband's affiliation. He was a U.S. Army officer named William Rouch. They lived at various army posts and had three children, all of whom had died by late 1860.

She Became a Male Soldier

At the outbreak of the Civil War in 1861, Rouch resigned from Federal service and joined the Confederate army. Loreta wanted to accompany him, disguised as a man, but he objected and instructed her to remain at their home in Arkansas.

In June, Rouch departed with his troops for Pensacola, Florida. Loreta, then nineteen, did not want to be left out of the action. Fulfilling her childhood dream, she disguised herself as a man by cutting her hair short, adding a false moustache and goatee, and staining her face, neck, and hands a tan color. With the help of a friend, she adopted a manly swagger and perfected the ability to spit. She assumed the name of Lt. Harry T. Buford, put on a man's suit, and ordered two uniforms from a German tailor.

"As he took my measurements he eyed me pretty close, and seemed to imagine that something was not quite right," she wrote in her memoir. "I was dreadfully afraid he would discover me as a woman but resolved, if he did, to silence him with a handsome bribe for a few days, until he got my uniforms finished."

She then recruited and equipped an infantry battalion in four days, shipped them to Pensacola, and presented them to her husband as his command.

Loreta Velazquez as Harry T. Buford

The battalion was known as the Arkansas Grays.

Rouch was not pleased. He was, in fact, furious. She had disobeyed him. He angrily told her she could not stay in Pensacola and be part of the regiment. Before the issue was resolved, Rouch was killed when a weapon exploded in his hands while he was demonstrating its use to his troops.

Determined to continue her work for the Confederacy, Loreta remained disguised as Buford. She turned her men over to a friend and began to search for more things to do. But first she needed to alter her attire.

The padding she had added to conceal her femininity had become very uncomfortable, so she visited a French army tailor and ordered six wire-net shields, specifying sizes and shapes. The tailor looked puzzled but didn't ask any questions. Wearing them next to her skin, she used them to flatten her breasts.

"They proved very satisfactory," she said, " in concealing my true form and in giving me something of the shape of a man."

Over the shields she wore a close-fitting silk undershirt held in place by straps across her chest and shoulders, similar to shoulder braces worn by men.

Then she stood before a mirror to examine herself. "Ah," she said, "I'm an uncommonly good-looking fellow." All evidence of a beautiful, slender woman had vanished.

Loreta then struck out on her own as Lt. Harry T. Buford. Proceeding to Virginia that summer of 1861 she took part in the First Battle of Manassas on July 21 and the Battle of Ball's Bluff on October 20 and 21. Although the Yankees were routed at Manassas, the battle was ferocious, and Loreta was sickened by the sight of nearly two thousand Confederates killed and wounded. At Ball's Bluff, she claimed to have been appointed commander of a company after the officer in charge was assumed to have been killed. Once the battle was over and won, the officer mysteriously appeared, saying he had been taken by Yankees but had managed to escape. Convinced he had been hiding in fear of fighting, Loreta wrote: "He had a very sheepish look, as if he was ashamed of himself for playing a cowardly trick."

"The spy must, of necessity, perform her work amid the most perilous environments. Self-preservation is the first law of nature and of armies; and it is the duty of a general to make it an exceedingly dangerous business for the secret emissaries of the enemy to penetrate his lines to pick up useful bits of knowledge."—Loreta Velazquez

After these battles, Loreta sought a diversion. She admitted that "being a second Joan of Arc was a mere girlish fancy, which my first experience as a soldier dissipated forever." It wasn't just the fighting and dying that bothered her. It was also the idleness between battles, conversations among men that were generally "revolting and vile," and discussions about women that were "thoroughly despicable."

"I needed no model," she realized. "My experience convinced me that a courageous and resolute woman who had a talent for assuming disguises could perform important services that a man could not even attempt." She concluded that "the secret of success consisted in watching the flow of events and in taking advantage of circumstances as they arose."

She had "an insatiable desire to see and to hear for myself what was going on within enemy lines. That would give me the excitement I craved and prove my ability to obtain reliable intelligence. Then those in authority could not ignore me."

On her own initiative—without authority from anyone and telling no one—she engaged in an exploratory reconnaissance of Washington.

Her first step was to visit an aged black woman at Leesburg, whom she knew. Leesburg was just beyond Ball's Bluff, about thirty-two miles from the capital. Adopting a philosophy that "lying is as necessary as fighting" in warfare, she told the woman she was going to visit the Yankees and try to convince them to free all slaves. Loreta asked her for women's clothes so she could get through the lines without being stopped. A twenty-dollar Confederate note provided adequate motivation, and the woman attired Loreta in a calico dress, a woolen shawl, a sunbonnet, and a pair of shoes a couple of sizes too big. Loreta left her uniform with the woman and asked her to hide it. "I should be back within ten days," she said.

Loreta returned to the river, where she paid a black man twenty-five dollars to row her across the Potomac to Maryland. He was eager to get the money, but he warned her of the risks: a strong current, icy water, and the danger of being fired upon by pickets on either bank. They started after midnight and did not reach the opposite shore until three hours later.

In Washington, she went directly to Brown's Hotel and learned that a prewar friend of her late husband—a Federal army officer—was in the city. She sent him a note, inviting him to call on her at the hotel. Pretending to be pro-Northern, Loreta said she had just arrived from New York and was behind on news about the war. The officer, lamenting recent Federal defeats, began to talk freely. He told her there would be a major undertaking in the western theater to gain control of the Mississippi River and that the operation would include a blockade of the river and an attack on New Orleans.

The next day the officer called on Loreta again and offered to take her to several Federal facilities, including the patent office, the treasury, and the War Department.

"While at the War Department I saw and heard all I could," Loreta wrote in her memoir. "I took particular pains to note the movements of everyone, and to observe exactly how things were done, so that if I returned on any special assignment, I should feel reasonably at home, and be able to go about my work with as little embarrassment as possible."

While her friend was transacting business at the post office, Loreta said she found out many things she wanted to know simply by listening to the conversations around her. In her memoir she expressed surprise that military officers and others talked openly and loudly about top-secret matters. "I wondered how the Federal authorities ever expected to prevent Confederates from finding out their plans if this kind of thing was going on all the time," she noted.

Having fulfilled her reconnoitering expedition, Loreta left Washington for Leesburg and retrieved the uniform hidden away for her. The next day, attired again as Lt. Harry Buford, Loreta boarded a train for Columbus, Tennessee. There she joined Rebel forces under the command of Maj. Gen. Leonidas Polk. Her sojourn in Washington had rekindled her resolve "to do my share of the fighting."

Initially, Loreta was assigned to the detective corps operating on trains. She examined passes, furloughs, and leaves of absence and arrested anyone who did not have the right papers. Nearly every day Loreta was amused by "little controversies between myself and ladies whose papers were not in order. I often laughed heartily to myself at the feminine wiles used to beguile me from the strict line of my duty. How embarrassed they would have been if they had known I was a woman!"

That duty was followed by her transfer to the Confederate army at Fort Donelson, Tennessee, in February 1862. Shortly after her arrival, Brig. Gen. Ulysses S. Grant attacked and surrounded the fort by land and water, forcing the surrender of the entire Rebel army there. In the mass confusion of processing nearly thirteen thousand prisoners, some Confederates walked unchallenged through the lines and escaped to Nashville. Among them was Lt. Harry Buford.

Buford would see further action in April at Shiloh, in West Tennessee, close to the Mississippi border. It was the bloodiest battle ever fought in America up to that time. One out of every four who had gone into battle had been killed, wounded, or captured. Federal casualties exceeded thirteen thousand; the Confederates lost at least ten thousand. More than three thousand lost their lives. It was a Union victory, but a costly one.

At Shiloh, Lieutenant Buford reported to Capt. Charles DeCaulp, a friend of her late husband. DeCaulp and Loreta had become lovers after Rouch's death and planned to marry after the war. DeCaulp did not know he had fought alongside her at Manassas and Shiloh. He assumed that Buford was a man.

The two came together again at a hospital in Atlanta, where DeCaulp was recovering from an illness and Buford needed treatment for foot and shoulder

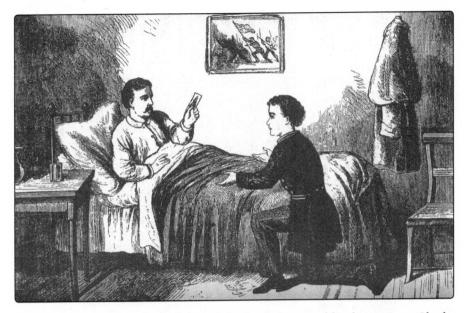

Loreta, dressed as Harry Buford, visited the hospital room of her lover, Capt. Charles DeCaulp. Her disguise was so good, he did not recognize her.

wounds sustained at Shiloh. Buford dropped in to see DeCaulp. During their conversation, DeCaulp showed Buford a photo of Loreta and said: "This is the woman I love. What do you think of her?"

"She is a fine-looking woman," Buford replied. "What would you give if you could see her now?"

"Oh," he said, "I would almost give my existence in heaven."

Loreta asked, "Well, captain, don't you think that the picture resembles me somewhat?"

He looked puzzled.

Raising himself, DeCaulp stared at Buford's face. Grasping her hand tightly, he exclaimed, "Can it be possible that you are she?"

"Yes," she said. "I am. Can you love me a little for doing a soldier's work for the Confederacy? Can you love me a little for that as well as for myself?"

When DeCaulp regained his composure, he replied: "I love you ten times more than ever for this, Loreta! And I cannot consent to part from you again until I have called you by the endearing name of my wife."

Taking into their confidence two physicians to act as witnesses and the post chaplain to perform the ceremony, they were married about a week later in

Atlanta. After a short honeymoon, DeCaulp returned to duty and persuaded Loreta to remain at home.

On his way to rejoin his unit, DeCaulp was taken prisoner by Union troops. His illness returned, and he was transferred to a Federal hospital in Chattanooga, Tennessee. He died there.

"This was a terrible blow to me," Loreta wrote in her memoir, "for I tenderly loved my husband, and was greatly beloved by him. Our short married life was a happy one, and its sudden ending brought to naught all the pleasant plans we had formed for our future. It left me nothing to do but to launch once more on a life of adventure. I would devote my energies to the advancement of the Confederate cause."

A "Bold Stroke" as a Spy

Her secret was now known to many persons, and she concluded that she should not wear a man's uniform again. "I believed," she wrote, "that, as a woman, I could perform very efficient service if I were only afforded proper opportunity."

For her, that meant something with intrigue—like covert activity. "I was convinced that the Secret Service was what I was best suited for." Making use of her talent for disguise, she wanted to go behind Union lines, find out what she could, and relay it to Confederate officials.

It was the autumn of 1863, and Loreta was about to become a spy.

First, she had to appeal to Brig. Gen. John H. Winder, the provost marshal of Richmond who also was the Confederacy's chief of counterespionage, a field about which he was basically ignorant. Loreta apparently wasn't savvy enough about ways to soften up the old man. She made her request, and he rejected it. He said he saw no opportunity for her. She asked if he would, at least, give her a letter of recommendation to the commanding officer of Confederate forces in the south and west. Reluctantly, he agreed.

Traveling through Confederate-occupied territory, she took up quarters in Mobile, Alabama, on the Gulf Coast. She resolved to make "a bold stroke of some kind" and on her own responsibility if necessary.

It wasn't necessary. She soon received a mysterious note in masculine handwriting. "Meet me this evening at the corner of the square," it declared. "I hesitated, not knowing what I might be getting into," Loreta wrote in her memoir, "but then I decided to meet this gentleman. The fact that I was traveling under credentials from General Winder, and was in a manner an attaché of the Secret Service Department, suggested to me that perhaps the man wanted me to undertake an important enterprise."

She was right. The man was a Confederate lieutenant. His name was Shorter.

"I have a job that will require both skill and nerve," he told her, "and I would like for you to undertake it, especially as you seem to have a talent for disguising yourself. I am in the Secret Service, and I want you to take a dispatch through the lines and give it to a certain party. You must succeed, for there will be the devil to pay if the Yankees discover what you are up to."

He told her to meet him the next night at Meridian, Mississippi, 120 miles north of Mobile. "I will have everything ready for you, and will give you detailed instructions. Be prepared for a long journey. In the meantime, keep quiet, and don't whisper a word to anyone."

At Meridian, Lieutenant Shorter explained the mission: "We have captured a Federal spy. He had papers giving accurate accounts of the movements of the forces of four Confederate generals—James Chalmers, Nathan Bedford Forrest, Robert Richardson, and Samuel Wragg Ferguson....We have changed the data on these papers to make them fictitious. To throw the enemy on the wrong scent, I want you to take these bogus papers to Memphis and deliver them to the Federal general, Cadwallader Washburn. Make him believe that the spy gave them to you."

Shorter also had a dispatch to be delivered to a Confederate secret agent in Memphis, for transmittal to General Forrest. Shorter described the agent, told Loreta where to find him, and gave her the password enabling her to communicate with him.

"Just don't let the Federals get their hands on this dispatch," Shorter warned, "or it will be all up for you."

She was to deliver the bogus papers to General Washburn first, so that the Federals would think she was on their side; then, at the earliest moment, she was to contact the agent.

Shorter advised Loreta to impersonate "a poor country woman who had lost her husband in the war and was running to Federal lines for protection." He gave her $136 in greenbacks and letters to Confederate commanders she might meet on the road—letters that directed them to assist her.

"Be vigilant and careful," Shorter reminded her.

Loreta was given an escort, a horse, and a pistol, and was told to dispose of the pistol before entering Federal lines. The escort was to conduct her by rail and horseback to a point near Holly Springs, Mississippi—165 miles north of Meridian. Then she would have to make her way alone to Memphis, a short distance of about 40 miles.

After traveling all night and most of the next day, they rode up to a black family's cabin, seeking shelter.

"It was a poor shelter, but better than nothing," Loreta wrote, "and feeling too ill to proceed any further without rest and refreshments, I persuaded my escort to stop for the night."

By paying for a night's lodging and food, they secured the black family's cooperation and learned that they were close to Federal lines. Asking for directions, they received none, but the oldest man in the cabin agreed to guide them to the area where he had seen Federal pickets. With Loreta in safe hands, her escort headed back to Meridian.

Loreta's new guide led her several miles down the road, and then he stopped and pointed to a church.

"Is that the church where you saw Yankee soldiers?" she asked him.

"Yes, miss, dat's de place; dey's jes' beyond dat church a bit, or dey was las' week."

She handed him a ten-dollar Confederate bill, and he darted off. Loreta rode up to the church, dismounted, and walked inside. Her first thought was to get rid of the pistol, lest she be suspected of being a spy. She raised a plank in the flooring, put the pistol under it, and covered it with dirt.

She continued on for a couple of miles before a picket saw her, stepped out of the woods into the road, and halted her. Loreta asked to see the captain. "It's very important," she asserted.

The picket called to his officer, and a young lieutenant came forward. Loreta repeated her request: "I want to go to Memphis to see General Washburn. I have important papers for him."

"Where are you from?" inquired the lieutenant.

"I am from Holly Springs. A man there gave me these papers, and told me that if I would get them through, he would pay me a hundred dollars."

"Who was he? What did he look like?"

"I mustn't tell you that sir; the man said not to tell anyone about him, except General Washburn."

The lieutenant agreed to take her to headquarters. On the way the officer queried her about the number and position of Confederate troops. She said that there seemed to be a large force near Holly Springs, but she did not tell him anything of significance.

In the town of Moscow, on the Memphis and Charleston Railroad, Loreta was cross-examined by the colonel in command, and he tried to induce her to give him the dispatch. She refused, insisting that she must see the general and that she needed a pass from him to go north to Ohio.

The colonel finally allowed her to board the train to Memphis, but he required the lieutenant to ride in the same car "and keep an eye on her movements." He requested permission to sit next to her, and she said she'd be glad to have his company.

"I will be greatly pleased if you accompany me all the way to the general's headquarters. It has been a long time since I have met any agreeable gentlemen, and I particularly admire officers." As she said this she gave him a killing glance, and then dropped her eyes as if half ashamed of having made such a bold advance to him. But he took the bait.

At Memphis, the lieutenant procured a carriage and took her to the office of the provost marshal. She again repeated her request, and he said: "Madam, I am sorry, but General Washburn is very much indisposed and cannot see you. I will be glad to receive anything you may have for him, and to give him any message from you."

> "I was justified in inflicting all the damage to the enemies of my cause, [I could] even by encouraging treason within their own ranks. That I associated with traitors, and strove to make men betray the cause to which they were bound by every tie of honor and duty, did not render them less despicable to me; and I even now shudder to think of the depravities of human nature revealed to me."— Loreta Velazquez

After a few moments' consideration, she decided that the best thing to do was to get the bogus dispatch off her hands and thus be free to attend to her other mission.

She said: "If the general won't see me, I suppose I will have to write to him."

She sat down at a desk and scribbled a brief note to the general, telling him enough about the source of the dispatch to make him believe it was genuine.

She enclosed her note and the dispatch in the same envelope, handed it to the provost marshal, and told him where she'd be staying in case the general desired to see her.

The lieutenant accompanied her to the Hardwick House Hotel, where she registered as Mrs. Fowler. Then, as a broad hint that she didn't want to see him anymore that day, she said she was tired from the journey and planned to retire after dinner. She asked the lieutenant to call in the morning, if he wished.

She still had to deliver a dispatch to a Confederate agent to carry to General Forrest. Not wanting to be recognized by a Union officer, Loreta gave five dollars to a hotel servant to borrow "more presentable articles of attire" so she could go out and "make some purchases." She then went to the address of the agent. He opened the door without saying a word. She gave the password. That changed his countenance. He smiled and invited her in. She handed him the dispatch for Forrest, emphasizing the need to get it to him as quickly as possible.

The agent replied that he would, but that he had just heard a rumor about a possible movement of Federal troops.

"Could you," he asked, "find out exactly what the plans are? That shouldn't be too difficult since you are on good terms at Union headquarters. And once you have the information, don't bring it to me. Write me a note. Deposit it in the place indicated on this map." He put the map in her hands and said it would be best if they did not meet again.

The next morning Loreta's Union friend made his appearance bright and early and gave her a hundred dollars as payment for bringing important information into the lines. During the day other Union officers and an officer's wife visited her. The officers hoped she might have more information about what was going on within the Rebel lines; the wife brought her a dress to wear.

In these discussions, Loreta later wrote: "I did not have any trouble in learning very nearly everything that my Confederate contact wanted to know about the number and disposition of troops along the line of the Memphis and Charleston Railroad, and also that the force at Collierville was being materially strengthened in apprehension of an attack in that quarter."

She promptly communicated this information to her confidant, and he started for Forrest's headquarters without further delay.

Col. *Lafayette Baker*

The Federal concentration at Collierville (east of Memphis) resulted from the bogus dispatch to General Washburn. It created a gap in the Federal line for Forrest to gallop through. Two days later, Loreta learned that Forrest was on "a grand raid" through western Tennessee. She wrote, "I knew that my covert activities had succeeded."

Double Agent at High Risk

By 1864 Loreta was a bona fide Confederate spy assigned to the Secret Service by General Winder. She described him as "a pleasant-looking old gentleman with white hair and an air of general benevolence that masked the hardness of his heart and his cunningly laid traps." She added that "his eyes were hard, cold, and piercing, and there was a wicked twist about his mouth that was far from being reassuring. I do not believe he had a conscience; he was utterly unscrupulous with regard to the means he used to accomplish his ends. He was a most valuable officer, however, and I doubt whether another individual in the whole Confederacy could have been found who would have commanded the Secret Service corps with the signal ability he did."

Back in Washington later that year, Loreta looked for prominent military friends she had known before the war. With her good looks and cunning, she soon made contact with a general and a captain. They were completely loyal to the Union, and neither of them gave her any information of consequence.

During her conversations with the general, he talked about the work of Col. Lafayette Baker, the chief government detective officer. He was "uncommonly expert" in hunting down Rebel spies, the general said. Loreta was determined to meet this spymaster. She asked the general if he would introduce her to him. He complied. They met the next day, and the general spoke of her in glowing terms. She now had a foot in the door of the man who ran the Union's spy organization.

Baker had come to Washington from California, where he had been a member of the famous vigilance committee that decimated the rogues of that city in 1856. His hair was dark and thick, and he wore a heavy beard. Loreta wrote in her memoir: "His eyes were a cold gray, and they had a peculiarly sharp and piercing expression. He had an abrupt manner of speaking at times. More than once, when I had reason to think that he might have knowledge of some of my transactions as a Confederate Secret Service agent, I felt cold creeps all over me as he looked me straight in the eyes and spoke in that cutting tone of voice."

Without wasting any time, Loreta asked Baker for a job in his detective corps. "I've lost everything in the rebellion," she said, "and I am in urgent need of employment by which I can support myself." She, of course, expressed hatred for the Rebels and a desire "to engage in spy duty to seek revenge on them."

Baker delayed a response for several weeks, during which time both the general and Loreta called on him to seek the appointment. Finally, he made an offer, and she accepted. "Baker fell into the trap laid for him as innocently and unsuspectingly as if he had never heard of such a thing as a spy," Loreta wrote.

She was now a double agent.

Baker immediately sent her on an expedition into the northwestern states (now the Midwest). The Confederacy was attempting to cripple the Union from within by instilling mass panic in the Northwest. Operating out of the Canadian office of the Confederacy, terrorists would strike across the border in a series of raids. Two major attacks were planned, but neither succeeded. Based on spy intelligence, Baker anticipated more trouble somewhere in the Northwest. Loreta's mission was to find out exactly what was brewing so that Baker could nip it in the bud.

Not far from the Canadian border was a large Union prisoner-of-war camp at Johnson's Island, near Sandusky, Ohio, on Lake Erie. Conspirators in the Canadian office came up with an elaborate plan. Agents would slip out of Canada, take over Lake Erie river steamers, and use them as impromptu warships for the boarding and seizure of the USS *Michigan*, which guarded the lake for the Union. The Confederates would then attack Johnson's Island and free and arm its twenty-five thousand prisoners. The freed Confederate soldiers, allied with the Sons of Liberty, then were to take over the region, forcing the North to consider Southern peace terms.

Loreta was in an interesting position. Richmond authorities had called upon her to convey funds and dispatches to their Canadian office supporting the proposed raid on the lakeshore. But she had to go to Richmond to get them, and she had to complete the Canadian trip before going to the Northwest for Baker. Loreta, lying to get results, told Baker that a Confederate spy had been captured and apparently imprisoned on Johnson's Island, where he could doubtless find means to communicate with Confederates outside. She requested permission to go to Richmond and impersonate a loyal Confederate (which she was) and attempt to find out who the spy was, where he was, what he and his people were trying to do, and when they were going to do it.

"You would be hanged if you were caught," Baker cautioned. "But you are a plucky little woman, and if you are willing to take the risk, I am willing to give you a chance." He gave her the necessary passes through Federal lines, $5,000 in bogus Confederate bills, and $150 in Federal greenbacks to see her through.

On her way to Richmond, she reached Confederate outposts and explained the true nature of her trip to the sentinels. They allowed her to pass through their lines. In Richmond, she was given several small packages, important dispatches and letters, and funds totaling eighty-two thousand dollars—all for the Canadian office. She then began the long journey to Canada. She carried the money in her satchel and concealed the dispatches in her clothing.

In New York City, Loreta was met at the ferry by a Confederate associate. He warned her that a Federal detective was in the area, looking for a female spy who was carrying dispatches to Canada.

"I know him," he said, "and I told him I thought I knew the person he was after. I gave him a photograph of a very different-looking woman. If this is the only picture he has, I think you will be safe."

Baker had not photographed Loreta before hiring her.

Regardless, the news startled Loreta. Any moment, a Federal detective might tap her on the shoulder. The story continues in Loreta's words from her memoir published in 1876 by T. Belknap in Hartford, Connecticut:

Upon approaching the depot, my companion pointed to a man in the crowd and said: "There, that is the fellow. He is looking for you, so beware of him."

Then, thinking it best that we not be seen together, my companion wished me good luck and said goodbye, leaving me to procure my ticket and to carry my heavy satchel to the train.

I watched the Federal detective as well as I could without attracting his attention. His eyes scanned the crowd of people passing into the depot. I was curious to know how he tracked me down. He obviously had accurate information about my movements. I also wondered whether Colonel Baker had any suspicion of me; but I made up my mind that he scarcely could have, or else this officer would have been better posted.

After boarding the train I lost sight of the detective until the train arrived at Rochester. Then, to my infinite horror, he entered the car where I was and took a seat near me.

When the conductor came through to collect tickets, the detective spoke to him in a low tone and showed him a photograph. The conductor shook his head, but I could not hear what he said. I did, however, hear the detective say, "I'll catch her yet," to which I mentally replied, "Perhaps."

This whispered conversation reassured me. Clearly, the officer was keeping his eyes upon the photograph, while the woman he was really after was sitting but a few feet from him. Since he did not suspect me, I decided to converse with this gentleman....because I thought I could say something to make him even more bewildered than he already was.

So, I picked up my shawl and satchel and moved to the seat immediately behind him. The window was up, and I made a pretense of not being able to put it down. This attracted his attention, and he came to my assistance. When he had closed the window I thanked him with a rather effusive politeness. He, probably feeling a little lonesome and also perhaps a bit discouraged, seated himself beside me and opened a conversation.

He was a short, thickset man with a dull heavy expression, deep set eyes, thick eyebrows, and a coarse and rather scrubby mustache.

I attempted to speak with an Irish brogue, hoping he would think I was a foreigner. I would have addressed him with a Spanish accent, but feared it could betray me. Baker and others were aware of my Spanish extraction. I did not know if he was one of Baker's men, nor did I know what Baker might have learned about me. I was playing a rather desperate game. But I felt *tolerably sure of being able to deal with this gentleman. I confess, however, of having high anxiety, although I strove to conceal it from him.*

"You are going to Canada, aren't you?" inquired my newmade friend.

"Yes sir."

"Do you live there?"

"Oh no sir. I live in England. I am going to Canada to visit some friends."

"Have you been in America long?

"Only about eight months."

"How do you like this country? Do you prefer it to England?"

"Oh I like living in England much better, and I expect to go back after visiting my friends. There is too much fighting going on here to suit me."

"Oh you need not mind that. Besides, the war will soon be over."

"Do you think so? I will be glad when the fighting is over. It is terrible to hear every day of so many being killed."

"Oh that is nothing. We get used to it."

"Yes," I mentally added, "it may be nothing to such as shark as you, for you will take precious good care to keep your carcass out of danger."

The detective took from his pocket the photograph my associate in New York had given him. Handing it to me, he asked: "Have you seen anybody resembling her? I would like very much to find her."

"She is very attractive," I replied. "Is she your wife?" I asked, looking him straight in the eye.

"Wife, no," said he, apparently disgusted at the suggestion that he was pursuing a faithless spouse.

"What has she done?" I asked. "She looks like a very nice lady, and I don't think she would do anything wrong."

"Well, she has been doing a lot of clandestine work for the Confederacy, and we are determined to stop it. She is one of the smartest of the whole gang." (This, I thought, was rather complimentary.) "I am on her track now, and I am bound to catch her."

"Well, if she has been doing anything against the law, I suppose she ought to be punished, but I hope you will treat her kindly if you do succeed in catching her."

"We won't show any mercy to these she-devils. They give us more trouble than all the men together."

"But perhaps this lady really isn't a spy. She looks too pretty and nice for anything of that sort. How do you know about her?"

"Oh, some of our force have been tracking her for a long time. She has been working for these Copperheads and with Rebel agents here in the North, and she has been running through the lines with dispatches and goods. She came through from Richmond only a short time ago, and she is now on her way to Canada with a lot of dispatches and a big sum of money—all of which I would like to capture."

"Doubtless you would," I thought, and then said aloud: "I wonder how you can find out so much when there must be many people coming and going all the time. Supposing that this lady is a spy as you say, how do you know that she has not already reached Canada?"

"Maybe she has, but I don't think so. I have got her down pretty fine and feel certain of taking her before she gets to the line."

"A spy must have a quick eye, a sharp ear, a retentive memory, and a talent for taking advantage of small, and apparently unimportant points, as aids for the accomplishment of the mission."—Loreta Velazquez

This was a highly edifying and entertaining conversation to me, and I would willingly have prolonged it indefinitely to learn things from him that might prove useful. But he changed the subject, and I was afraid to seem too inquisitive.

He was very polite. On leaving the cars he carried my satchel containing $82,000 belonging to the Confederate government and those important packages. After we boarded the boat, I took the satchel from him and thanked him for his attention. I then got out of his sight as expeditiously as I could.

When the customs-house officer examined my luggage, I winked at him and whispered the password I had been instructed to use. He merely turned up the shawl on my arm and briefly looked into my satchel.

On reaching the Canadian shore, I was met by Mr. L. (last name not used to protect his identity). He gave me a very hearty greeting, but I cautioned him to say as little as possible as we might be watched. Glancing back, I saw the detective surveying the passing crowd, and I called Mr. L's attention to him. I said: "Do you see that large man who looks as though he has lost something?"

"Yes. What of him?"

"He has been traveling with me all day and has been exceedingly attentive. But he is a Yankee detective, and I am the person he is after. He just doesn't have enough information to identify me."…

On my arrival in Canada, I was welcomed with great cordiality by the Confederates. They were eager to know about my relationship with Col. Lafayette Baker and to receive the letters, dispatches, and funds from Richmond. After reviewing these materials, one of the agents asked me if I could take on one more assignment. I said I would try. He said they needed to transmit information to a certain prisoner on Johnson's Island. "Could you possibly manipulate Colonel Baker into allowing you to get inside the prison?" "That's already in the works," I said. "It should not be a problem."

Returning to Washington, I hurried to Colonel Baker's office. I was apprehensive. Perhaps I was walking into a lion's den. But I believed that the detective I met on the train was working somewhat in the dark. It was of great importance, however, that I gain immediate admittance to the military prisons and that was only possible if I went to the prisons as an agent in Baker's corps. So, stifling my fears I walked boldly into the colonel's office and announced that I had just gotten back from Richmond.

He congratulated me on my safe return. There was nothing whatever in his manner to indicate that he had the slightest suspicion of me. [Lying], I told him I had obtained the name of the spy whom he was anxious to discover, as well as a description, and that I should be able to identify him without any difficulty, if I could get to see him. I added: "From what I learned, I believe he is on Johnson's Island, but I cannot be certain."

I indicated that Richmond authorities understood that the spy—wherever he was—had found ways to communicate with the Copperheads and with Confederate agents. This was not entirely true, but it was the story my Confederate contacts told me to tell Baker. A little truth mingled with fiction was likely to throw Baker off the scent.

Baker seemed hesitant about my going to Johnson's Island, but said he would think about it overnight.

He expressed concern about not hearing from me for such a long time. I replied by telling him how and why I had been detained—lies, of course— but my explanation appeared to be entirely satisfactory, for he said no more about it.

"You can rely upon me, sir," I emphasized, *"and I think you will find me as shrewd as most of your detectives are."*

"If you will only keep your eyes and ears attentive, and open your mouth only when you have business to talk about, I will most likely find you a good deal shrewder."

"Why, colonel, you don't appear to have the best opinion of some of your detectives."

"They do pretty well; some of them are really first-rate men; but they are not as smart as they ought to be for the kind of service they are in."

"I suppose some of those Rebel spies give you a good deal of trouble in keeping the run of them."

"Oh, you haven't any idea of it. Some of my people are after a spy now who has been traveling between Richmond and Canada, but they don't seem to be able to lay their hands on her. If they don't catch her soon, I have half a mind to let you try what you can do."

With that, I changed the subject....

The next morning Colonel Baker greeted me with a pleasant smile and said: *"Well, I have made up my mind to let you try your skill as a detective once more, if you are in the same mind you were in yesterday."*

"Yes," I replied. *"I am just as anxious now as I was then. I can at least try."*

"If you find that Confederate Spy at Johnson's Island, telegraph me immediately. If he is not there, try and find out if any of the prisoners know anything about him. At all events, make every effort to find him."

"I will, colonel."

Baker had fallen into the trap.

I went to Johnson's Island in Lake Erie as a Union agent. I showed my letter from Colonel Baker to the commanding officer. I explained that I was searching for a Rebel spy supposedly engaged in a plot against the Union, and that Washington authorities desired to learn more specifics about it. My credentials were verified, and I was admitted into the enclosures and permitted to speak freely with the prisoners.

Once inside the prison I reverted to my real work as a Confederate agent. My greatest fear was that some of the Confederates would recognize me and say or do something that would lead to my detection. I was known to a great many in the Confederate service, both as a man and as a woman. Some *prisoner might have been heedless enough to claim acquaintance with me and thus spoil everything.*

Glancing around the enclosure I could see no signs of recognition on any of the faces of the prisoners, although several of them were gazing curiously at me. After a bit I began to breathe a little freer. I inspected the men closely in an effort to pick out one to communicate with.

At length, I saw a young officer I had known slightly when I was fighting as Lt. Harry T. Buford and whom I knew to be a particularly bright, intelligent fellow. Calling him to me I asked him a few immaterial questions until we had walked out of earshot of the others. Then I said: "I am a Confederate and got in here under false colors. I have something important to say to you."

"I hope you have good news for us."

"Yes, it is good news, at least I hope you will think it is, for it concerns your liberation."

"Well, that is good if it can be done. We are mighty tired of this, I can tell you."

"It will depend a great deal upon yourselves whether anything can be done, but if the prisoners will cooperate in the right spirit, at the right moment, with our friends outside, not only will the prisoners be released, they also will be able to hit the Yankees a staggering blow."

His eyes sparkled at this. Obviously, he was willing and able to engage in almost any enterprise that promised to secure his liberation. I was only fearful that, in his excitement, he would do something incautious that would interfere with the successful prosecution of the scheme.

"You must be very careful," I said. "Keep cool and above all things don't give a hint as to who I really am. Say that I am a Yankee, if anybody asks you, and pretend that this conversation was only about how you are treated and matters of that kind."

"I will fix that all right. What is it that the boys outside are going to do for us?"

"I have a dispatch here which will describe the arrangements, explain what the signals outside will be, and instruct you on what to do when you see the signals. Give this dispatch to the person it is addressed to and consider yourself under his orders until your liberation is effected. When you are once outside of the prison, you will find plenty of people to help you."

"Well, don't you want to see the person that the dispatch is for?"

"No, it is better for a number of reasons for me not to be seen conversing with him."

I then dropped on the ground a package containing $800 and said: *"The package contains some money. Conceal it as quickly as you can, and distribute it among the men as far as it will go."*

He sat down upon a block of wood in front of me and commenced whittling a stick. I stood close to him with my back to the guard and with my skirts covering the package. When the guards were looking another way, he seized the package and slipped it into his boot. He then went on whittling in as unconcerned a manner as possible.

I told him I would leave Sandusky the next day. I shook his hand, and as I did so I passed to him another dispatch containing detailed directions. *"My mission is finished,"* I told him. *"Carrying out the scheme will depend on yourself and the others."* I cautioned him to be exceedingly wary. *"Take none of the prisoners into your confidence unless you are sure they are reliable. Goodbye and good luck."*

With the precious paper in his possession, he whistled and whittled as he walked away, while I hurriedly returned to the office. I told the commander I was unable to find the man I sought and would have to visit other prison camps.

Before leaving Sandusky I wrote to Colonel Baker and said that the man I was looking for was not at Johnson's Island, and that I was going to Indianapolis to visit the prison camp there.

I desired very much, however, to remain in Sandusky to observe the progress of events and, perhaps, take part in any fighting that might occur.

The great drama was ready for the curtain to go up. The two principal characters and their supporters had prepared their roles well. They were ready to capture a Federal gunboat, free the prisoners of war on Johnson's Island, and fire upon and burn Toledo, Sandusky, Cleveland, and Buffalo. They were supplied with thousands of dollars by the Confederate government. President Jefferson Davis had given his blessing. It was all for "the cause."

The lead characters were John Yates Beall and Capt. Charles H. Cole. Beall's naval background on the Chesapeake Bay prepared him well for the plot on Lake Erie. On the Chesapeake he led a guerrilla band that cut a Union telegraph cable, blew up a lighthouse, and captured several ships, including one carrying supplies to a Union force at Port Royal, South Carolina.

"I do not know that we ever accomplished any great things," Beall later wrote, "but we deviled the life out of the gunboats of the Chesapeake trying to catch us."

In November 1863, he and his comrades were arrested for piracy and imprisoned for several months before being exchanged. He then slipped into Canada and worked with Jacob Thompson on the project about to get underway. Thompson, a former U.S. congressman, headed all clandestine operations.

Captain Cole had been part of the command of the famous Confederate cavalry leader Nathan Bedford Forrest. To carry out his role in the great mission on Lake Erie, Cole took up residence in the lakeshore city of Sandusky. There he pretended to be a young Philadelphia millionaire. With his easy, affable manner and his apparently unlimited wealth, he had no difficulty in developing friendships with important military officers and upper-crust socialites. He entertained at lavish dinners and sumptuous banquets, and Federal officers reciprocated by entertaining him on Johnson's Island and on the USS *Michigan*, which, watchdoglike, guarded the island.

On the island he was allowed to mingle with the prisoners, and after revealing his true identity to some of them, he learned that there had existed for some time an escape plan—a plan thwarted only by the presence of the USS *Michigan* but recently rekindled by the visit of Loreta Velazquez. The *Michigan* had been the stumbling block. News from Velazquez and Cole about the impending assault had reassured the prisoners that stepping-stones to freedom were in the making.

The plan called for Cole to host his most elaborate entertainment ever on Monday night, September 19, 1864. Some of the guests would be his secret agents. The others were to be every Federal officer Cole could induce to attend. With free-flowing wine, Cole wanted all of them to get drunk. Those who remained sober were to be drugged, including the captain of the *Michigan*. Cole had already secured employment on the *Michigan* for many of his own men, and they would be on the ship that night instead of at the party.

Early that day, Beall and two of his men boarded the *Philo Parsons*, a small steamer that made daily trips down the Detroit River to Lake Erie and Sandusky. At Beall's request, the captain made an unscheduled stop at the mouth of the river on the Canadian side, and sixteen more of Beall's men boarded, paid their fare, and mingled with the other passengers. The only piece of baggage in the whole party was one old, very heavy, roped trunk.

When the *Philo Parsons* was well on the way once more, Beall and several of his men strolled into the pilothouse, and Beall put a pistol to the helmsman's head. At the same moment, three men approached the ship's acting captain and leveled revolvers at him. Beall's men brought out the heavy trunk, which held two revolvers and hatchets for each man. They then rounded up the eighty passengers—nearly half of them women—and marched them into the cabin and set a guard over them.

Beall had captured the ship.

The *Philo Parsons* was put about and steamed in a great half circle back to Middle Bass Island. As she drew up to the wharf, the *Island Queen*, a Sandusky-to-Toledo steamer, approached and came alongside. Suddenly, Beall and his cohorts leaped onto the *Island Queen*. Among the passengers were more than twenty-five unarmed Federal infantrymen on their way to Toledo to be mustered out. Beall and men charged into the crowd of passengers on deck, wielding hatchets and revolvers. Women shrieked. Men yelled. Shots were fired. The engineer was wounded. Then the *Queen*'s captain surrendered. The passengers from both ships were set ashore on the island, marooned, so that they could not warn authorities.

Night had come. But a full moon provided light and visibility. The crew lashed together the *Philo Parsons* and the little *Island Queen* and steamed out across the lake. Then the *Island Queen* was unlashed and sunk. The *Philo Parsons* steamed on to attack the *Michigan*. All were silent. Way off in the distance were the unseen lights of Sandusky.

Excited about what he expected to happen within minutes, Beall ran through the plan in his mind. From Sandusky Captain Cole would send a signal to the organized prisoners on Johnson's Island to indicate all was ready. The prisoners then would show a signal to Beall. The approach of the familiar *Philo Parsons* would arouse no notice; she would be alongside the *Michigan* before its bewildered sailors, hesitating in the absence of their officers, would take action. In an instant, Beall and his men would be aboard and at the sailors' throats. Then they would fire a cannon shot through the officers' quarters on the island. At this signal, the twenty-five thousand waiting prisoners would rise against their surprised guards and by sheer weight of numbers overpower them.

Meanwhile, on shore, the noise of the gun from the *Michigan* would be the signal for the secret agents at Cole's party to take all the Federal officers as prisoners. Some of Cole's other agents, scattered throughout the city, would cut every telegraph wire. Others would seize the arms of the National Guard and take over every stable in the city. Thus, when the escaping prisoners landed, they would find arms and horses with which to fight their way through the militia across the state and into Virginia.

Beall waited impatiently for the signal from the island. It was past time for it. Then, eight bells on the *Michigan* announced the hour of midnight. The signal should have been sent at least thirty minutes earlier. Beall strained his eyes, watching and waiting. Something was terribly wrong. Beall's crew knew it.

"Women have the reputation of being bad secret-keepers. That depends on circumstances. I have always succeeded in keeping mine, when I have had any worth keeping; and I have always found it more difficult to beguile women than men into telling me what I wanted to know. The truth seems to be, that while women find it often troublesome, and well nigh impossible, to keep little and inconsequential secrets, they are first-rate hands at keeping great ones."—Loreta Velazquez

"Captain Beall!" cried out a longtime associate and friend. "The men have mutinied! Only two of them will go on."

Stunned, Beall went into the cabin. His men awaited him. They believed that the plot had been discovered, that it would be madness to go on. Beall pleaded with them. He cursed them. But the men refused. Having control of the *Philo Parsons*, they steamed away from the *Michigan* and returned to the Canadian shore, where they abandoned the ship and burned it. The great plan to save the Confederacy had gone up in smoke.

The signal from Johnson's Island had not been given because the plot had been exposed. On the morning of September 19, the *Michigan's* captain had returned to his ship one day earlier than expected. Shortly he received a telegram from officials in Detroit. The telegram apprised him of the whole plot.

That afternoon, about the time Beall and his men took over the *Philo Parsons*, Federal officers walked into Cole's elegant suite in Sandusky, handcuffed him, and locked him up. Almost immediately he confessed and voluntarily incriminated his Sandusky accomplices. Later, John Beall was captured and hanged. Cole was acquitted of all charges.

Loreta later wrote: "Cole should have permitted himself to have been torn limb from limb before revealing the plot, as I would have done. The failure of this raid caused much disappointment....The Confederates in Canada, to whom its execution was entrusted, were greatly censured, and were accused of treachery and lack of courage."

Afraid to return to Washington, Loreta sent a letter of resignation to Colonel Baker, stating she had obtained a position with a better salary. But after Lincoln's assassination, Loreta eventually did return to the capital. During her visit, Colonel Baker ran into her in the lobby of a hotel.

"Could we talk privately?" he inquired.

"Certainly," she replied. They sat down in a parlor.

"I have a job on hand now which I want you to undertake," Baker said, "and which I think you can manage if you will do your best. If you succeed, you shall be paid handsomely....I want you to find a woman who is traveling as a Confederate agent. Some of my people have been on her track for a long time, but she is a slippery customer, and they have never been able to lay hands on her."

Loreta knew he was talking about her, especially when he showed her a photograph similar to the one the detective on the train had shown her several months earlier.

Wondering what made him so eager to capture her now, she inwardly resolved that the best thing would be to leave the country at the earliest possible moment.

Baker gave her until nine o'clock the next day to decide whether or not to accept the mission—a mission to find herself! Before Baker came the next morning, Loreta received a letter from her brother, whom she had not seen for some time. He expected to be in New York in a few days with his wife and child. He proposed that since they and she were the last remnants of their family, "We should continue with each other in the future and perhaps go to Europe until things quiet down in America."

Loreta wrote in her memoir: "This letter determined what course I would pursue. I would accept the commission from Baker, thinking by so doing I would more effectually prevent any of his detectives discovering my identity."

So when Baker called, she told him she would undertake the mission. She wrote in her memoir: "I started for New York on a search for myself ostensibly, but in reality to wait anxiously for the coming of my brother. In his company I proposed to proceed across the Atlantic without further delay, and remain there until the time should come when no one would have any reason to trouble us." She reportedly took one hundred thousand dollars in cash with her.

A year later Baker was relieved of his duties by President Andrew Johnson for spying on him and on a female friend. Baker's dismissal relieved Loreta of any worries about returning to the United States.

After the War

A year or so after the war, Loreta was back in the States and married to a Confederate officer named Major Wesson. They soon moved to Venezuela to investigate a colonization plan for Confederate soldiers. It was not to their liking, and sadly, while in South America, Wesson caught black fever and died.

Loreta resettled in Nevada in 1868 and married for the fourth time, but she never took any of her husbands' names. In 1876 she completed a six-hundred-page book about her four years of service to the Confederacy. Much of this chapter is based on that book, *The Woman in Battle: A Narrative of the Exploits, Adventures, and Travels of Madame Loreta Janeta Velazquez.* The description of the plot to free Confederate prisoners on Johnson's Island is drawn primarily from the highly regarded *On Hazardous Service: Scouts and Spies of the North and South*, written by historian William Gilmore Beymer in 1912.

The accuracy of Loreta's memoir continues to be an issue with scholars. Some claim it is all fiction, but in doing so they ignore a newspaper report about the arrest of a Lieutenant Bensford (undoubtedly Buford) when it was discovered that he was actually a woman. The article gives her name as Alice Williams, one of the aliases Loreta used.

Other scholars have noted that the details in Loreta's memoir show a familiarity with the times that would be difficult to completely simulate. In 2007, the History Channel broadcast "Full Metal Corset." The program presented details of Loreta's story as genuine.

The two persons who could have vouched for Loreta and verified her story died in the 1860s. Brig. Gen. John H. Winder, provost marshal for Richmond, died of a heart attack in February 1865. Col. Lafayette Baker, head of the National Detective Police, died mysteriously at his home on July 3, 1868. Only forty-two, he suffered symptoms typical of arsenic poisoning.

Beyond the Call of Duty

More Heroines

Early in the war President Lincoln was concerned about the scarcity of Union spies. Writing to his western generals in the spring of 1862, he emphasized that knowledge of enemy movements was "the most difficult" of problems.

That fall Gen. Ulysses S. Grant selected Maj. Gen. Grenville Mellen Dodge to be his intelligence chief for western operations. Dodge became a superb spymaster, with a cadre of nearly 120 spies and scouts who were known only by numbers, not names. On long missions, couriers accompanied spies so they could take back critical information swiftly. Dodge preferred to use women as couriers because he thought they had a better chance of getting through Confederate lines.

Two of his favorite female spies were Mississippians Jane Featherstone and Molly Malone. Very little is known about them or their work, and that is to their credit. Molly was illiterate, but she was very successful as a spy. Both women reportedly brought back important intelligence from Mississippi and Alabama.

Dodge was very protective of his female operatives. When Mary Mainard, one of his agents, was arrested by Confederate officials, he considered abducting a Confederate officer's wife and holding her hostage until his spy was released. Dodge ultimately did not pursue this course, and Mary remained in jail for the rest of the war.

When Grant moved east to assume command of all Union armies, he named Brig. Gen. George H. Sharpe as the first head of the Bureau of Military

Information. By mid-1863 Sharpe managed the most professional spy organization in the U.S. military since the days of George Washington. For the first time in the war, the Union army surpassed the Confederates in knowledge of opposing forces, thereby fulfilling Lincoln's objective. By the end of the war, Sharpe had some two hundred agents throughout the Confederacy, many of them women. Like Dodge, he never revealed their names. Given the secrecy imposed on names by both Dodge and Sharpe, many exciting stories will never be told. What follows are a few gems, not widely known, from both North and South.

Mary Caroline Allan

Mrs. Mary Caroline Allan's sensational arrest in 1863 shocked the Confederate capital because she had betrayed her friends. She was the Cincinnati-born wife of Patterson Allan, a respected Virginian. At the time of her arrest she was a guest in the home of Mrs. Moses Drury Hoge, whose husband, the Reverend Hoge, was in Europe. Mrs. Allan, it seems, had written letters to friends in the North urging the arrest of Dr. Hoge before he could return to the Confederacy. She also was accused of sending a list of Southern sympathizers in the North to the Reverend Morgan Dix, father of Union Maj. Gen. John A. Dix, and recommending their arrest. Further, she forwarded maps to the North showing "commanding locations" on the James River where Federal guns should be placed.

She confessed to all of these acts but pleaded ill health and was sent to a hospital instead of the despicable prison, Castle Thunder. Her mild punishment irritated Southern women who were aware of the harsh treatment that captured Rebel spies received in the North.

Mrs. Allan was freed on a bail of one hundred thousand dollars in December 1863. Through the skills and connections of her lawyer, former Confederate Secretary of War George W. Randolph, her trial was delayed several times. After the war ended, she was freed.

Fannie Battle

Mary Frances "Fannie" Battle grew up on her family's plantation near Nashville, Tennessee. When the Civil War started in 1861, she was nineteen. Her father and two brothers enlisted in the Confederate army. Both brothers were killed at the battle of Shiloh, and her father was taken prisoner.

Thus motivated to help the Confederate cause, Fannie and a friend, Harriet Booker, began dating Federal soldiers after the Union army occupied Nashville in March 1862. Other girls joined in this scheme. They formed a ring of spies determined to obtain information about Federal defenses and troop movements. They smuggled what they learned to Confederate troops.

While attempting to carry documents to Rebels near Tullahoma, Tennessee, in April 1863, Fannie and Harriet were arrested and imprisoned in the Tennessee State Penitentiary before being transferred to the Old Capitol Prison in Washington, D.C.

Two years later, just before the end of the war, Fannie's two sisters, Dolly and Sallie, were taken into custody on the charge of being part of a family of "spies and harborers of rebels and guerrillas."

After the war Fannie became a social reformer in Nashville. She organized the Nashville Relief Society to help impoverished victims of the 1881 flood of the Cumberland River; she was a leader in the creation of United Charities of Nashville; and she founded a day home for at-risk children, believed to be the oldest child care center in the United States.

Louisa Buckner

Federal Postmaster General Montgomery Blair, a loyal member of Lincoln's cabinet, was tricked by his niece, Louisa Buckner, into giving her money to buy supplies in Washington to take back to Virginia.

She bought the supplies, but they were not the kind that Blair expected. When Louisa was stopped and searched on the way home, Federal agents found more than a hundred ounces of quinine sewed in her skirt—medicine Southern forces badly needed.

Louisa wound up in the Old Capitol Prison, but through Blair's intervention she was soon released. Blair's political enemies, the Radical Republicans, attacked him mercilessly. Blair maintained that she had promised to spend the money on groceries.

Mary Dodge

By 1863, the Federals controlled Little Rock, Arkansas. Camden, a small town eighty miles south, was held by the Confederates. In Camden, on December 24, 1863, Andrew Dodd sent his seventeen-year-old son David to Little Rock to deliver letters to former associates. Dodd hoped they would invest in a plan to buy tobacco and store it for later sale at a higher price. Since the boy was underage, he was considered neutral in the war and should not have had any problems making the deliveries and returning home. Confederate Brig. Gen. James F. Fagan issued him a pass, and he made the deliveries and stayed over Christmas with an aunt.

Teenage boys were scarce in Little Rock, so the hormones in teenage girls fired up when they saw David. At least two girls—Mary Swindle and Minerva Cogburn—invited him to holiday dances. Another girl, sixteen-year-old Mary Dodge, invited him to spend considerable time with her at her home, where Union officers were quartered. Mary Dodge, like David, was pro-Southern. Her father, R. L. Dodge, was a Vermont native on friendly terms with Northern troops.

One or more of these three girls served as Rebel spies and made copious notes about Federal strength and locations in Little Rock. The notes were written in Morse code and hidden in secret pockets in clothing and in false handles of parasols. One girl, probably Mary Dodge, asked David if he would take the information to Confederate officials in Camden. Reluctantly, he agreed. She transferred the messages in code to a small leather notebook he carried.

On December 28 David visited the provost marshal's office and obtained a pass through Union lines to rejoin his family in Camden. As he left Union territory, the guard tore up David's pass, believing he would no longer need it since he was in Confederate territory.

To break up the trip, David went toward Hot Springs, southwest of Little Rock, to spend the night with an uncle. The next day he traveled through the woods and found himself behind Union lines without a pass. Stopped by a sentry, David showed him his small leather notebook. Leafing through it, the sentry found David's birth certificate and a page with dots and dashes. A Union officer translated the code. It revealed Federal positions. They arrested David. He was formally charged as a spy and taken to a military prison.

For two days Union officers grilled him: "Who gave you this information? Who is your source?" He refused to tell.

On the third day, the commander of Union occupation forces, Maj. Gen. Frederick Steele, ordered Mary Dodge and her father to be escorted under armed guard to a Union gunboat on the Arkansas River and transported to Vermont. Mary remained in Vermont until the end of the war. General Steele apparently had discovered that Mary headed the spy ring, but he would not hang a sixteen-year-old girl.

David, on the other hand, received no mercy. The seventeen-year-old boy was tried by a military tribunal and found guilty of treason. He was hanged for his crime on January 8, 1864.

There are more monuments to David O. Dodd in Arkansas than to any other of its war heroes, including Gen. Douglas MacArthur of World War II fame. David is often referred to as the "Boy Martyr of the Confederacy." In 1984, the Sons of Confederate Veterans awarded him the Confederate Medal of Honor. He is one of only twenty-two persons so honored.

As for the young female spies responsible for his death, nothing further is known about them.

Belle Edmondson

Belle Edmondson, alias Brodie West, was a warmhearted and loving twenty-one-year-old lady from Memphis, Tennessee, who did her part for her beloved Confederacy.

Belle smuggled pharmaceutical drugs and basic necessities across Yankee picket lines and also carried hundreds of letters back and forth between Rebel soldiers and their families. One night she worked until three o'clock in the morning to prepare packages of three hundred letters for the soldiers. On another occasion Belle carried under her clothes eight yards of cloth, two hats, one pair of boots, one dozen buttons, two cords, eight tassels, and numerous letters. She could not walk because of the weight, so she hired a carriage to ride across picket lines. She also concealed messages in her elaborate hairdo.

Belle wrote in her diary: "God bless the Rebels. I would risk my life a dozen times a day to serve them—think what they suffer for us."

The Rebels blessed her too. Maj. Thomas H. Price wrote to her in 1863: "God speed you in your angelic mission of imparting comfort and happiness to the soldiers of the South…with whom the name of Belle Edmondson will ever be a household word."

Jane Ferguson

Jane Ferguson was a pro-South Tennessee teenager with a face "frank and simple as a child's." She disguised herself as a Union soldier and infiltrated Union lines for information to pass to Confederate officers. She was caught and sentenced to be hanged, but the sentence was commuted to time in prison.

Hattie Lawton

Hattie Lawton, who was twenty-four at the start of the war, worked for Allan Pinkerton's National Detective Agency in Chicago before joining him in the Federal Secret Service. She traveled throughout the South and gathered information of a strategic nature and "wormed out secrets" by means unavailable to male detectives. She was often accompanied by another Pinkerton operative, John Scobell, an African American who posed as her servant.

Hattie was arrested in Richmond while nursing Pinkerton's most famous agent, Timothy Webster, who suffered from inflammatory rheumatism. When Pinkerton hadn't heard from Lawton or Webster for three weeks, he sent two other agents, Pryce Lewis and John Scully, to find out what was wrong. Unfortunately, they were recognized as Union agents, arrested, and sentenced to hang. To save himself, Scully betrayed Webster and Hattie in exchange for a commutation of his sentence to a year in prison, and Lewis apparently did the same.

Webster and Hattie were both found guilty of spying. His sentence was death by hanging; her sentence, as his accomplice, was a year in prison. Hattie's assistant, John Scobell, was not arrested. Confederate officials believed that no slave was smart enough to be a spy.

Hattie appealed Webster's sentence to Mrs. Jefferson Davis, but she refused to intervene. President Lincoln sent a message to the Confederate president threatening to hang Confederates then held as spies if Webster were executed. Davis ignored the threat. Webster was hanged on April 29, 1862. He was the first spy in the Civil War to be executed.

While Hattie was in prison, she was visited by Richmond's most accomplished Union spy, Elizabeth Van Lew, who also pleaded in vain for Hattie's release. Apparently, neither woman knew that the other was a spy for the Union.

On December 13, 1862, Hattie was freed as part of a prisoner-exchange program. She was one of four Federals exchanged for Confederate spy Belle Boyd.

Jeanette Laurimer Mabry

Jeanette Laurimer Mabry was a staunch Unionist married to a Confederate colonel. She lived in East Tennessee and was in constant contact with Federal guides, spies, and envoys. She fed information to them throughout the war.

Hattie Lawton pleads unsuccessfully for the life of Timothy Webster.

Mary and Sophia Overstreet

These nineteen-year-old twin sisters from Tennessee carried messages and documents for Capt. John W. Headley, a spy for Confederate Gen. Braxton Bragg.

They made a mistake when they tried to help Sallie and Dollie Butler, who had been mistakenly arrested by the Federals. In the process, Union officials searched Mary and Sophia's home and found incriminating materials. The twins were arrested in May 1865 after the war was over, and they were released shortly thereafter. Mary then got another happy ending—she married Captain Headley.

Ann and Kate Patterson

These sisters-in-law shared the same home overlooking a major turnpike in Nashville, Tennessee. They signaled Confederate agents and troops by raising and lowering window shades. When the shades were raised, it was safe for agents to be in the area and to come to their home. The women also smuggled secrets, maps, and supplies in the false bottom of their father's buggy.

Emeline Piggot

Emeline Piggot, aged twenty-five, and her parents lived near the coast of North Carolina, defended by Confederate soldiers in the 26th North Carolina. They were stationed just across the creek from the Piggot home. Emeline served as a Confederate spy, passing food, clothing, and information to them in designated hollow trees.

After Federals occupied the area, she made numerous clandestine trips to New Bern, an important shipping port, to gather intelligence about Union forces and the blockade. Her informants included local fishermen who reeled in military secrets from Yankees who purchased their fish. She also obtained information by entertaining and flirting with Union soldiers in her home. She reportedly carried to Rebel forces as much as thirty pounds of supplies and intelligence in large pockets under her hoopskirt.

In 1865, Union officials arrested Emeline and her brother-in-law, Rufus Bell. She ate some of the evidence, but the Federals found numerous items hidden in her hoopskirt. Two months later the war ended, and they were released.

Antoinette Polk

This teenager was from a well-to-do family who lived in an estate called Ashwood Hall near Columbia, Tennessee, a Union-occupied city. One day Antoinette and a female cousin rode into town to buy supplies. While there, they saw a division of Union cavalry and asked a storekeeper about them. He said they were preparing to search the area for Confederate sympathizers.

At the time, Confederate officers were visiting her father at the estate, and Antoinette realized they were in danger. Being skilled riders, like many Tennessee girls, she and her cousin raced to Ashwood Hall and gave the alert. The Confederate soldiers made a safe retreat just before the Union troops rode up to the estate.

Sallie Pollock

This seventeen-year-old Maryland girl attempted to carry Confederate secrets in her vegetable basket down the Shenandoah Valley to Staunton, Virginia. She was arrested on April 12, 1864, and served several months in the Old Capitol Prison in Washington, D.C.

Lola, Panchita, and Eugenia Sanchez

The alertness and swift action of these three daughters of a Cuban immigrant in Florida prevented a Federal attack on Confederate fortifications in their area.

When several Union officers chatted on the front porch of the Sanchez home, Lola eavesdropped near an open window and heard them discuss plans to use a gunboat to attack the fortifications. Lola then ran upstairs to report this information to her sisters. They quickly developed a plan. The two prettiest girls—Panchita and Eugenia—sauntered to the front porch and introduced themselves to the soldiers, who were quite taken by them. A lengthy conversation ensued. Meanwhile, Lola saddled her horse and rode through the dark woods lying between her home and the Confederate lines.

When she reached Confederate pickets, she was escorted to an officer. Her information enabled the Rebels to surprise and capture the Union gunboat. They renamed the boat *The Three Sisters* in honor of their service.

Sarah Jane Smith

Sarah Jane Smith began her acts of sabotage and smuggling in Missouri when she was fourteen. Her most serious offense was cutting four miles of Federal telegraph wires in the southeastern part of the state. Caught in 1864, the then-sixteen-year-old girl was sentenced to be hanged. Union Maj. Gen. William S. Rosecrans commuted the sentence to imprisonment for the rest of the war.

Molly Tatum and Carrie Gray

As residents of Petersburg, Virginia, Molly Tatum and Carrie Gray pretended to be Unionists but were actually hard-core Confederates. They provided intelligence for Confederate Sgt. George D. Shadburne, chief of scouts for the cavalry corps of Robert E. Lee's Army of Northern Virginia. They once saved Shadburne from capture by hiding him in an upstairs bedroom while one of the girls had a screaming fit. The Yankees pursuing Shadburne decided not to intrude upon a domestic squabble and did not search the house.

During the summer of 1864, Shadburne became one of Maj. Gen. Wade Hampton's notorious Iron Scouts. They hid along the Blackwater River just two miles from Grant's lines near City Point, Virginia. While wearing Yankee uniforms, they skillfully eluded capture while they killed or captured Union pickets and couriers and interfered with wagon supply trains and telegraph lines.

Shadburne was captured on March 6, 1865, near Fredericksburg and charged with being a spy. He would have been hanged had he not escaped on March 10. After the war he practiced law in San Francisco.

Kate Jones Thompson

Kate Jones had it all. She was one of the most beautiful girls in Mississippi, and her father, Peyton Jones, was a wealthy plantation owner. Jacob Thompson, a young congressman and lawyer, was a friend of Peyton and a frequent visitor in his home. When he first saw Kate, she was only fourteen, but he was impressed with her queenly grace, beauty, and personal charm. Kate greatly admired the handsome, young politician too, and in a matter of weeks their friendship ripened into love.

Although Thompson was more than twice her age, he called upon Kate's father to ask for the hand of his daughter. Jones, however, insisted that Kate be well educated before thinking of marriage and moving to Washington as a congressman's wife. Thompson offered a solution. He proposed to marry Kate immediately and place her in school in France. When she finished her education, they would begin their life together as man and wife. Kate's father accepted the deal. Kate remained in France for four years, until she was eighteen, and then joined Jacob in Washington, where she quickly became a social leader.

After Lincoln's election, Thompson resigned his position as secretary of the interior under President James Buchanan and became an aide-de-camp to Confederate Gen. P. G. T. Beauregard. Then, in the spring of 1864, Jefferson Davis chose Thompson to head the Confederate operation in Canada—a terrorist organization focused on clandestine actions against Northern civilians.

Kate remained in Mississippi until 1865, near the end of the war, living in a palatial mansion Thompson had built while she was in Europe. Thompson, desperately needing to communicate with Kate, paid a Canadian girl five thousand dollars to deliver a message to her. The message urged Kate to bury all of their treasured articles and come through the Federal lines to Montreal. She was to bring with her a receipt for one hundred thousand pounds in British stock investments he had made from cotton profits.

Kate concealed the receipt in the lining of her corset, but getting through Federal lines was a major challenge. She used a bogus pass to board a steamboat going up the Mississippi River. At Memphis, Federal officials brought ashore for inspection all persons they suspected of being spies. The group included Kate. With a lady attendant at her side, Kate was required to undress to her bare skin. The attendant tossed her corset, with the secret paper inside, over a screen to examining officials. To distract them, Kate told funny stories she had learned in France. They must have enjoyed them, because they returned the corset without disturbing the contents.

At Cairo, Illinois, Kate had to go through another inspection. This time she removed an upper dental plate and folded the document until it fit snugly against the roof of her mouth. She then placed the dental plate back in position. She was cleared within an hour and able to resume her journey to Montreal.

With the Federals offering a $25,000 reward for Thompson's arrest, he and Kate escaped to the British Isles. In 1869, they returned to the States and established their home in Memphis, Tennessee. They became engaged in numerous philanthropic and charitable activities.

Mary Touvestre

After Virginia seceded, Union forces in Norfolk were in a precarious situation. The best strategy seemed to be to leave and destroy the Federal supplies. So, on April 21, 1861, they set fire to the navy yard and several ships, including a steam-powered frigate called the *Merrimack*. It burned to the waterline and sank. Confederates later raised the ship and began repairing her in secrecy. They renamed the vessel the CSS *Virginia*.

A freed slave, Mary Touvestre, worked as a housekeeper for one of the engineers making repairs and modifications. Other engineers met with him at his home to discuss the project—the conversion of this ship to an ironclad that could destroy the wooden-hulled Federal blockaders. They talked in her presence because they considered slaves too ignorant to understand their conversations. Union cannonballs, they said, would leave hardly a scratch on the *Virginia*'s iron sides, which were up to four inches thick.

Mary realized the significance of this new vessel. She stole the plans the engineer brought home and hid them in her dress. At great risk, she made her way to Washington and met with Navy Secretary Gideon Welles. Welles later wrote that she reported "the ship was nearly finished, had come out of dock, and was about to receive her armament." Surprised by the momentum of the Confederate project, Union officials sped up the building of the Union ironclad, the *Monitor*.

Meanwhile on March 8, 1862, the battle of Hampton Roads began. The *Virginia* rammed and sank the USS *Cumberland*, set ablaze the surrendered USS *Congress*, and damaged the USS *Minnesota*. That night the *Monitor* arrived, under tow from Brooklyn, at Union-held Fort Monroe and rushed to Hampton Roads. When the *Virginia* returned the next day to finish off the *Minnesota* and attack other blockaders, the *Monitor* sortied to stop her. In the first-ever naval battle between two ironclad warships, they fought for about four hours, neither one sinking or seriously damaging the other. While the battle was a draw, it was a strategic victory for the *Monitor* because it had stopped the *Virginia*'s mission to break the Union blockade.

If the former slave had not carried her warning to Washington, the *Virginia* might have remained unchallenged for several weeks as she waged a rampage against vulnerable Union ships. Such action probably would have thwarted the blockade long enough for the South to receive desperately needed supplies from Europe.

Robbie Woodruff

Robbie Woodruff was a beautiful Mississippi farm girl who walked ten miles to town to collect Confederate dispatches. She placed them into a designated hollow stump where the regular Confederate couriers, who always knew where to look, picked them up at their leisure. Although she was stopped many times by Yankee pickets for not having a pass, Robbie overpowered them with her sweet Mississippi drawl and good looks. She was never arrested or even suspected of being a spy.

19

DID SHE DIE FOR THEIR SINS?

Mary Surratt

As the war came to an end, no female spy had been executed, even though many had been found guilty, and some had been sentenced to hang. In a time of chivalry, their gender saved them. It was not considered morally right to hang women.

For Southern spies, their great sacrifices, daring bravery, and heroic fortitude had been in vain. But no Southerner would ever forget what they did for their cause: Belle Boyd's nocturnal ride of thirty miles in the Shenandoah to warn Stonewall Jackson of the Union plan to capture his army; Antonia Ford's intelligence that saved Southern troops from certain disaster at the Second Battle of Manassas; Laura Ratcliffe and Roberta Pollock, who foiled Union plots to capture Col. John Singleton Mosby; and Rose Greenhow, whose amazing network of spies kept Confederate generals informed about Federal plans and troop movements.

A Federal official who didn't forget such actions was the irascible Secretary of War, Edwin M. Stanton. Reportedly, he hated Southern women and, not surprisingly, despised Southern female spies with a vengeance that expressed itself in pungent temper tantrums. Stanton also hated Catholics. And after Lincoln's assassination, his hatreds seemed to focus on one woman: a Catholic Southerner named Mary Surratt. What happened, and how it happened, is an American tragedy.

On Friday, July 7, 1865, Mary Surratt became the first woman in American history to be executed by the Federal government. Joining her on the scaffold were three male collaborators of John Wilkes Booth in the plot to kill President Lincoln and other members of his administration.

Why was Mary Surratt on the scaffold with these villains, waiting to be hanged? She was not a spy, and she played no role on the night of the assassination. A deeply religious, forty-two-year-old widow, Mary ran a boardinghouse in Washington and a tavern at Surrattsville, Maryland. Put simply,

Mary Surratt

she would be hanged primarily because of the dogged determination, vindictiveness, and unforgiving actions of three men: ringleader and mastermind Secretary of War Edwin Stanton, Judge Adv. Gen. Joseph Holt, and President Andrew Johnson.

Mary Surratt was one of eight conspirators charged by the government in the crimes committed against Lincoln and Secretary of State William H. Seward (who was attacked in his home on the night that the president was shot). The conspirators were tried before a nine-member military commission. In a peculiarity of military justice, the prosecutors (but not the defense attorneys) sat with and advised the judges in their deliberations. They participated not only in the verdicts but also in the determination of the sentences delivered.

The evidence against Mary Surratt was inconclusive. It was supplied by an alcoholic and by a family friend who may have betrayed her to save himself. While she may have been part of—or at least aware of—the earlier conspiracy to kidnap Lincoln, there was no proof that she was part of the conspiracy to kill the president. Most observers expected her sentence to be a light prison term or a pardon.

Based on the specification read against her, to find her guilty, the military commission had to prove that she knew about the conspiracy to kill Lincoln, assisted in its execution, and aided the conspirators in escaping. This they could not do. A two-thirds majority (six votes) was required for the death penalty. But according to reliable sources, only four of the nine judges favored execution for Mary Surratt.

In an 1880 article published in the *North American Review*, one of her attorneys, John Clampitt, asserted (on what he called "the most credible authority") that "it was at first proposed to acquit Mrs. Surratt, or at least to spare her life." But, he said, the judge advocate and chief prosecutor, Joseph Holt, strongly objected. Clampitt later confirmed this information, quoting the commission's chairman, Maj. Gen. David Hunter, that the commission had voted *against* capital punishment for Mary Surratt. That should have ended the matter and saved her life. But it didn't. The decision was changed after Holt demanded that the testimony be reinterpreted—an act Hunter supposedly condemned as a violation of "all principles of law and equity." Holt was determined to hang Mary Surratt, no matter what.

In a sneaky maneuver, Holt submitted a motion to hang her and, as a compromise, to attach to the findings a recommendation for mercy. Through Holt's inducement, the commission concurred, and Hunter and four other judges (a majority of the court) signed the petition favoring life imprisonment in consideration of her age and gender—further proof of their objection to hanging her. The decisions were given to Holt to deliver to President Johnson for final approval. To avoid public discourse, the petition was kept secret.

Such tomfoolery and political chicanery were too much for attorney and former Democratic Congressman David DeWitt. In his book *The Judicious Murder of Mary E. Surratt* (1895), he asked pointedly: "Where can we look in the history of the world for a parallel to such a spectacle?" According to DeWitt, the prosecutors probably reasoned that "with the petition in their custody and the president under their domination," they could still hang Mary Surratt, even though the majority of the commission was against it.

That's exactly what happened. DeWitt placed the blame on Stanton and accused him of pressuring the prosecutors and/or the commission to make an example of Mary Surratt as a warning to all women who had aided the enemy. DeWitt believed that Holt, with Stanton's encouragement, emphasized that female spies for the South had been more troublesome than a hundred times as many men and should be taught their places, beginning with Mary Surratt.

Others have argued that some members of the court probably decided death and imprisonment penalties based on one simple point. Those who dealt with Booth through the day of the assassination were executed; those who backed away after the failed kidnapping attempt a month earlier went to prison. The latter included Dr. Samuel Mudd, Samuel B. Arnold, Michael O'Laughlin, and Edman Spangler.

Mary Surratt, however, appeared to a minority of the court to be doing Booth's bidding within hours of the assassination. Thus, from their perspective, she should be hanged.

And what did she do? She ran an errand for Booth, at his request. She took field glasses and a message to John Lloyd, the man who leased her tavern at Surrattsville. The message instructed Lloyd to retrieve two Spencer carbines that had been concealed earlier at the tavern, because they would be called for that night. Booth did call for one of them after the assassination, but it was never used to shoot anyone or to commit a crime.

The key question for the court to resolve was this: Did Mary Surratt know that Booth was contemplating murder rather than kidnapping? Some argued that regardless of the answer to that question, she must have known that something terrible was in the offing. And if she had notified the Federal authorities, she might have saved the president's life.

Then, too, her boardinghouse in Washington and her tavern at Surrattsville were havens, or safe houses, for Confederate spies, smugglers, and dispatch carriers, and her son, John, was a close associate of Booth. In fact, two of the three men hanged with her—George Atzerodt and Lewis Paine—were among her houseguests. The third man, David Herold, had visited the Surratt Tavern and was a close friend of John Surratt. Booth himself visited both establishments on several occasions, primarily to consult with John Surratt and to meet with one or more of the others, but he never stayed overnight at either venue.

This information was circumstantial at best, and none of it enabled the military commission to prove that Mary Surratt knew about the conspiracy to kill Lincoln, assisted in its execution, or aided the conspirators in escaping—the court's necessary requirements to convict her.

If David Hunter's reported communication to Mary's attorney, John Clampitt, is correct, the court had decided that Mary should not be executed.

Their ruling would have held, except for pressure from Holt and, undoubtedly, Stanton, to whom Holt reported.

Even though the commission issued its decision on June 30, 1865, Holt did not meet with President Johnson until July 5. The delay was apparently because Johnson was ill. At that meeting, Holt reviewed the commission's deliberations. It consisted of a five-and-a-half-page summary and eighteen pages of documents containing the formal findings and sentences. The papers were held together by a thin yellow ribbon. The petition on behalf of Mary was not noted on her sentencing pages, but it was attached at the back, folded under the other leaves, and positioned so it was upside down and difficult to find.

Only Holt and Johnson were present at this meeting. The judge advocate general briefed the president, and Johnson signed the papers, approving the sentences, but he did not sign the clemency plea. His signature condemned four prisoners, including Mary Surratt, to death by hanging and the other four to terms of imprisonment.

Holt, after conferring with Johnson, walked to Stanton's office, where another prosecutor, Brig. Gen. Henry L. Burnett, was already with the war secretary. According to Burnett, Stanton asked what the president did, and Holt replied that he "approved the findings and sentence of the Court."

Stanton, revealing his own knowledge of the secret petition, then inquired, "What did he say about the recommendation of mercy for Mrs. Surratt?"

Holt replied (according to Burnett): "He said that she must be punished with the rest....He said her sex furnished no good ground for his interfering; that women and men should learn that if women committed crimes they would be punished; that if they entered into conspiracies to assassinate, they must suffer the penalty; that were this not so, hereafter conspirators and assassins would use women as their instruments; it would be mercy to womankind to let Mrs. Surratt suffer the penalty of her crime."

Burnett's statement may be suspect because of his loyalty to Stanton and Holt. Interestingly, shortly before Stanton's death in 1869, he secured a promise from the other prosecutor, Ohio Representative John A. Bingham, to keep forever secret what they knew about the Mary Surratt case.

The exact nature of the discussion between Holt and Johnson about Mary Surratt's fate is unknown. When the petition became public knowledge two years later at the trial of her son, the news sparked a public furor, and Johnson scrambled to save his political life. He emphatically denied ever seeing the petition, but Holt insisted that he did. One of them lied.

Johnson later pointed out that the authorized published proceedings of the commission contained no reference to the petition for clemency. He accused Stanton and Holt of deliberately omitting it. Johnson was right. The petition could not have been omitted without Stanton's knowledge and consent. The petition, which should have saved Mary's life, had simply faded away for two years.

In 1873, when Johnson was back in politics, he again attacked Stanton and Holt. In a speech, he stated unequivocally that Mary Surratt had been executed by trickery. He also let it be known through others that he would have commuted her sentence to life in prison if he had seen the petition. He shifted all onus from himself to Stanton and Holt.

Noted historians Benjamin Thomas and Harold Hyman concluded that Holt "willfully concealed the contents of the petition from the president" and that he did so because he wanted Mary Surratt to die. These historians emphasized that Holt would not have deceived Stanton in a matter of such importance. Stanton had no sense of humor. He wore an undeviating mantle of severity. Men trembled in his presence. No member of Lincoln's and Johnson's cabinets—save William H. Seward and Salmon P. Chase—ever spoke kindly or favorably of Stanton. He was so tough and merciless that he once told a general: "When you think a man deserves it, shoot him on the spot!" No trial, no hearing, just shoot him.

Congressman DeWitt had no doubts about it; he was convinced that Stanton connived with the three prosecutors—Holt, Bingham, and Burnett—to secure the death sentence and to keep Johnson from seeing the petition for clemency. In a scalding indictment, David DeWitt wrote that Stanton, Holt, and Bingham "procured the death sentence by a trick." He added: "They cheated their own court. They cheated their own president. They sneaked a woman into the arms of death by sleight-of-hand....The execution of Mary Surratt is the foulest blot on the history of the United States." Even Stanton's biographers have accepted DeWitt's assertion that the petition was withheld from Johnson by trickery.

But whether or not Johnson was tricked, he showed no interest in sparing Mary Surratt's life. He refused to see a delegation consisting of Mary's daughter Anna, a congressman, and a Catholic priest. They were denied access by two

Radical Republican senators and backed up by soldiers with rifles and bayonets. Through an assistant, Johnson advised the delegation to see Judge Advocate Holt, "for he had authority over the case." But at Holt's office they were told: "These matters are in the hands of the president. Whatever he says will be final."

Johnson did see the widow of Stephen A. Douglas, the noted Democratic senator and presidential candidate, who came to try to persuade Johnson to save Mrs. Surratt. Johnson declared he would not interfere with the execution. His later attempts to place all blame on Stanton and Holt, compounded by his own suggestion that he would have commuted her sentence if he had seen the petition, can only be interpreted as political backtracking by a weak president.

During a social call, Johnson told the Reverend J. George Butler, a Washington pastor who was on the scaffold to comfort George Atzerodt, that "very strong appeals had been made for the exercise of executive clemency," but he could not be moved, for Mrs. Surratt "kept the nest that hatched the eggs." By that, Johnson strongly implied that a landlady should be held responsible for the crimes of her tenants or visitors. Besides the irrationality of that thought process, the plot was more likely hatched at the Parker House in Boston, where Booth met with three men from Canada on July 26, 1864, or at the St. Lawrence Hotel in Montreal, where Booth and the Confederates' Canada cabinet conferred in October 1864. Would Johnson also have hanged the managers and owners of these hotels?

Aside from what one writer called "the judicial murder" of Mary Surratt, one other fact towers above all others and should have saved Mary Surratt from the gallows. Under the rules of procedure in a military court, the prosecution must present all evidence bearing on both the guilt and innocence of the accused. But it did not.

None other than Radical Republican Congressman Benjamin F. Butler brought this out on the floor of the House of Representatives in the spring of 1867. After Congressman Bingham (one of the prosecutors in the trial) attacked Butler for a military failure as a general, Butler accused Bingham and his associates of hanging an innocent woman, saying that she was "convicted without sufficient evidence in my judgment."

Bingham responded, "What does the gentleman know of the evidence in the case, and what does he care?"

Butler asserted that it was Bingham's duty "to present to the commission all the evidence bearing upon the case," but he did not. He was referring to Booth's diary, which proved "that up to a certain hour Booth contemplated capture and abduction," and Mary Surratt may or may not have known that he had changed his purpose to assassination. "And if Mrs. Surratt did not know of this change of purpose, there is no evidence that she knew in any way of the assassination and ought not, in my judgment, to have been convicted of taking part in it."

Clearly, the prosecutors had obstructed justice by deliberately and illegally withholding material physical evidence so that they could hang or imprison legally innocent persons who apparently had been involved only in the failed plot to capture the president.

Johnson, Holt, and Stanton obviously stacked the deck against Mary Surratt to secure the outcome they desperately craved. And while doing so, they spared many others who had aided Booth, such as Thomas Jones and Samuel Cox, who had hidden Booth for six days after the assassination.

The Execution of Mary Surratt

On July 7, 1865—the day of the execution—most of Washington expected Mary Surratt to be spared the gallows. The commandant of the military district, Maj. Gen. Winfield Scott Hancock, even delayed the proceedings, expecting a stay of execution from the president. After waiting two hours in an oppressive heat, he realized that no reprieve would be forthcoming. The general walked into the prison yard and issued instructions for the guards to "get everything ready."

Around noon, Mary was brought out of her cell and allowed to sit on a chair at the doorway. Father Jacob A. Walter, her Catholic priest, stood at her side. Solemnly she declared her innocence to him. Walter years later stated that her "exact words...the last confession of an innocent woman whilst she stood on the verge of eternity [were that she] was innocent of any complicity in that great crime." He asserted, "She died as innocent of that crime as a babe unborn."

The four prisoners mounted the thirteen steps to the gallows and were seated in chairs positioned before the dangling ropes. Umbrellas shaded them from the blazing sun. Maj. Gen. John F. Hartranft, governor of the military prison, read the death warrants and ordered the executioner to proceed.

"Her too?" asked hangman Capt. Christian Rath.

Most Washington observers expected Mary's sentence to be lightened to a prison term; instead, she was hanged with three of Booth's conspirators.

"Yes," replied Hartranft.

Mary wavered a little. It was feared she would faint. At one point she said to those standing by her, "Please don't let me fall."

A colonel then removed Mary's bonnet and veil and fastened her hands tightly behind her back. He bound her skirts about her knees, placed a noose around her neck, and covered her face and head with a long white hood. The others were similarly bound.

With everything in place, Rath clapped his hands three times—the death signal. Four soldiers knocked the props from beneath the platform, and the four prisoners catapulted downward. Mary Surratt died instantly.

With her death, every woman who ever served as a spy for the South must have shed a few tears. And every person who believed in equal justice under law must have bowed his or her head in disgust.

SELECTED SOURCES

Alexander, John H. *Mosby's Men*. New York: Neale Publishing Co., 1907.

Allen, Thomas B. *Harriet Tubman, Secret Agent: How Daring Agents and Free Blacks Spied for the Union during the Civil War*. Washington, DC: National Geographic, 2006.

Andrews, Matthew Page. *The Women of the South in War Times*. Baltimore: Norman, Remington, 1920.

Ashby, Thomas A. *Life of Turner Ashby*. New York: Neale Publishing Co., 1914.

Axelrod, Alan. *The War Between the Spies: A History of Espionage during the American Civil War*. New York: Atlantic Monthly Press, 1992.

Bakeless, John. *Spies of the Confederacy*. Philadelphia: J. B. Lippincott Co., 1970.

Bakeless, Katharine, and John Bakeless. *Confederate Spy Stories*. Philadelphia: J. B. Lippincott Co., 1973.

Baker, Lafayette C. *History of the United States Secret Service*. Philadelphia: L. C. Baker, 1867.

———. *Spies, Traitors, and Conspirators of the Late Civil War*. Philadelphia: J. E. Potter & Co., 1894.

Banks, Leo. *Stalwart Women: Frontier Stories of Indomitable Spirit*. Phoenix: Arizona Highways, 1999.

Barton, George. *The World's Greatest Military Spies and Secret Service Agents*. Boston: Page Co., 1917.

Beymer, William Gilmore. *On Hazardous Service: Scouts and Spies of the North and South*. New York: Harper & Brothers, 1912.

Blackman, Ann. *Wild Rose: Rose O'Neale Greenhow, Civil War Spy*. New York: Random House, 2005.

Blackwell, Sarah E. *A Military Genius: The Life of Anna Ella Carroll*. 2 vols. Washington, DC: Judd & Detweiler, 1891–95.

Boyd, Belle. *Belle Boyd in Camp and Prison*. New York: Blelock & Co., 1865.

Bradford, Sarah Hopkins. *Scenes in the Life of Harriet Tubman*. Auburn, NY: W. J. Moses, 1869.

Brock, Sally A. *Richmond during the War: Four Years of Personal Observation*. New York: G. W. Carleton & Co., 1867.

Brockett, Linus Pierpont. *Scouts, Spies and Heroes of the Great Civil War: How They Lived, Fought and Died for the Union*. Philadelphia: National Publishing Co., 1911.

Bryan, George S. *The Spy in America*. Philadelphia: J. B. Lippincott Co., 1943.

Burger, Nash Kerr. *Confederate Spy: Rose O'Neal Greenhow*. New York: Franklin Watts, 1967.

Burwell, Sally. "Famous 'Blue Dog' Haunts Rose Hill Every February." *Charles County (MD) Times Crescent*, March 15, 1956.

Caravantes, Peggy. *Petticoat Spies: Six Women Spies of the Civil War*. Greensboro, NC: Morgan Reynolds, 2002.

Carlton, Eileen M. "Friends of Laura Ratcliffe Gala." *Loudoun Times*, May 27, 2008.

Cheney, Edna. "Moses." *Freedmen's Record* 1 (March 1865): 34–38.

———. *Reminiscences of Edna Dow Cheney*. Boston: Lee & Shepard, 1902.

Christen, William. *Pauline Cushman: Spy of the Cumberland*. Roseville, MN: Edinborough Press, 2006.

Civil War Times Staff. "The Loyal Girl of Winchester." *Civil War Times* 2, no. 3 (June 1960): 15.

Clinton, Catherine. *Harriet Tubman: The Road to Freedom*. New York: Back Bay Books, 2005.

Collins, Denis. *Spying: The Secret History of History*. New York: Black Dog & Leventhal Publishers, 2004.

Colman, Penny. *Spies! Women in the Civil War*. Cincinnati: Betterway Books, 1992.

Conrad, Earl. *Harriet Tubman*. New York: Paul S. Eriksson, 1943, 1969.

Cooke, John Esten. *Surry of Eagle's Nest*. New York: G. W. Dillingham, 1894.

Crouch, Richard E. "Endangered by County Priorities." *Fairfax Chronicle*, May 2, 2005.

———. "Rebel General Smitten by Virginia Beauty's Charm." *Washington Times*, December 22, 2001.

Cushman, Pauline. *An Inside View of the Army Police: Thrilling Adventures of Pauline Cushman, the Distinguished American Actress and Famous Federal Spy of the Department of the Cumberland*. Cincinnati: Rickey & Carroll, 1864.

———. *The Romance of the Great Rebellion: The Mysteries of the Secret Service: Pauline Cushman: The Famous Federal Scout and Spy in the Department of the Cumberland*. New York: Wynkoop & Hallenbeck, 1864.

Dannett, Sylvia. *Noble Women of the North*. New York: Thomas Yoseloff, 1959.

———. *She Rode with the Generals: The True and Incredible Story of Sarah Edmonds Seelye*. New York: Thomas Nelson, 1960.

Douglas, Henry Kyd. *I Rode with Stonewall*. Chapel Hill: University of North Carolina Press, 1940.

Edmonds, Sarah Emma. *Memoirs of a Soldier, Nurse, and Spy: A Woman's Adventures in the Union Army*. Hartford, CT: W. S. Williams & Co., 1865.

Eggleston, Larry G. *Women in the Civil War: Extraordinary Stories of Soldiers, Spies, Nurses, Doctors, Crusaders, and Others*. Jefferson, NC: McFarland & Co., 2003.

Emert, Phyllis Raybin, ed. *Women in the Civil War: Warriors, Patriots, Nurses, and Spies*. Auburndale, MA: History Compass, 2008.

Eskew, Garnett Laidlaw, *Willard's of Washington*. New York: Coward-McCann, 1954.

Feis, William B. *Grant's Secret Service*. Lincoln: University of Nebraska Press, 2002.

Fishel, Edwin C. *The Secret War for the Union: The Untold Story of Military Intelligence in the Civil War*. Boston: Houghton Mifflin, 1998.

Fladeland, Betty. "Alias Frank Thompson." *Michigan History* 42 (1958): 435–62.

Freeman, Douglas Southall. *Lee's Lieutenants*. 3 vols. New York: Charles Scribner's Sons, 1942.

Garrison, Webb. *Amazing Women of the Civil War*. Nashville: Rutledge Hill Press, 1999.

Gray, Wood. *The Hidden Civil War: The Story of the Copperheads*. New York: Viking, 1942.

Greenhow, Rose O'Neal. *My Imprisonment and the First Year of Abolition Rule at Washington*. London, England: Richard Bentley & Son, 1863.

Hall, James O. "The Lady in the Veil." *Maryland Independent*, June 25, 1975, and July 2, 1975.

Hall, Richard. *Patriots in Disguise: Women Warriors of the Civil War*. New York: Paragon House, 1993.

Harper, Judith E. *Women during the Civil War: An Encyclopedia*. New York: Routledge, 2007.

Hazelton, Joseph Powers. *Scouts, Spies, and Heroes of the Great Civil War*. Washington, DC: National Tribune, 1899.

Headley, John W. *Confederate Operations in Canada and New York*. New York: Neale Publishing Co., 1906.

Hemingway, Edith Morris, and Jacqueline Cosgrove Shields. *Rebel Hart*. Shippensburg, PA: White Mane Books, 2000.

Hoehling, Adolph A. *Women Who Spied*. New York: Dodd, Mead, 1967.

Hoffert, Sylvia D. "Madame Loreta Velazquez: Heroine or Hoaxer." *Civil War Times Illustrated* 17, no. 3 (June 1978): 24–26.

Humez, Jean M. *Harriet Tubman: The Life and the Life Stories*. Madison: University of Wisconsin Press, 2003.

Humphreys, David. *Heroes and Spies of the Civil War*. New York: Neale Publishing Co., 1903.

Jones, C. Irwin. "The Nice, Little Old Witch." Unidentified clipping, April 16, 1948.

Jones, Catherine M. *Heroines of Dixie: Confederate Women Tell Their Story of the War*. New York: Greenwood Publishing Group, 1955.

Jones, Wilmer L. *Behind Enemy Lines: Civil War Spies, Raiders, and Guerrillas*. New York: Cooper Square Press, 2001.

Kane, Harnett T. *Spies for the Blue and Gray: A Composite Biography of Those Courageous and Extraordinary Men and Women Who Became the Famous Spies of the Civil War*. Garden City, NY: Hanover House, 1954.

Kerner, Marion H. "The Lady Guerilla and the Telegrapher." *(Summersville) West Virginia Hillbilly*, December 11, 1982, reprinted from *Leslie's Weekly*, May 26, 1910.

Kinchen, Oscar A. *Women Who Spied for the Blue and the Gray*. Philadelphia: Dorrance & Co.,1972.

King, Julia, Christine Arnold-Lourie, and Susan Shaffer. *Pathways to History, Charles County, Maryland, 1658–2008*. Mount Victoria, MD: Smallwood Foundation, 2008.

Larson, Kate Clifford. *Bound for the Promised Land: Harriet Tubman: Portrait of an American Hero*. Toronto: One World/Ballantine, 2004.

Larson, Rebecca D. *Blue and Gray Roses of Intrigue*. Gettysburg, PA: Thomas Publications, 1993.

Leonard, Elizabeth D. *All the Daring of the Soldier: Women of the Civil War Armies*. New York: W. W. Norton & Co., 1999.

Lewis, Thomas A. *The Shenandoah in Flames: The Valley Campaign of 1864*. The Civil War. Alexandria, VA: Time-Life Books, 1987.

McCracken, Lawrence. "Thrilling Civil War Story of Girl Spy Revealed at Last; Novel Heroine Actually Lived." *Detroit Free Press*, October 6, 1935.

Mahoney, M. H. *Women in Espionage: A Biographical Dictionary*. Santa Barbara: ABC-CLIO, 1993.

Markle, Donald E. *Spies and Spymasters of the Civil War*. New York: Hippocrene Books, 1994.

Maslowski. Peter. "Military Intelligence Sources During the American Civil War: A Case Study." In *The Intelligence Revolution and Modern Warfare*, edited by James E. Dillard and Walter T. Hitchcock. Military History Symposium Series of the United States Air Force Academy, vol. 3. Chicago: Imprint Publications, 1996.

Massey, Mary Elizabeth. *Bonnet Brigades*. New York: Knopf, 1966.

Mauro, Charles. *A Southern Spy in Northern Virginia: The Civil War Album of Laura Ratcliffe*. Charleston, SC: History Press, 2009.

Miller, Francis T. *The Photographic History of the Civil War*. 10 vols. New York: Review of Reviews Co., 1912.

Milton, David Hepburn. *Lincoln's Spymaster: Thomas Haines Dudley and the Liverpool Network*. Mechanicsburg, PA: Stackpole Books, 2003.

Moore, Frank. *Women of the War: Their Heroism and Self-Sacrifice: True Stories of Brave Women in the Civil War*. 1866. Reprint, Alexander, NC: Blue Gray Books, 1997.

Morn, Frank. *The Eye That Never Sleeps: A History of the Pinkerton National Detective Agency*. Bloomington: Indiana University Press, 1982.

O'Toole, G. J. A. *Honorable Treachery: A History of U.S. Intelligence, Espionage, and Covert Action*. New York: Atlantic Monthly Press, 1991.

Phillips, Larissa. *Women Civil War Spies of the Confederacy*. New York: Rosen Publishing Group, 2004.

Pinkerton, Allan. *The Spy of the Rebellion*. New York: G. W. Carleton & Co., 1883.

Pittenger, William. *Capturing a Locomotive: A History of the Secret Service in the Late War*. Philadelphia: J. B. Lippincott Co., 1882.

Pratt, Fletcher. *Secret and Urgent: The Story of Codes and Ciphers*. Indianapolis: Blue Ribbon Publishing, 1939.

Ramage, James A. *Gray Ghost: The Life of Colonel John Singleton Mosby*. Lexington: University Press of Kentucky, 1999.

Raskin, Joseph, and Edith Raskin. *Spies and Traitors: Tales of the Revolutionary and Civil Wars*. New York: Lothrop, Lee & Shepard Co., 1976.

Reit, Seymour. *Behind Rebel Lines: The Incredible Story of Emma Edmonds, Civil War Spy*. Orlando: Harcourt Brace Jovanovich, 1988.

Robertson, James I., Jr. *The Stonewall Brigade*. Baton Rouge: Louisiana State University Press, 1963.

Ross, Ishbel. *Rebel Rose: Life of Rose O'Neal Greenhow, Confederate Spy*. New York: Harper & Brothers, 1954.

Rust, Jeanne J. *A History of the Town of Fairfax*. Washington, DC: Moore & Moore, 1960.

Ryan, David D. *Cornbread and Maggots, Cloak and Dagger: Union Prisoners and Spies in Civil War Richmond*. Richmond: Dietz Press, 1994.

———, ed. *A Yankee Spy in Richmond: The Civil War Diary of "Crazy Bet" Van Lew*. Mechanicsburg, PA: Stackpole Books, 1996.

Sakany, Lois. *Women Civil War Spies of the Union*. New York: Rosen Publishing Group, 2004.

Sandburg, Carl. *Abraham Lincoln: The War Years*. New York: Harcourt, Brace, & Co., 1939.

Sarmiento, Ferdinand L. *Life of Pauline Cushman, the Celebrated Union Spy and Scout*. Philadelphia: J. E. Potter & Co., 1865.

Savage, Douglas J. *Women in the Civil War*. Philadelphia: Chelsea House, 2000.

Scarborough, Ruth. *Belle Boyd, Siren of the South*. Macon, GA: Mercer University Press, 1983.

Schoof, Heidi. *Elizabeth Van Lew: Civil War Spy*. Mankato, MN: Compass Point Books, 2005.

Scott, John. *Partisan Life with Col. John S. Mosby*. New York: Harper & Bros., 1867.

Sheridan, Philip H. *Personal Memoirs of P. H. Sheridan, General, United States Army*. 2 vols. New York: Webster, 1888.

Sigaud, Louis A. *Belle Boyd, Confederate Spy*. Richmond: Dietz Press, 1945.

Simkins, Francis B., and James W. Patton. *The Women of the Confederacy*. St. Clair Shores, MI: Scholarly Press, 1977.

Simmons, Linda J. "The Antonia Ford Mystery." *Northern Virginia Heritage*, October 1985, 3–6, 20.

Smith, Ophia D. *Oxford Spy: Wed at Pistol Point*. Oxford, OH: Cullen Printing Company, 1962.

Statement by Clara Judd, U.S. Military Prison, Alton, IL, May 11, 1863.

Statement from Maj. T. Hendrickson, prison commander at Alton, Illinois, to Col. W. Hoffman, commissary-general of prisoners, Washington, DC, May 15, 1863.

Statement of testimony against Clara Judd, from John Fitch, provost-judge, to Capt. William M. Wiles, provost-marshal-general, 14th Army Corps, Nashville, Tennessee, January 13, 1863.

Stern, Philip Van Doren. *Secret Missions of the Civil War: First-Hand Accounts by Men and Women Who Risked Their Lives in Underground Activities for the North and South*. Chicago: Rand McNally & Co., 1959.

Stutler, Boyd B. *West Virginia in the Civil War*. 2nd ed. Charleston, WV: Education Foundation, 1966.

Taussig, Betty Carvey. *Windfall of Inherited Treasures*. Annapolis, MD: Windfall Publishing, 1983.

Tidwell, William A., James O. Hall, and David Winfred Gaddy. *Come Retribution: The Confederate Secret Service and the Assassination of Abraham Lincoln*. Jackson: University Press of Mississippi, 1988.

Time-Life, Editors of. *Spies, Scouts and Raiders: Irregular Operations*. The Civil War. Alexandria, VA: Time-Life Books, 1985.

U.S. War Department. *The War of the Rebellion: A Compilation of the Official Records of the Union and Confederate Armies*. 128 vols. Washington, DC: Government Printing Office, 1880–1901.

Varon, Elizabeth R. *Southern Lady, Yankee Spy: The True Story of Elizabeth Van Lew, a Union Agent in the Heart of the Confederacy.* New York: Oxford University Press, 2003.

Vaughan, Gladys. "Colorful Nicholas County Civil War Mata-Hari Revenged in Daring Escapade." N.d. West Virginia Archives Library, West Virginia Division of Culture and History, Charleston, WV.

Velazquez, Loreta Janeta. *The Woman in Battle: A Narrative of the Exploits, Adventures, and Travels of Madame Loreta Janeta Velazquez, Otherwise Known as Lieutenant Harry J. Buford, Confederate States Army.* Edited by C. J. Worthington. Hartford: T. Belknap, 1876.

Wert, Jeffery D. *Mosby's Rangers.* New York: Simon & Schuster, 1990.

Wheeler, Linda. "A Confederate Spy, at Home in Virginia." *Washington Post,* April 15, 2007.

Wiley, Bell I. *Confederate Women.* Westport, CT: Greenwood Press, 1975.

Williamson, James J. *Prison Life in the Old Capitol and Reminiscences of the Civil War.* West Orange, NJ: n.p., 1911.

Winkler, H. Donald. *Lincoln and Booth: More Light on the Conspiracy.* Nashville: Cumberland House, 2003.

Wise, Winfred E. *Lincoln's Secret Weapon.* Philadelphia: Chilton Co., 1961.

Wood, Leonara W. *Belle Boyd: Famous Spy of the Confederate States Army.* Keyser, WV: L. W. Wood, 1940.

Wormser, Richard. *Pinkerton: America's First Private Eye.* New York: Walker & Co., 1990.

Internet Sources

Central Intelligence Agency. "Intelligence in the Civil War." https://www.cia.gov/library/publications/additional-publications/civil-war/index.html. See especially Black Dispatches, Conspiracy in Canada, and Intelligence Collection—The South.

"Nancy Hart." About.com: Women's History. http://womenshistory.about.com/od/womenspiescivilwar/p/nancy_hart.htm.

"Nancy Hart: The Lady Guerrilla." Mid-Missouri Civil War Round Table. http://mmcwrt.missouri.org/2001/default0106.htm.

Willard Family Papers. Library of Congress. http://www.loc.gov/rr/mss/text/willardf.html.

Manuscripts

Antonia Ford. Letters from 1861 to 1863 (4/21/61, 10/7/61, 11/25/61, 4/13/63, 4/63, 7/18/63, 6/26/63, 9/18/63, 12/31/63), Library of Congress, Manuscript Division, Willard Papers, Boxes 1, 198, 201, 202, 203, 204.

———. Various letters and documents from 1863 to 1864 (11/12/63, 11/30/63, 12/63, 1/11/64, 1/12/64, 1/15/64, 1/30/64, 2/1/64, 2/2/64). City of Fairfax Historic Collections, Fairfax, VA.

Sarah Thompson Papers. "Sarah Thompson's Account of Morgan's Defeat, September 3, 1864." Special Collections Library, Duke University.

Television Programs

Fischer, Steve. *Now & Forever Yours: Letters to an Old Soldier.* Annandale, VA: Northern Virginia Community College, NVCC-TV, 2007.

Full Metal Corset: Secret Soldiers of the Civil War. San Rafael, CA: Indigo Films for the History Channel, 2007.

Image Credits

Photographs on the following pages courtesy of the Library of Congress: 12, 72, 18, 23, 30, 41, 52, 58, 61, 65, 81, 83, 90, 97, 106, 120, 131, 139, 144, 202, 224, 228, 230, 254, 271, 307. Photographs courtesy of the author's collection: 2, 73, 136, 157, 170, 176, 207, 225. Photographs courtesy of the National Archives: 9, 16, 35, 72, 196. Photographs courtesy of Harper's Weekly: 72, 152, 182. Photographs from *The Woman in Battle*: 261, 265. Photographs from *Union Spy and Scout*: 123, 130. Photographs courtesy of St. Albans Historical Museums: 43, 44. Photographs courtesy of Karla Vernon: 170, 180. Photograph courtesy of the North Carolina Office of Archives and History: 27. Photograph courtesy of the University of North Carolina Library, North Carolina Collection: 32. Photograph courtesy of the Society for the Restoration of Port Tobacco: 40. Photograph courtesy of Constance Stuart Larrabee: 41. Photograph courtesy of the Museum of the Confederacy, Richmond, VA: 79. Photograph courtesy of Smith Library of Regional history: 98. Photograph courtesy of Cambridge Democrat: 144. Photograph Courtesy of West Virginia State Archives: 160. Photograph courtesy of Susan Block: 171. Photograph courtesy of Surratt House Museum: 300. Photograph from *Memoirs of a Soldier*: 232. Photograph courtesy of Lewis Leigh Jr.: 174. Photograph from *The Spy of the Rebellion*: 293.

Photograph from *The Shadows of Silver*: 60. Photograph from *The Soldiers in our Civil War*: 71. Photograph courtesy F.O.C. Darby: 10.

INDEX

About the Author

H. Donald Winkler is a professional journalist, historian, and retired university public affairs executive. He has received eighty-four national awards and was inducted into the Virginia Communications Hall of Fame. He has written three highly acclaimed books on Lincoln and on the Civil War: *Lincoln's Ladies* (also issued as *The Women in Lincoln's Life*); *Lincoln and Booth: More Light on the Conspiracy*; and *Civil War Goats and Scapegoats*. He has been a featured speaker at Ford's Theatre, the Carl Sandburg Home National Historic Site, and other venues across the nation.

Earlier in his career Winkler founded and edited an international issues magazine, *East-West Perspectives*, which was chosen as the nation's outstanding educational magazine. He has been cited by the Council for Advancement and Support of Education for "professional endeavors that have strengthened the entire fabric of American education."